LESSONS

IN

ELOCUTION;

WITH

Numerous Selections, Analyzed for Practice.

A TEXT BOOK

IN READING AND SPEAKING, FOR SCHOOLS, SEMINARIES, AND PRIVATE LEARNERS.

By ALLEN A. GRIFFITH,

PROFESSOR OF ELOCUTION, AND PRINCIPAL OF BATAVIA INSTITUTE.

SECOND EDITION -- REVISED AND ENLARGED.

CHICAGO:
ADAMS, BLACKMER, & LYON;
NEW YORK: BARNES & BURR;
MILWAUKEE: A. WHITTEMORE.

1865.

HORTON & LEONARD,
PRINTERS,
CHICAGO.

CHICAGO TYPE FOUNDRY:
J. CONAHAN,
STEREOTYPER.

PREFACE.

An attempt is made in this book to reduce the principles of Elocution to a system, and present them to the student in an analytical and progressive form. It is believed that more of our young men and misses would be interested in the exercise of reading and recitation if they could have placed in their hands a work which would supply the place of the living teacher in showing them how. Many educators have taken it for granted that any one could learn a piece and recite it, and have allowed those under their immediate charge to follow their own ideas in this department, and hence there have been monotony, indifference, and, too frequently, failure.

The analysis referred to is elaborated, with such models in Position and Gesture, and such illustrations of the principles of Vocalization, that it is thought the teacher or pupil can prepare himself to utter the chosen selection with entertaining power, and correct any faults he may have in Tone, Gesture, or Position. One thing the pupil *must do* — he must commit to memory the words he would recite, or have their meaning clearly defined in his own mind if he is to read with expression. No knowledge of principles will supply this neglect. The student can do this; then all the energy can be d'rected to the expression of the sentiment.

M. . . ' he matter herein is new, and embodies the spirit of the t. . . several choice gems of eloquence, brought out by the terrible death of our loved President, having more than a temporary value to the youth of the Nation, are inserted as models for practice.

Many of the most prominent teachers and professors in the schools of the Northwest have repeatedly urged the publication of the analysis herein, with the selections which have been given in my public readings; and if we are to be censured for adding another to the large list of works on Elocution, they must share the censure.

Hoping the young people will take courage in this special department, and prepare themselves for the clear and perfect expression of their thoughts, and the gems of our language, I submit this Hand-Book to their keeping.

BATAVIA, July, 1865.

CONTENTS.

————•◦•————

DEFINITIONS AND DIRECTIONS.

CONTENTS.

SELECTIONS.

SUGGESTIONS TO TEACHERS.

With a little preparation before recitation, the principles of the "Analysis of Elocution" contained in this book may be taught to a class or school in such a manner as to awaken a genuine interest in the subject. The teacher should lead the exercise, or give the model, and the pupil should follow, without hesitation, as directed. For instance: if the drill is upon Position or Gesture, the teacher will place himself in such a position as to be easily seen by all who take part, (or he may place a student in this conspicuous position, who will repeat the model from the teacher to the class,) and commence with the *first position.* All having taken it promptly, he will pass to the second. Great care should be taken that all have just the position required; feet separated alike, body at rest, and the same self-control exhibited by each. The ungraceful should be corrected and encouraged. These positions should be repeated every day, in recitation. Whenever the student rises to recite, he may practice position, and, as he proceeds with the recitation, he may practice gesture and vocalization. Having practiced the positions, proceed to the fifteen systematic gestures with the right hand, as represented by the cuts; first to the *lower* horizontal circle, then the *middle,* then to the *upper,* and vary the pitch of voice and force as you progress. Before repeating the sentences have the gestures given in concert, after the teacher, by *number,* then by the use of the *vowel* elements, and then by *sentences.* This exercise may be extended with profit until the school or class, will repeat after the teacher a whole selection, like the "Charge of the Light Brigade," or "Excelsior," with appropriate gestures. For the purpose of cultivating an easy, graceful manner, practice *walking* and *turning* until the student can come to rest in the proper position. The teacher will discourage all mannerism, affectation or strutting. If these first principles are successfully introduced, the remainder of the analysis will follow naturally in the order laid down in the book—the teacher always leading the class in a good model. It is not intended in the foregoing drills that the pupils will have books. They follow the teacher.

For conducting a reading exercise the following plan has been very successful in our experience. Every member of the class should be made to understand the object of loud reading; that it is to *convey the thoughts of an author to some person or persons who are supposed to be listening.* The reader must understand an author himself before he can make another understand; hence a series of inquiries like the following, before reading, are important:

What is the spirit of this selection?

Is it Plaintive, Animated, Grave, Declamatory, or Humorous?

What quality of voice predominates?

Repeat the qualities of voice with their corresponding emotions.

Does this selection contain personations?

What is the author's object in this selection?

Can you say anything about the author?

After the selection has been read with the teacher in concert, request the different members of the class, separately, to step out and read until called to stop; and while one reads the others listen, with books closed, and show the hand or make some sign, as soon as there is anything that is not understood. Place the class as far from you as is possible, and require them to read standing, with the book in the left hand, the upper part of it held below the chin so as to show the countenance, and permit the free use of the eyes, which should frequently be cast from the book to those who listen. Practice holding the book in concert. 1st. Book in the right hand by the side — first position. 2d. Raise it and open it to place. 3d. Pass it to left hand. 4th. Right hand drop by the side. Great precision and promptness should be insisted on in this drill. In teaching Emphatic Force, let one of the students read alone until the emphatic word or sentence is reached, and then have all the class join their voices to give the expression desired. The students will soon be able to give the required force themselves, individually, by this method. Before every reading exercise, the class should give in concert and individually, if time permits, the elements of the language, exploding the vowels to acquire variety of *Force* and *Pitch*, and facility in the inflection of voice.

ELOCUTION.

ELOCUTION is the utterance of words, in reading or speaking, in such a manner as to express their meaning. To do this well, a person requires a knowledge, —

1st. Of the vocal organs and the muscles which act on them.

2d. A clear conception of the meaning of the words to be read or spoken.

3d. Extensive practice in the application of the principles of elocution to the delivery of the best models of composition.

ANALYSIS OF PRINCIPLES.

The following arrangement will indicate how the subject may be progressively studied:

ATTITUDE OF BODY.

Learn how to sit, how to stand, how to use the hands and arms, and how to breathe.

THE VOCAL ORGANS.

THE LARYNX, — ITS MUSCLES AND APPENDAGES.

Articulation of elements, syllables, words, and sentences.

THE VOICE.

1st. Modulation.　　2d. Quality. $\begin{cases} \text{Pure,} \\ \text{Impure.} \end{cases}$

VARIATIONS OF VOICE.

3d. Pitch. $\begin{cases} \text{High,} \\ \text{Middle,} \\ \text{Low.} \end{cases}$　　4th. Force. $\begin{cases} \text{Loud,} \\ \text{Medium,} \\ \text{Gentle.} \end{cases}$　　5th. Time. $\begin{cases} \text{Quick,} \\ \text{Moderate,} \\ \text{Slow.} \end{cases}$

6th. Emphasis. $\begin{cases} \text{Radical,} \\ \text{Vanishing,} \\ \text{Median,} \\ \text{Compound.} \end{cases}$　　7th. Inflection. $\begin{cases} \text{Rising,} \\ \text{Falling,} \\ \text{Circumflex,} \\ \text{Monotone.} \end{cases}$

PAUSES.

Grammatical — Rhetorical.

PERSONATION.

In Voice — Countenance — Gesture.

EXPRESSION.

Application of principles to emotional utterances, and to the exhibition of the passions.

DEFINITIONS AND DIRECTIONS.

ATTITUDE.

The student should be careful to keep the body erect. A good voice depends upon it. An instrument, to produce a good tone, must be kept in tune.

The practice of *Position* and *Gesture* will prove a valuable aid in physical
culture, and in acquiring a graceful address.

We have but two *Primary* positions of the feet:

First—The body rests on the
right foot, the left a little advanced, left knee bent.

Second—The body rests on the
left foot, right a little advanced,
right knee bent.

FIRST POSITION.

SECOND POSITION.

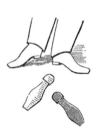

We have two other posi-
tions which are called *Secondary.*   They are assumed
in argument, appeal, or persuasion.   The first secondary
position is taken from the
first primary, by advancing
the unoccupied foot, and resting the body upon it, leaning
forward, the *right* foot brought
to its support.

THIRD POSITION, OR FIRST
SECONDARY.

FOURTH POSITION, OR SECOND
SECONDARY.

The second secondary position is the same as the first, the body resting
upon the right foot.

In assuming these positions, all movements should be made with the
utmost simplicity, avoiding "the stage strut and parade of the dancing
master."

Advance, retire, or change, with ease, except when the action demands
energy, or marked decision.   Adopt such positions only as consist of manly
and simple grace, and change as the sentiment or subject changes, or as
you direct attention to different parts of the audience.   Avoid moving
about, or "weaving," or moving the feet or hands while speaking.

We subjoin a few models of position and gesture, showing how to use the hands and arms. Second position before commencing address; arms at ease. The fingers may be relaxed or partly closed.

Arm pointing to the zenith. The dotted lines show the direction of the gesture, and its point or place in the curve, for less animated address. The arm leaves its point of rest in curved lines.

To give a better idea of the place of the gesture, we introduce a diagram of the sphere, bounded by circles. It should be carefully studied, until the student has a clear idea of the direction and point of gesture.

ARMS AT EASE.

SECOND POSITION.

THE SPHERE BOUNDED BY CIRCLES, SHOWING THE PLACE OF GESTURE.

The human figure is supposed to be so placed within the sphere that the centre of the breast shall coincide with its centre.

The motions and positions of the arms are referred to and determined by these circles and their intersections.

It will be noticed that there are fifteen positions, or points, in the circles reached by the arms. These fifteen systematic positions of the arms may be multiplied by *three*. If the utterance is moderate and unimpassioned, the gestures will correspond; but if the utterance is animated and impassioned, the gesture must also correspond. If an individual is referring to some scene in nature—a landscape, the clouds, the woods, or a body of water—the arm will be extended forward, or toward the object; but if a general is pointing to a company or regiment, which he desires shall be charged upon, he will incline forward; the arm will be stretched out toward the men with energy and expression. And, again, if the object referred to in the gesture is frightful, or to be shunned, or dreaded, then the body will shrink back, the arm will point, and then recoil, with marked decision. These three styles of gesture, corresponding with the expression, and constituting the *action* of the speaker, are well defined; and, for the sake of classification, may be styled *Conversational, Energetic*, and *Recoiling*. Now, if we notice that they may be given with the *right* hand, with the *left*, or with *both* hands, we shall have a series of gestures, amounting to *one hundred and thirty-five* in all.

The practice of these gestures, with proper positions, after a living model, is as beneficial as the free gymnastic drill, and secures grace and ease of movement in the positions and movements of the arms.

We know that gesture cannot be made by rule, in speaking; and, in the practice, mechanical precision is not to be enforced, though exactness and uniformity should be insisted upon.

Some insist that all gestures shall be made with the right hand and arm. We find no good authority, either *ancient* or *modern*, for thus limiting the gesture.

We give the first fifteen systematic gestures of the right arm, with appropriate positions. The student may correct any faults he may have by studying these models. The first five are directed to the lower circle, next to the middle, and last to the circle above.

"Here sleeps he, now, alone!"

" See! the earth is cover'd with snow."

" Around me are the beautiful things of earth."

" The grass is withered, and the leaves are falling."

(The student will supply an appropriate sentence.)

"Before me is the flood, rolling in its might !"

" How frightful the scene !"

" Yonder a boat tossed high on the waves !"

" See! she reels !"

" Roll on, thou deep and dark blue ocean, ROLL."

"Behold how beautiful are the clouds !"

(Supply a sentence.)

"Nail to the mast her threadbare sails !"

A

"Give her to the god of storms—the lightning and the gale!"

"Arm, thou leader of the North.
O Thou that rollest above!"

CONVERSATIONAL GESTURE, No. 1.

CONVERSATIONAL GESTURE, No. 2.

CONVERSATIONAL GESTURE, No. 3.

ANIMATED GESTURE, No. 1.

ANIMATED GESTURE, No. 2.

RECOILING.   ARMS ENCUMBERED.   DEFENSIVE.

THE HANDS MAY BE PLACED ON

THE BREAST.   THE FOREHEAD.   THE LIPS.   THE HEAD.   THE CHIN.

MISCELLANEOUS GESTURES.

No. 1, THE FLOURISH.   No. 2. THE WAVE.   No. 3, STRIKING.

RECOILING, No. 1.   BOTH HANDS FORWARD, No. 2.   BOTH OBLIQUE, No. 3

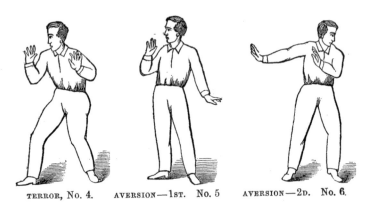

TERROR, No. 4.   AVERSION—1ST. No. 5   AVERSION—2D. No. 6.

HORROR, No. 7.   FEAR—LISTENING, No. 8.   ADMIRATION, No. 9.

VENERATION—SUB-
MISSION.

APPEAL TO HEAVEN.

DEPRECATION.

The motions of the arms appear awkward, unless the expression of the hand corresponds with the thought, and is natural. We introduce a few diagrams from life, for study:

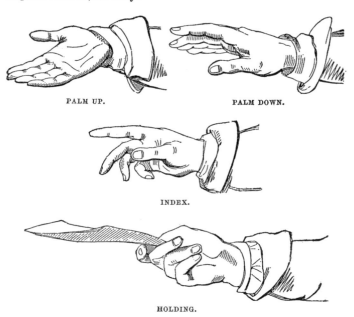

PALM UP.

PALM DOWN.

INDEX.

HOLDING.

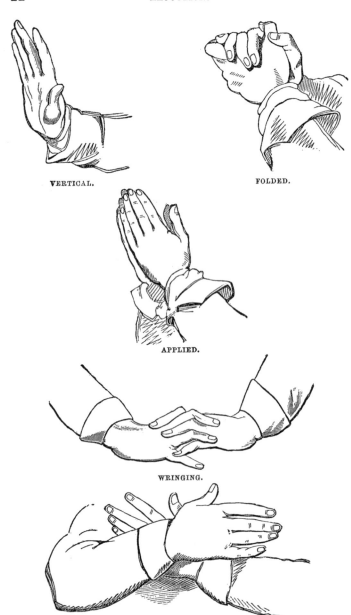

VERTICAL.

FOLDED.

APPLIED.

WRINGING.

CROSSED.

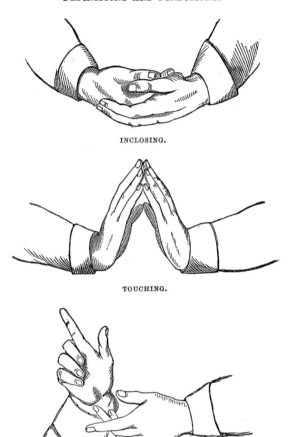

INCLOSING.

TOUCHING.

ENUMERATING.

The expressions and positions of the hands may be taught in concert, the teacher or one of the pupils giving the model and leading by number.

The sitting position for reading aloud and singing, may be learned from the Cut.

SITTING POSTURE — PROPER AND IMPROPER.

Sit erect with the head thrown back, that the chest may expand and contract freely in the operation of breathing. Place the feet upon the floor. Do not sit with the limbs crossed in reading, speaking, or singing.

How to Breathe.

Deep breathing with the lips closed, inhaling as long as possible and exhaling slowly, is very beneficial. Having inflated the lungs to their utmost capacity, form the breath into the element of long *o*, in its escape through the vocal organs. This exercise should be frequently repeated as the voice will be strengthened thereby, and the capacity of the chest greatly increased. Do not raise the shoulders or the upper part of the chest alone when you breathe. Breathe as a healthy child breathes, by the expansion and contraction of the abdominal and intercostal muscles. Such breathing will improve the health and be of great assistance in continuous reading or speaking. Great care is necessary in converting the breath into voice. Do not waste breath; use it economically, or hoarseness will follow. Much practice on the vocal elements, with all the varieties of pitch, then the utterance of words, then of sentences, and finally, of whole paragraphs, is necessary in learning to use the breath, and in acquiring judgment and taste in vocalizing. Never speak when the lungs are exhausted. Keep them well inflated.

THE VOCAL ORGANS.

THE LARYNX—ITS MUSCLES AND APPENDAGES.

Having learned how to stand, how to use the hands and arms, how to sit, and how to breathe, we now proceed to the VOCAL ORGANS and their *use*.

At the root of the tongue lies a semilunar shaped bone, which, from its resemblance to a certain Greek letter, is called the hyoid or u-like bone; and immediately from this bone arises a long cartilaginous tube which extends to the lungs and conveys the air backward and forward in the process of respiration. This tube is called the trachea, or wind-pipe; and the upper part of it, or that immediately connected with the hyoid bone, the larynx, and it is this upper part or larynx which constitutes the seat of the voice. The tube of the larynx is formed of five distinct cartilages, the largest and apparently lowermost of which, together with two other cartilages of a smaller size and power, form the ring or glottis, which is the aperture from the mouth into the larynx. The fourth cartilage lies immediately over the aperture and closes it in the act of swallowing, so as to direct the food to the œsophagus, which leads to the stomach. These four cartilages or membranes are supported by a fifth, which constitutes their basis. The larynx is contracted and dilated in various ways, by different muscles, and the elasticity of its different coats. It is covered internally with a very sensitive, vascular, and mucous membrane similar to the membrane of the mouth.

We see then that the *organ* of the voice is the *larynx, its muscles and appendages,* and the voice itself is *the sound of the air propelled through and striking against the sides of the glottis,* or opening into the mouth. The *modulation* of the voice depends upon the internal diameter of the glottis, its elasticity and mobility, and the force with which the air is propelled.

Speech is the modification of the voice into intelligible articulations in the cavity of the glottis itself, or in that of the mouth or the nostrils.

ARTICULATION.

Sheridan says: "A good articulation consists in giving every letter in a syllable its due proportion of sound, according to the most approved custom of pronouncing it; and in making such a distinction between the syllables of which words are composed, that the ear shall, without difficulty, acknowledge their number, and perceive at once to which syllable each letter belongs. Where these particulars are not observed the articulation is defective."

A good articulation may be acquired by carefully repeating aloud, and in a whisper, the elements of the language. These elements are divided into three classes. *Vocals, Sub-Vocals, and Aspirates.*

The vowels, or vocal sounds, are arranged in the following table for individual and class practice:

A long, as in ale, fate, state, lave, gale.

A short, as in at, hat, sat, mat, plaid, charity.

A Italian, as in arm, far, star, heart, mart.

A broad, as in all, fall, water.

  { *A long, before R,* as in fare, dare, rare, stare, air.

  { *A intermediate, as in* fast, branch, class, mastiff.

E long, as in eve, mete, speed, degree, theme.

E short, as in end, bend, leopard, special, yes.

E like A long, before R, as in heir, there.

I long, as in ice, child, sky, smile, flight.

I short, as in it, pin, whip, cynic, ring.

O long, as in old, dome, bourn, more, poet, glow.

O short, as in ox, not, got, fond, from, fossil.

O long, as in move, prove, food, remove.

U long, as in few, duty, music, tube.

U short, as in up, tub, must, rug, tongue, sum.

U middle, as in pull, push, puss, should.

U short and obtuse, as in burn, murmur.

Oi, as in oil, choice, noise, coin, toy, boil.

Ou, as in out, sound, town, thou, around.

Speak the word distinctly and then the element, exploding it with variety of force and on different notes of the scale. For flexibility of voice and good articulation, there is no better exercise than the utterance of the vowel elements with the different inflections, first rising, then falling, then the circumflexes. The practice of exploding the Vocal elements with a Consonant prefixed, first a Sub-Vocal Consonant, then an Aspirate, is of great value in acquiring control of the mouth, teeth, and lips.

Sub-Vocals, or Vocal Consonants should be treated, in the practice, as the Vocals in the preceding table. They are formed by the vibration of the Vocal chords, modified by the organs of speech:

B, as in bat, bag, beet, babbler, beggar, bound.

D, as in dun, debt, dated, deed, need, did.

G, as in gun, gag, gog, gew-gaw, give.

J, as in jib, joy, judge, June, jury.

L, as in let, lull, wall, isle, lark, loll.

M, as in man, main, mound, mammon, drum.

N, as in nun, nay, noun, name.

Ng, as in sing, king, ring, flinging, lynx, monkey.

R, (*trilled,*) run, rap, Richard, France, round.

R, as in nor, far, border, appear, forbear, ear.

Th, as in thine, thus, thy, beneath, wreathe.

V, as in vent, valve, vine, veer, weave.

W, as in went, wall, one, woo, worn.

Y, as in yes, young, year, yawl, use, you.

Z, as in zeal, as, was, breeze, maze, arise.

Zh, or Z, as in azure, leisure, osier, vision.

Prolong the Sub-Vocal Consonants as follows: b——at d————un, and then pronounce the Sub-Vocal without uttering the word. Then give the Sub-Vocals with the Inflections.

$$b' \; b^{\backslash} \; d' \; d^{\backslash} \; g' \; g^{\backslash} \; j' \; j^{\backslash} \; l' \; l^{\backslash} \; \&c$$

The Aspirate Consonants should be repeated according to the table. Be careful not to waste breath, and utter them with no more power than they require in words:

F, as in fit, fame, fife, fanciful, futile, phantom.

H, as in hat, hope, hay, hap-hazard, hot-house.

K, as in kid, car, coil, king, talk, chasm, chorus.

P, as in pit, pin, pupil, piper, stop, steep, rapid.

S, as in suit, dose, sinless, science, steep, scene.

T, as in top, time, tune, matter, debt, titter, better.

Ch, as in chat, church, churn, child, satchel, chirp.

Sh, as in shun, shade, gash, rash, sash, mansion.

Th, as in thin, thank, thick, breath, thankful.

Wh, as in when, whit, whale, what, why, while, where.

The Elements, we repeat, afford a better exercise in Articulation than words connected to form sense. The drill on the Elements should form a daily exercise in all our primary schools. Change the pitch and force often in reciting them. The student will be well repaid for his trouble if he would study Webster's and Worcester's Dictionaries, especially the introduction in regard to the Elements of the English Language.

If we give the Elements properly we shall have no trouble with their construction into words and sentences.

In exploding the vocals, be careful to breathe deeply, and use the whole of the upper part of the system, not confining the utterance to the upper part of the larynx, or to any one class of the vocal organs.

We here give a table of cognates, which are produced by the same organs in a similar manner, and only differ in one being a half tone, the other a whisper.

Cognates.

ATONICS.		SUBTONICS.	
li*p*	*p*	or*b*	*b*
*f*i*f*e	*f*	*v*ase	*v*
*wh*ite	*wh*	*w*ise	*w*
*s*ave	*s*	*z*eal	*z*
*sh*ade	*sh*	a*z*ure	*z*
*ch*arm	*ch*	*j*oin	*j*
*t*ar*t*	*t*	*d*i*d*	*d*
*th*ing	*th*	*th*is	TH
*k*in*k*	*k*	*g*i*g*	*g*

For combinations of these Elements and difficult exercises, we refer the student to the selections in the body of this work. To be critically exact in pronunciation, frequent reference must be made to Webster's or Worcester's Dictionary.

We give another classification of the Elements—the Phonetic—which is, perhaps, better adapted to class drill than any other. Let the pupils, singly or in concert, give the Elements in the order in which they are arranged, commencing with the long vowels. This natural arrangement of the elements enables scholars to fix them in their minds readily and permanently. In many of our best Normal, and High Schools, this classification is adopted.

The Phonetic Alphabet.

LONG VOWELS.

E, as in eel, me.   *A, as in* all, talk.
A, as in ale, fate.   *O, as in* ope, note.
A, as in arm, palm.   *OO, as in* food, moon.

SHORT VOWELS.

I, as in ill, fin.   *O, as in* on, not.
E, as in ell, met.   *U, as in* up, tub.
A, as in am, fat.   *OO, as in* foot, good

SHADE VOWELS.

E, as in ermine, her.   *A, as in* ask, dance.
A, as in air, share.

DIPHTHONGS.

I, as in ice, fine.   *Ow, as in* owl, towel.
Oi, as in oil, join.   *U, as in* use, mule.

COALESCENTS.

Y, as in year, yet.   *W, as in* way, wit

ASPIRATE.

H, as in hay, he.

EXPLODENTS.

P, as in pope, post.   *Ch, as in* etch, chest.
B, as in robe, boast.   *J, as in* edge, jest.
T, as in fate, teem.   *K, as in* lock, can.
D, as in fade, deem.   *G, as in* log, gain.

CONTINUANTS.

F, as in safe, fear.   *S, as in* buss, seal.
V, as in save, veer.   *Z, as in* buzz, zeal.
Th as in wreath, thigh.   *Sh, as in* vicious, sure.
Th, as in wreathe, thy.   *Zh, as in* vision, jour. **(Fr.)**

LIQUIDS.

L, as in fall, lull.   *R, as in* for, roar

NASALS.

M, as in sum, met.   *Ng, as in* sing, ring.
N, as in sun, net.

THE VOICE.

Voice is the sound of the breath, *propelled* through the larynx, striking against its glottis or opening into the mouth.

Its *modulation* depends upon the control of the larynx, the internal diameter of the glottis, its elasticity and mobility, and the force with which the air is expelled.

To modulate or change the voice from one key to another, with proper degrees of power to each, as the subject demands, is as beautiful in its effect as it is difficult in its performance or acquirement.

Poets, to produce variety, alter the structure of their verse and rather hazard uncouthness and discord than sameness. Prose writers change the style, time, and structure of their periods, and sometimes throw in exclamations, and sometimes interrogatories, to rouse and keep alive the attention; but all this art is entirely thrown away, if the reader does not enter into the spirit of the author, and by a similar kind of genius, render even variety itself more various; if he does not, by an alteration in his voice, manner, tone, gesture, loudness, softness, quickness, slowness, adopt every change of which the subject is susceptible.

We have never yet found a person who could not acquire proficiency in modulating the voice. It is the mind's instrument of communication. Some are obliged to practice more than others, but none need give up the work as useless.

QUALITY OF VOICE.

We should understand the different qualities of voice and the ideas they express. We make two general divisions of Quality, PURE and IMPURE. These may again be sub-divided into Pure, deepened or Orotund Quality, Tremor Quality, Guttural Quality and Aspirate Quality. We represent these Qualities by a diagram, together with the emotions or ideas they express when used naturally.

The following diagram will help the student to remember the Qualities of voice:

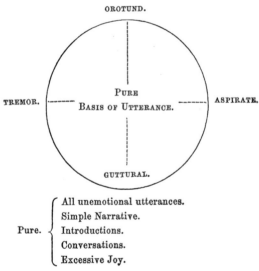

Pure, Deepened, Orotund Quality.	Sublime Utterances. Bold Declamation. Animated Appeals. Apostrophe.
Guttural Quality.	Expressions of Hatred, Contempt, Etc. Denunciation. Revenge. Scorn and kindred Emotions.
Aspirate Quality.	Fear. Horror. Despair. Remorse and kindred Emotions.
Tremor Quality.	Pity, Tenderness. Grief, (excessive.) Joy, (excessive.) Hope.

The emotions help to define the voices. It is difficult to separate these Qualities of voice. Like the Emotions, they shade into each other so much, that it requires long and patient study to express, with exactness, the ideas of an author.

The Pure Quality is most used, and should be most zealously cultivated. It introduces all the other Qualities.

We now give several selections which require, in their proper reading, all the Qualities of voice. By giving whole selections, we hope the student will discover the Quality of voice, and understand the reason of its use from the connection and sense.

The Pilot—A Thrilling Incident.

BY JOHN B. GOUGH.

a John Maynard was well known in the lake district as a God-fearing, honest and intelligent pilot. He was pilot on a steamboat from Detroit to Buffalo, one summer afternoon—at that time those steamers seldom carried boats—smoke was seen ascending from below, and the captain called out:

b "Simpson, go below and see what the matter is down there."

----

a Begin with pure voice, as in simple narrative. Increase, moderately, in pitch until the personation is reached. *b* High pitch; orotund voice.

c Simpson came up with his face pale as ashes, and said, *d* "Captain, the ship is on fire."

e Then "Fire! fire! fire!" on shipboard.

f All hands were called up. Buckets of water were dashed on the fire, but in vain. There were large quantities of rosin and tar on board, and it was found useless to attempt to save the ship. The passengers rushed forward and inquired of the pilot:

g "How far are we from Buffalo?"

h "Seven miles."

"How long before we can reach there?"

"Three-quarters of an hour at our present rate of steam."

i "Is there any danger?"

"Danger, here—see the smoke bursting out—go forward if you would save your lives."

Passengers and crew—men, women and children—crowded the forward part of the ship. John Maynard stood at the helm. The flames burst forth in a sheet of fire; clouds of smoke arose. The captain cried out through his trumpet:

j "John Maynard!"

k "Aye, aye, sir!"

"Are you at the helm?"

"Aye, aye, sir!"

"How does she head?"

"South-east by east, sir."

"Head her south-east and run her on shore," said the captain.

l Nearer, nearer, yet nearer, she approached the shore. Again the captain cried out:

"John Maynard!"

The response came feebly this time, "Aye, aye, sir!"

"Can you hold on five minutes longer, John?" he said.

"By God's help, I will."

The old man's hair was scorched from the scalp, one hand disabled, his knee upon the stanchion, and his teeth set, with his other hand upon the wheel, he stood firm as a rock. He beached the ship; every man, woman, and child was saved, as John Maynard dropped, and his spirit took its flight to its God.

---

c Pure voice; low pitch. *d* Aspirate voice, with fear. *e* Give the alarm of "fire" as if it was real, and in the immediate vicinity. Aspirate voice; high pitch. *f* Pure voice; narrative; increase. *g* Aspirate voice with earnestness. *h* Orotund; low pitch, with firmness. The Pilot's answer will all be given in the same voice, and passengers in aspirate with increased feeling. *i* Narrative; pure voice. *j* Orotund; commanding, as if to a person at a distance; high pitch. *k* Orotund; low pitch, and so change until the colloquy is ended. *l* Orotund; low pitch to begin with. Change the pitch as the word nearer is repeated. Change the voice in Pitch and Quality to represent the Captain and Pilot, and give the closing paragraph with intense feeling; low pitch and impassioned utterance.

We give another selection from the same author, which contains **variety** of voice and expression. The student will complete the analysis.

THE POWER OF HABIT.

a I remember once riding from Buffalo to the Niagara Falls, and said to a gentleman, *b* "What river is that, sir?"

c "That," said he, "is the Niagara River."

d "Well, it is a beautiful stream," said I; "bright, and fair, and glassy; how far off are the rapids?"

"Only a mile or two," was the reply.

"Is it possible that only a mile from us we shall find the water in the turbulence which it must show when near the Falls?"

"You will find it so, sir." *e* And so I found it; and the first sight of Niagara I shall never forget. Now, launch your bark on that Niagara river; it is bright, smooth, beautiful, and glassy. There is a ripple at the bow; the silver wake you leave behind adds to your enjoyment. Down the stream you glide, oars, sails, and helm in proper trim, and you set out on your pleasure excursion. Suddenly some one cries out from the bank, *f* "Young men, ahoy!"

"What is it?"

"The rapids are below you."

"Ha! ha! we have heard of the rapids, but we are not such fools as to get there. If we go too fast, then we shall up with the helm and steer to the shore; we will set the mast in the socket, hoist the sail, and speed to the land. Then on, boys; don't be alarmed; there is no danger."

"Young men, ahoy there!" ·

"What is it?"

"The rapids are below you!"

NOTE. — It is difficult to give illustrations of the several qualities of voice *separately*. In the expression of mixed emotions the voices shade into each other so frequently that success in reading or speaking is only gained by a thorough acquaintance with the meaning of the author, and the power over the vocal instrument to change the tone and pitch at pleasure. We know that writers upon this subject have given illustrations of these voices separately. But unless the teacher or elocutionist gives the model quality, the student reads them with but little variety, or neglects them altogether; but as they follow each other in a varied selection, if the student enters at all into the spirit of the author, he sees the necessity of them, and is eager for the practice that will enable him to give them.

a Pure, narrative voice. *b* Pure, high pitch. *c* Low; pure; "said he," in very low pitch. *d* High; pure. *e* Pure; narrative; animated. *f* Orotund; very loud. The reply will be given with low pitch, and with impatience at the interruption; then with laughter and an expression of fearlessness.

B

"Ha! ha! we will laugh and quaff; all things delight us. What care we for the future! No man ever saw it. Sufficient for the day is the evil thereof. We will enjoy life while we may; will catch pleasure as it flies. This is enjoyment; time enough to steer out of danger when we are sailing swiftly with the current."

"Young men, ahoy!"

"What is it?"

"Beware! Beware! The rapids are below you!"

g Now you see the water foaming all around. See how fast you pass that point! Up with the helm! Now turn! Pull hard! quick! quick! quick! pull for your lives! pull till the blood starts from your nostrils, and the veins stand like whip-cords upon your brow! Set the mast in the socket! hoist the sail! ah! ah! it is too late! Shrieking, cursing, howling, blaspheming; over they go.

Thousands go over the rapids every year, through the power of habit, crying all the while, "when I find out that it is injuring me I will give it up!"

THE PILOT.

BY COCHRAN.

1. *a* The waves are high, the night is dark,
　　Wild roam the foaming tides,
　　Dashing around the straining bark,
　　As gallantly she rides.
　b "Pilot! take heed what course you steer;
　　Our bark is tempest driven!"
　c "Stranger, be calm, there is no fear
　　For him who trusts in Heaven!"

2. *d* "O pilot! mark yon thunder cloud,—
　　The lightning's lurid rivers;
　　Hark to the wind, 'tis piping loud,—
　　The mainmast bends and quivers!
　　Stay, pilot, stay and shorten sail,
　　Our stormy trysail's riven!"
　e "Stranger, what matters calm or gale
　　To him who trusts in Heaven?"

---

g Very quick; aspirate.

a One voice, (which?) *b* Another voice, (which?) *c* Another voice, (which?) *d* Change the voice; increase. *e* Change; diminish.

3. *f* Borne by the winds, the vessel flies
  Up to the thundering cloud.
 Now tottering low, the spray-winged seas
  Conceal the topmast shroud.
 g " Pilot, the waves break o'er us fast,
  Vainly our bark has striven ! "
 h " Stranger, the *Lord* can rule the blast,—
  Go, put thy trust in Heaven ! "

4. *i* Good hope ! good hope ! one little star
  Gleams o'er the waste of waters ;
 'Tis like the light reflected far
  Of Beauty's loveliest daughters ;
 j " Stranger, good hope He giveth thee,
  As He has often given ;
 Then learn this truth—whate'er may be,
 k To put thy trust in Heaven ! "

LIBERTY AND UNION.

a 1. I profess, sir, in my career hitherto, to have kept steadily in view, the prosperity and honor of the whole country, and the preservation of our federal union. It is to that union we owe our safety at home, and our consideration and dignity abroad. *b* It is to that union that we are chiefly indebted for whatever makes us most proud of our country. That union we reached only by the discipline of our virtues, in the severe school of adversity. It had its origin in the necessities of disordered finance, prostrate commerce, and ruined credit. Under its benign influences, these great interests immediately awoke, as from the dead, and sprang forth with newness of life. Every year of its duration has teemed with fresh proofs of its utility and its blessings ; and although our territory has stretched out wider and wider, and our population spread farther and farther, they have not outrun its protection or its benefits. It has been to us all a copious fountain of national, social, and personal happiness.

c 2. I have not allowed myself, sir, to look beyond the union, to see what might lie hidden in the dark recess behind. I have not coolly weighed the chances of preserving liberty, when the bonds that unite us together shall

---

f Pure, *g* Orotund; high. *h* Orotund; low. *i* Pure and tremor, (the tremor is given only on certain words,) with animation. *j* Orotund; full; joyous. *k* Diminish; slow

a Pure voice; unemotional. *b* Orotund; increase. *c* Pure, deepened; more boldly,

be broken asunder. I have not accustomed myself to hang over the precipice of disunion, to see whether, with my short sight, I can fathom the depth of the abyss below; nor could I regard him, as a safe counsellor in the affairs of this government, whose thoughts should be mainly bent on considering, not how the union should be preserved, but how tolerable might be the condition of the people, when it shall be broken up and destroyed. *d* 3. While the union lasts we have high, exciting, gratifying prospects spread out before us, for us and our children. Beyond that I seek not to penetrate the veil. God grant that in my day, at least, that curtain may not rise. God grant that on my vision may never be opened what lies behind. *e* When my eyes shall be turned to behold, for the last time, the sun in heaven, may I not see him shining on the broken and dishonored fragments of a once glorious union; on states dissevered, discordant, belligerent; on a land rent with civil feuds, or drenched, it may be, in fraternal blood! Let their last feeble and lingering glance, rather, behold the gorgeous ensign of the republic, now known and honored throughout the earth, *f* still full high advanced, its arms and trophies streaming in their original luster, not a stripe erased or polluted, not a single star obscured, bearing for its motto no such miserable interrogatory as — *g* What is all this worth? Nor those other words *h* of delusion and folly — *i* Liberty first and union afterward; *j* but everywhere, spread all over, in characters of living light, blazing on all its ample folds, as they float over the sea and over the land, and in every wind under the whole heavens, that other sentiment, dear to every true American heart, — Liberty AND Union, now and forever, one and inseparable!

VARIATIONS.

PITCH, — FORCE, — TIME.

The voices depend, for expression, upon *Pitch*, which refers to the key note, *Force*, which refers to the degree of loudness or volume, and *Time*, which refers to the rate of utterance or degree of rapidity with which words are uttered. We have anticipated these variations in the examples under voice.

We mark *three* divisions of *Pitch: High*, as in shouting, or calling to persons at a distance, or giving commands; *Low*, as in solemn utterances, or emotions requiring the aspirate voice; and *Middle*, as in ordinary address and unimpassioned expressions.

---

d Pure, deepened; high pitch; joyous. *e* Pure, deepened; low pitch; grave. *f* Positive; higher. *g* Bold; orotund; harsh. *h* Slightly guttural. *i* Full, orotund; long quality slide. *j* Much animation and dignified expression with the close.

The degrees of *Force* are almost without limit, but we make three general divisions: *Loud* and *full Force*, as in bold declamation and impassioned address; *Medium Force* for unemotional utterances; and *Soft* or *gentle Force* in pathetic or subdued emotions.

The time or movement of utterance depends upon the sentiments delivered, and the kinds are as numerous as the styles of thought, but we make three general divisions: *Quick, Moderate* and *Slow*, or we might have quick, and very quick, moderate and slow, and very slow.

We may remark that we cannot read or speak a line or paragraph, correctly, without applying all the principles of elocution. We analyze different selections, with some one or more of these principles.

The following poem, by Longfellow, contains examples in almost every variety of Pitch, Force, and Time. Let it be carefully studied.

EXCELSIOR.

1. *a* The shades of night were falling fast,
   As through an Alpine village passed
   A youth, who bore, 'mid snow and ice,
   A banner with the strange device,
        Excelsior!

2. *b* His brow was sad; his eye beneath,
   Flashed like a falchion from its sheath,
   c And like a silver clarion rung
   The accents of that unknown tongue,
        Excelsior!

3. *d* In happy homes he saw the light
   Of household fires gleam warm and bright;
   Above, the spectral glaciers shone,
   And from his lips escaped a groan,
        e Excelsior.

4. *f* "Try not the Pass!" *g* the old man said;
   "Dark lowers the tempest overhead,
   The roaring torrent is deep and wide!"
   And loud that clarion voice replied,
        h Excelsior!

---

a Moderate pitch; pure; narrative; low. *b* Moderate; pure. *c* High pitch; increase; orotund on "Excelsior." *d* Moderate pitch; slow. *e* Low pitch; prolonged quality. *f* High pitch; personation. *g* Low; narrative. *h* High; loud.

5. *i* "Oh stay," the maiden said, "and rest
 Thy weary head upon this breast!"
 A tear stood in his bright blue eye, *j*
 But still he answered, with a sigh,
   Excelsior!

6. *k* "Beware the pine-tree's withered branch!
 Beware the awful avalanche!"
 This was the peasant's last good-night,
 A voice replied, far up the height,
   l Excelsior!

7. *m* At break of day, as heavenward
 The pious monks of St. Bernard
 Uttered the oft-repeated prayer,
 n A voice cried through the startled air,
   Excelsior!

8. *o* A traveller, by the faithful hound,
 Half buried in the snow was found,
 Still grasping in his hand of ice
 That banner with the strange device,
   Excelsior!

9. *p* There in the twilight cold and gray,
 Lifeless, but beautiful, he lay,
 And from the sky, serene and far,
 A voice fell, like a falling star,
   q Excelsior!

THE CHARGE OF THE LIGHT BRIGADE.

1. *a* Half a league, half a league,
 Half a league onward,
 All in the valley of Death
 Rode the six hundred.

---

i Moderate pitch. *j* Low; prolonged. *k* High and loud; long quality; personation. *l* High pitch; head tone; ventriloqinal; requiring much practice. *m* Moderate; narrative. *n* High; quick; increase. *o* Moderate; narrative; slow. *p* Moderate; slow time. *q* High pitch; terminating low; diminish.

a Narrative; pure voice; increase.

b " Forward, the Light Brigade!
" Charge for the guns!" he said:
c Into the valley of *Death*
   Rode the six hundred.

2. *d* " Forward, the Light Brigade!"
   Was there a man dismay'd?
   Not tho' the soldier knew
      Some one had blunder'd:
   Theirs not to make reply,
   Theirs not to reason why,
   Theirs but to do and die,
   Into the valley of Death
      Rode the six hundred.

3. *e* Cannon to right of them,
   Cannon to left of them,
   Cannon in front of them
      Volley'd and thunder'd;
   Storm'd at with shot and shell,
   Boldly they rode and well,
   Into the jaws of Death,
   Into the mouth of Hell
      Rode the six hundred.

4. *f* Flash'd all their sabres bare,
   Flash'd as they turn'd in air,
   Sabring the gunners there,
   Charging an army, while
      All the world wonder'd:
   Plunged in the battery-smoke
   Right thro' the line they broke;
   Cossack and Russian
   Reel'd from the sabre-stroke
      Shatter'd and sunder'd.
   Then they rode back, but not,
      Not the six hundred.

b Personation; orotund; high; bold. *c* Low pitch; aspirate, on the word "death."
d Orotund; high; increase through the stanza. *e* Bold; orotund; measured. *f* Guttural;
full of passion and action, as if in battle.

5. *g* Cannon to right of them,
   Cannon to left of them,
   Cannon behind them
     Volley'd and thunder'd;
   Storm'd at with shot and shell,
   While horse and hero fell,
   They that had fought so well
   Came thro' the jaws of Death
   Back from the mouth of Hell,
   All that was left of them,
     Left of six hundred.

6. *h* When can their glory fade?
   O the wild charge they made!
     All the world wonder'd.
   Honor the charge they made!
   Honor the Light Brigade,
     Noble Six Hundred!

Examples in Very Quick Time.

1. Quick—man the boat. John, be quick. Get some water. Throw the powder overboard. "It cannot be reached." Jump into the boat, then. Shove off. There goes the powder. Thank heaven, we are safe.

2.   At length, o'er Columbus, slow consciousness breaks,
    "LAND! LAND!" cry the sailors; "LAND! LAND!"—he awakes—
    He runs,—yes! behold it! it blesseth his sight!
    The land! O! dear spectacle! transport! delight!

This selection contains a compendium of the principles of Elocution, by a master of the art. It requires variety of voice, pitch, force and time in its delivery. The student will analyze it:

Hamlet's Instructions.
SHAKESPEARE.

Speak the *speech*, I pray you, as I *pronounced* it to you, trippingly on the tongue; but if you *mouth* it, as many of your players do, I had as lief

---

g Orotund; moderate.   *h* Pure tone: joyous; long quality; orotund on the last words.

the *town crier* spoke my lines. Nor do not saw the air too much with your hand, *thus;* but use all gently: for in the very torrent, tempest, and (as I may say,) whirlwind of your passion, you must acquire and beget a temperance that may give it smoothness. O, it offends me to the soul, to hear a robustious, periwig-pated fellow tear a passion to tatters, to very rags, to split the ears of the groundlings; who, for the most part, are capable of nothing but inexplicable dumb shows and noise. I would have such a fellow whipped for o'erdoing Termagant; it out-herods Herod: pray you avoid it.

Be not too tame neither, but let your own discretion be your tutor: suit the action to the word, the word to the action, with this special observance, that you o'erstep not the modesty of nature; for anything so overdone is from the purpose of playing, whose end, both at the first, and now, was and is, to hold, as 'twere, the mirror up to nature, to show virtue her own feature, scorn her own image, and the very age and body of the time; his form and pressure. Now, this overdone, or come tardy off, though it make the unskillful laugh, cannot but make the judicious grieve; the censure of which the one, must, in your allowance, o'erweigh a whole theater of others. O, there be players that I have seen play,—and heard others praise, and that highly,—not to speak it profanely, that, neither having the accent of Christian, nor the gait of Christian, pagan, or Turk, have so strutted, and bellowed, that I have thought some of Nature's journeymen had made men, and not made them well, they imitated humanity so abominably.

DEFINITION OF ELOQUENCE.

WEBSTER.

When public bodies are to be addressed on momentous occasions, when great interests are at stake, and strong passions excited, nothing is valuable in speech, farther than it is connected with high intellectual and moral endowments. Clearness, force and earnestness are the qualities which produce conviction. True eloquence indeed does not consist in speech; it cannot be brought from far. Labor and learning may toil for it, but they toil for it in vain: words and phrases may be marshaled in every way, but they cannot compass it: it must exist in the man, in the subject, and in the occasion. Affected passion, intense expression, the pomp of declamation,— all may aspire after it; they cannot reach it: it comes, if it come at all, like the outbreaking of a fountain from the earth, or the bursting forth of volcanic fires, with spontaneous, original, native force.

EMPHASIS.

As in pronunciation we mark certain syllables with stress of voice which we call *accent*, so in reading we distinguish certain words by stress of voice, which is called emphasis. It is of three kinds, abrupt or radical, median or smooth, and vanishing Emphasis. By *radical*, we mean the sudden, emphatic force which is given to the first part of sound in speaking or reading; by *median*, that smooth or even sound applied to the middle of words; and *vanishing*, that last or ending sound. It is given with a sudden jerk or snap of the voice, on the last syllable of words in expressing revenge, scorn, defiance, anger, contempt.

Sometimes we have the radical and vanishing emphasis united; we distinguish that emphasis as compound.

We append a few selections and extracts for practice in Emphasis, and at the same time, would remind the student that this department of our subject cannot be learned from books. It is that natural variation in the utterance of sentences which exhibits thought, and gives the agreeable variety to the speech of those who understand its application. It is more than stress of voice. It requires feeling. The greatest emphasis is frequently exhibited, when there is least voice. It is both expressive and impressive utterance.

To apply Emphasis correctly, in reading or speaking, it is necessary to understand thoroughly the sentiments uttered, and to enter fully into the spirit of them. This is the only suggestion or rule that we give for Emphasis, and we are assured that the student will rarely fail in its application, if he observe this rule.

Let the student enter into the spirit of each quotation and selection, and emphasis will take care of itself.

The American Boy.

SON.

a Father, look up, and see that flag!
How gracefully it flies!
Those pretty stripes, they seem to be
A rainbow in the skies.

---

a Pure voice; high pitch; childlike; median emphasis.

FATHER.

b It is your country's flag, my boy,
And proudly drinks the light,
O'er ocean's wave, in foreign climes,
A symbol of our might.

SON.

Father, what fearful noise is that,
Now thundering in the clouds?
Why do they wave their hats,
And rush along in crowds?

FATHER.

It is the voice of cannonry,
The glad shouts of the free;
This is a day of memory,
'Tis FREEDOM'S JUBILEE!

SON.

I wish that *I* was now a man,
I'd free my country too,
And cheer as loudly as the rest;
But father, why don't *you?*

FATHER.

I'm getting old and weak; but still
My heart is big with joy;
I've witnessed many a day like this.
Shout you aloud, my boy!

SON.

c HURRAH, FOR FREEDOM'S JUBILEE!
God bless our native land!
And may *I* live to hold the boon
Of *freedom* in my hand.

FATHER.

d Well done, my boy, grow up, and love
The land that gave you birth, —
A land where Freedom loves to dwell, —
A paradise on earth.

---

b Orotund; low; manly. Medium emphasis.   *c* High pitch; joyous; compound emphasis.
d Orotund; moderate pitch; slow but bold.

APPEAL FOR EAST TENNESSEE.

EXTRACT FROM A SPEECH BY ANDREW JOHNSON, —1861.

a The amendments to the Constitution, which constitute the bill of rights, declare that "a well regulated militia being necessary to the security of a free State, the right of the people to keep and bear arms shall not be infringed." Our people are denied this right secured to them in their own Constitution, and the Constitution of the United States. We ask the Government to interpose to secure us this constitutional right. *b* We want the passes in our mountains opened; we want deliverance and protection for a down-trodden and oppressed people, who are struggling for their independence without arms. If we had had ten thousand stand of arms and ammunition when the contest commenced, we should have asked no further assistance. We have not got them. We are a rural people; we have villages and small towns—no large cities. Our population is homogeneous, industrious, frugal, brave, independent; but now harmless, and powerless, and oppressed by usurpers. *c* You may be too late in coming to our relief; or you may not come at all, though I do not doubt that you will come; they may trample us under foot; they may convert our plains into graveyards, and the caves of our mountains into sepulchres; but they will never take us out of the Union, or make us a land of slaves—no, never! *d* We intend to stand as firm as adamant, and as unyielding as our own majestic mountains that surround us. Yes, we will be as fixed and as immovable as are they upon their bases. We will stand as long as we can; and if we are overpowered, and liberty shall be driven from the land, we intend before she departs, to take the flag of our country, with a stalwart arm, a patriotic heart, and an honest head, and place it upon the summit of the loftiest and most majestic mountain. We intend to plant it there, and leave it, to indicate to the inquirer who may come in after times, the spot where the goddess of liberty lingered and wept for the last time, before she took her flight from a people once prosperous, free, and happy.

THE ATTEMPT TO SUBVERT THE UNION.

D. S. DICKINSON, —1861.

a This effort to divide the Union, and subvert the Government, whatever may be the pretence, is, in fact, a daring and dangerous crusade against

---

a Bold, but pure tone of commencing address.   *b* Orotund; high pitch. Slow but firm   *c* Orotund; compound emphasis; increase.   *d* Gestures elevated to points in circle above the head.

free institutions. It should be opposed by the whole power of a patriotic people, and crushed beyond the prospect of a resurrection; and to attain that end, the Government should be sustained in every just and reasonable effort to maintain the authority and integrity of the nation; to uphold and vindicate the supremacy of the Constitution, and the majesty of the laws by all lawful means; not grudgingly sustained, with one hesitating, shuffling, unwilling step forward to save appearances, and two stealthy ones backward to secure a seasonable retreat; nor with the shallow craft of a mercenary politician, calculating chances, and balancing between expedients, but with the generous alacrity and energy which have a meaning, and prove a loyal, a patriotic, a willing heart. It is not a question of administration′, but of a Government‵—not of politics′, but of patriotism‵—not of policy,′ but of principles‵ which uphold us all′—a question too great for party′—between the Constitution and the laws on one hand′, and misrule and anarchy on the other‵.

INFLECTIONS.

Mr. Richard Culver introduces Walker's Theory of Inflection, with the following suggestions:

"All vocal sounds may be divided into two kinds; namely, speaking sounds and musical sounds. Musical sounds are such as continue a given time on one precise point of the musical scale, or leap, as it were, from one note to another; while speaking sounds, instead of dwelling on the note they begin with, slide either upwards or downwards to the neighbouring notes without any perceptible or decisive rest on any: so that speaking and musical sounds are essentially distinct; the former being constantly in motion from the moment they commence; the latter being at rest for some given time, in one precise note.

The continual motion of speaking sounds makes it almost impossible for the ear to mark their several differences; and the difficulty of arresting them for examination has made almost all authors suppose it impossible to give any such distinct account of them as to be of use in speaking and reading; but whether words are pronounced in a high or low, in a loud or soft tone; whether they are pronounced swiftly or slowly, forcibly or feebly, with the tone of the passion or without it, they must necessarily be pronounced either sliding upwards or downwards, or else go into a monotone

----

a Pure voice; slow; middle pitch, as important narrative. Notice inflections towards the close and give the last words in bold declamatory style.

or song. When we consider this, we shall find that the primary division of speaking sounds is into the upward and downward slide of the voice; and that whatever other diversity of time, tone, or force is added to speaking, it must necessarily be conveyed by these two slides.

These two slides, or inflections of voice, therefore, are the axis, as it were, on which the force, variety, and harmony of speaking turns. They may be considered as the great outlines of pronunciation.

By the rising and falling inflection of the voice is not meant the pitch in which the whole word is pronounced, or that loudness or softness which may accompany any pitch; but the upward or downward slide which the voice makes, when the pronunciation of a word is finishing; and which may, therefore, not improperly be called the rising and falling inflection.

So important is a just mixture of these two inflections, that the moment they are neglected, our pronunciation becomes forceless and monotonous: *if the sense of a sentence require the voice to adopt the rising inflection, on any particular word, either in the middle or at the end of a phrase, variety and harmony demand the falling inflection on one of the preceding words; and, on the other hand, if emphasis, harmony, or a completion of sense, require the falling inflection on any word, the word immediately preceding, almost always, demands the rising inflection;* so that these inflections of voice are in an order nearly alternate.

We see then, that there are two inflections of voice, *Rising* and *Falling*, and that these are united to form the circumflexes, which are *Rising* and *Falling*.

These inflections depend upon the style of the composition or address, for their length. If the composition is to be read in pure voice, unimpassioned style, the inflections are moderately long. If grand, or sublime, or bold, requiring the orotund voice, the inflections will be long. If plaintive, or subdued, requiring the tremor voice, low pitch, or slow time, the inflection will be short.

If we understand the principle of utterance, that inflections alternate, we require to know which leads, and then the following cadence will take care of itself. We can decide which is the leading inflection by applying the following rule:

All complete or positive assertions have the falling inflection at the close. All incomplete, or negative sentences have the rising inflection at the close.

Sometimes, the principal word, which has the emphasis and the inflection, will not be the closing word in the sentence.

The reason of the above rule, for the closing inflections, is found in emphasis which controls all other rules in expressive reading.

Some who know what inflection a sentence requires, cannot give it. They need to practice the slides of the voice; in counting, for instance, as 1′ 1′ 2′ 2′ 3′ 3′ 4′ 4′, changing the inflections at pleasure. Then the same with the Vowel Elements; then the sub-vocals, until the voice is disciplined.

We append numerous examples of inflections, marked for practice:

EXAMPLES OF INFLECTIONS.

1.

As we cannot discern the shadow moving along the dial-plate′, so the advances we make in knowledge are only perceivable by the distance‵ gone over.

2.

Although I fear it may be a shame to be dismayed at the entrance of my discourse in defence of a most valiant man′; and that it no ways becomes me, while Milo is more concerned for the safety of the state than for himself, not to show the same greatness of mind in behalf of him′; yet this new form of prosecution terrifies my eyes, which, whatever way they turn, want the ancient custom of the former, and the former manner of trials‵.

Although, son Marcus, as you have now been a hearer of Cratippus for a year, and this at Athens, you ought to abound in the precepts and doctrines of philosophy, by reason of the great character, both of your instructor and the city, one of which can furnish you with knowledge, and the other with examples′; yet as I always, to my advantage, joined the Latin tongue with the Greek, and I have done it not only in oratory, but likewise in philosophy, I think you ought to do the same‵, that you may be equally conversant in both languages‵.

3.

If impudence prevailed as much in the forum and courts of justice as insolence does in the country and places of less resort′; Aulus Cæcina would submit as much to the impudence of Sextus Æbutius in this cause, as he did before to his insolence when assaulted‵ by him.

4.

Natural reason inclines men to mutual converse and society`: It implants in them a strong affection for those who spring` from them : It excites them to form communities, and join in public assemblies: And, for these ends, to endeavor to procure both the necessaries´ and conveniences` of life.

5.

COMMENCING SERIES.

EXAMPLE.

Lóve, jóy, peàce; long-súffering, géntleness, gòodness; fáith, méekness, témperánce, are the fruits of the Spìrit, and against suòh there is no làw.

6.

CONCLUDING SERIES.

EXAMPLE.

But the fruit of the Spirit is lóve, jóy, peàce ; long-súffering, géntleness, goodnèss ; fáith, méekness, tèmperance : — Against such there is no law.

7.

COMMENCING SERIES.

EXAMPLE.

Métaphors , enígmas, móttoes, párables; fáfbles, dreáms, visìons ; dramátic writings, burlèsque, and all methods of allúsion are comprehended in Mr. Locke's definition of wit, and Mr. Addison's short explanation of it.

8.

CONCLUDING SERIES.

EXAMPLES.

Mr. Locke's definition of wit, with this short explication, comprehends most of the species of wit; as, mètaphors, enìgmas, mòttoes, paràbles ; fà-bles, drèams, visìons ; dramátic writings, burlésque, and allùsion.

9.

We are always complaining our days are féw, and acting as though there should be no ènd of them.

I imagined that I was admitted into a long spacious gallery, which had one side covered with pieces, of all the famous painters who are now lív-ing ; and the other with the greatest masters who are dèad.

The wicked may indeed taste a malignant kind of pleasure, in those actions to which they are accustomed whilst in this life; but when they are removed from all those objects which are here apt to gratify them, they will naturally become their own tormentors.

The pleasures of the imagination are not so gross as those of sénse, nor so refined as those of the understànding.

10.

It was necessary for the world, that arts should be invented and impróved books written and transmitted to postérity, nations cónquered and civilized.

All other arts of perpetuating our ideas, except writing and printing, continue but a short time: statues can last but a few thousands of yèars, edifices féwer, and colors still fewer than èdifices.

Our lives, says Seneca, are spent either in doing nothing at àll, or in doing nothing to the púrpose, or in doing nothing that we òught to do.

11.

I conjure you by that which you profess
(Howe'er you come to know it) answer me;
Though you untie the winds and let them fight
Against the chùrches; though the yesty waves
Confound and swallow navigàtion up;
Though bladed corn be lodg'd and trees blown dòwn;
Though castles topple on their warder's héads;
Though palaces and pyramids do slope
Their heads to their foundàtions; though the treasure
Of nature's germins tumble altogèther,
Ev'n until destruction sícken, answer me
To what I ask you.

12.

So when the faithful pencil has design'd
Some bright idea of the master's mìnd,
Where a new world leaps out at his command,
And ready nature waits upon his hànd;
When the ripe colours soften and unite,
And sweetly melt into just shade and lìght;
When mellowing years their full perfection give,
C

And each bold figure just begins to lìve;
The treacherous colours the fair art betrays′,
And all the bright creátion fades awày.

13.

When the gay and smiling aspect of things has begun to leave the passage to a man's heart thus thoughtlessly unguàrded; when kind and caress-
ing looks of every object without, that can flatter his senses, have conspired
with the enemy within, to betray him and put him off his dèfence; when
music likewise hath lent her aid, and tried her power upon the pàssions;
when the voice of singing men, and the voice of singing women, with the
sound of the viol and the lute, have broke in upon his soul, and in some
tender notes have touched the secret spring of rápture, —that moment let
us dissect and look into his hèart, —see how vàin, how wèak, how émpty a
thing it is‵!

14.

Where, amid the dark clouds of Pagan philosophy, can he show us such
a clear prospect of a future stàte, the immortality of the sòul, the resurrection of the deàd, and the general júdgment, as in St. Paul's first Epistle to
the Corìnthians?

But to consider the Paradise Lost only as it regards our present subject;
what can be conceived greater than the battle of àngels, the majesty of
Messíàh, the stature and behaviour of Satan and his pèers? what more
beautiful than Pandemonium, Pàradise, Heaven‵, ‵Angels, ′Adam, and‵ Eve?
what more strange than the creation of the wòrld, the several metamor-
phoses of the fallen ángels, and the surprising adventures their leader meets
with in his search after Pàradise?

15.

But should these credulous infidels after all be in the right, and this pre-
tended revelation be all a fable; from believing it what hàrm could ensue?
Would it render princes more tyránnical, or subjects more ungóvernable;
the rich more insolent, or the poor more disórderly? Would it make
worse parents or childrén, husbands or wíves; masters or sérvants, friends
or néighbors? Or would it not make men more vìrtuous, and, consequently
more happy in èvery situation?

16.

Consider, I beseech you, what was the part of a faithful citizen, of a prudent, an active, and an honest minister? Was he not to secure Euboea as our defence against all attacks by séa? Was he not to make Bœtia our barrier on the mídland side? The cities bordering on Peloponnesus our bulwark on thát quarter? Was he not to attend with due precaution to the importation of corn, that this trade might be protected through all its progress up to our own hárbors? Was he not to cover those districts which we commanded, by seasonable detachments, as the Proconesus, the Chersonesus, and Ténedos? To exert himself in the assémbly for this purpose? While with equal zeal he laboured to gain others to our interest and alliance, as Byzantium, Abydos, and Eubœá? Was he not to cut off the best and most important resources of our enemies, and to supply those in which our country was deféctive? And all this you have gained by my counsels and my administration.

17.

Presumptuous man! the reason wouldst thou find,
Why form'd so wéak, so líttle, and so blínd?
First, if thou canst, the hàrder reason guess,
Why form'd no wéaker, blìnder, and no lèss.
Ask of thy mother, earth, why oaks are made
Taller and stronger than the weeds they shàde?
Or ask of yonder argent fields above,
Why Jove's satellites are less than Jòve?

18.

A parenthesis must be pronounced in a lower tone of voice than the principal sentence, and conclude with the same pause and inflection which terminates the member that immediately precedes it.

EXAMPLES.

It is this sense which furnishes the imagination with its ideas; so that by the pleasure of the imagination or fáncy (which I shall use promiscuously) I here mean such as arise from visible objects.

Natural historians obsérve (for while I am in the country I must fetch my allusions from thénce) that only·male birds have voices; that their songs begin a little before breeding-time, and end a little after.

Notwithstanding all this care of Cicero, history informs us that Marcus proved a mere blockhead; and that náture (who it seems was even with the son for her prodigality to the fáther) rendered him incapable of improving, by all the rules of eloquence, the precepts of philosophy, his own endeavors, and the most refined conversation in Athens.

19.

But when the intervening member goes farther than these simple phrases, they must always be pronounced in a lower tone of voice, and terminate with the rising inflection.

EXAMPLE.

I had létters from him (here I felt in my póckets) that exactly spoke the Czar's character, which I knew perfectly well.

Young master was alive last Whitsuntide, said the coachman. Whitsuntide! alàs! cried Trim, (extending his right arm and falling instantly into the same attitude in which he read the sérmon,) what is Whitsuntide, Jónathan, (for that was the coachman's náme,) or Shrovetide, or any tide or time past, to this? Are we not here nów, continued the córporal, (striking the end of his stick perpendicularly upon the floor, so as to give an idea of health and stabílity,) and are we nót (dropping his hat upon the ground) gone in a móment?

20.

A company of waggish boys were watching of frogs at the side of the pond, and still as any of them put up their heads, they would be pelting them down again with stones: "Children," (says one of the frogs,) "you never consider, that though this may be play to you, it is death to us."

21.

My departure is objected to me, which charge I cannot answer without commending myself. For what must I sày? That I fled from a conscious-ss of guílt? But what is charged upon me as a crime, was so far from being a fault, that it is the most glorious action since the memory of màn. That I feared being called to au account by the péople? That was never tàlked of; and if it had been done, I should have come off with double hònour. That I wanted the support of good and honest mén? That is fàlse. That I was afraid of déath? That is a càlumny. I must, therefore, say what I would not, unless compelled to it´, that I withdraw to preserve the cìty.

THE CIRCUMFLEX.

The Circumflex is a union of the inflections, and is of two kinds, *Rising and Falling.* It is governed by the same principle; that is, positive assertions of irony, raillery, etc., will have the falling Circumflex, and all negative assertions of double meaning, will have the rising.

Doubt, pity, contrast, grief, supposition, comparison, irony, implication, sneering, raillery, scorn, reproach, and *contempt,* are expressed by them. Be sure and get the right *feeling* and *thought,* and you will find no difficulty in *expressing* them properly, if you have mastered the *voice.*

Both these circumflex inflections may be exemplified in the word *so,* in a speech of the Clown in Shakespeare's "*As You Like it.*"

1. I knew when seven justices could not take up a quarrel; but when the parties were met themselves, one of them thought but of an If; as if you said sŏ, then I said sô. Oh hô! did you say sŏ? So they shook hands and were sworn friends.

2. The queen of *Denmark,* in reproving her son, *Hamlet,* on account of his conduct towards his *step*-father, whom she married, shortly after the murder of the *king,* her *husband,* says to him, "*Hamlet,* you have your father *much* offended." To which he replies, with a circumflex on *you,* "*Madam, yôu*—have my father mŭch offended." *He* meant his *own* father; *she*—his *step*-father; he would *also* intimate, that she was *accessory* to his father's *murder;* and his peculiar reply was like *daggers* in her *soul.*

3. In the following reply of *Death* to *Satan,* there is a frequent occurrence of *circumflexes,* mingled with *contempt:* 'And recon'st *thou thyself* with *spirits* of heăven, hell-dŏomed, and breath'st *defiance here,* and *scorn,* where I reign kĭng? and, to enrage thee *more,* — *th*ᵛ*y* king, and *lŏrd!*' The voice is circumflexed on *heaven, hell-doomed, king,* and *thy,* nearly an octave.

HAMLET TO LAERTES.

3. Zounds! show me what thoul't do: woul't *wĕep?* woul't *fig*ᵛ*ht?* woul't fast? woul't *teăr* thyself? I'll do it. Dost thou come here to *whĭne?* to outface *mĕ,* with leaping in her *grăve?* be buried *quick* with her, and so will *I*ᐱ*;* and if thou prate of *moun*ᵛ*tains,* let them throw MIL^LIONS of acres on us, till our ground, singeing her pate against the burning *zone,* make *Ossa* like a *wart.* Nay, and thoul't mouthe, *I'll* rant as well as *thôu.*

FURTHER EXAMPLES IN CIRCUMFLEX.

1. They tell ûs to be moderate, but thĕy revel in profusion.
2. Most courteous tyrants! Româns! Râre patterns of humanity!
3. So evĕn ran his line of life, his neighbors thought it ôdd.
4. Is thy servant a dŏg, that he should do this great thing?

5. They will give us peăce! Yes; such pĕace as the wŏlf gives to the lămb—the kīte to the dôve.

6. Talk to me of danger? Death and shame! Is not my race as high, as ancient, aṅd as proud as thine?

7. Thêy follow an adventurer whom they fêar, and obey a power which they hate; wĕ serve a monarch whom we lŏve,—a God whom we adore.

THE MONOTONE.

The Monotone is sameness of sound, arising from repeating the several words or syllables of a passage in one and the same general tone.

The Monotone is employed in the delivery of a passage that is solemn or sublime.

EXAMPLES.

1. Măn thăt īs bŏrn ŏf wŏmăn, īs ŏf fĕw dăys ănd fŭll ŏf trŏuble. Hē cōmĕth fŏrth līke ā flōwĕr, ānd īs cūt dŏwn; hĕ flĕĕth ălsō ăs ā shădōw, ānd cōntīnūĕth nŏt.

2. Măn dīĕth, ănd wāstĕth āwāy: yĕā, măn gīvĕth ūp thĕ ghŏst, ănd whĕre īs hĕ? As thĕ wāters fāīl frŏm thĕ sĕā, ănd thĕ flōŏd dĕcāyĕth ānd drīĕth ūp, sŏ· măn līĕth dŏwn, ănd rīsĕth nŏt; till thĕ hĕāvĕns bĕ nō mōrē, thĕy shăll nŏt āwāke, ṅŏr bĕ rāīsed ŏŭt ŏf thĕīr slĕĕp.

3. Fŏr thūs sāith thĕ ·hīgh ănd lŏfty ōne that īnhăbītĕth ĕtērnīty, whōse nāme īs Hōly, I dwĕll īn thĕ hīgh ānd ·hōly plăce.

4. Lŏrd thŏu hăst bĕĕn ōūr dwĕllīng-plăce īn āll gēnērātīōns. Bĕfōre thĕ mōūntaīns wĕre brŏught fŏrth, ŏr ĕvēr thŏū hădst fŏrmed thĕ ēarth ănd thĕ wŏrld, ĕvĕn frŏm ĕvĕrlāstĭng tō ĕvĕrlāstīng, Thŏu ărt Gŏd.—*Bible.*

PAUSES.

We have seen that the art of Elocution is the application of that system of rules which teaches us to pronounce written composition with justness, energy, variety, and ease. Agreeably to this definition, reading may be considered as that species of delivery which not only expresses the sense of an author, so as barely to be understood, but which, at the same time, gives it all that force, beauty, delicacy, and variety of which it is susceptible; the first consideration depends upon *grammatical pauses* which separate clauses, sentences, and paragraphs according to their sense—the last depends much upon rhetorical pauses which are introduced to give expression to the words of an author.

Thus we have two kinds of pauses — *Grammatical* and *Rhetorical.* We have also pauses peculiar to poetry, and designed to increase the beauty and melody of verse; they are termed *harmonic.* These are usually considered as two; the one being called *cæsural,* and the other the *final* harmonic pause.

The length of pauses are not fixed and invariable, and so cannot be brought under precise rules. There are, however, a few general principles which may be safely observed as far as they have application.

One is that the pause should be proportioned to the rate of utterance — the intervals of rest being comparatively long when the rate is slow, and short when it is quick.

RULES FOR RHETORICAL PAUSES.

1. A long pause may be made before or after a word expressive of intense feeling.

2. A slight pause should mark an ellipsis or omission of a word.

3. After words, placed in opposition to each other, there should be a pause.

4. A pause is required between the parts of a sentence which may be transposed.

5. Before and after an intervening phrase, there should be a short pause.

6. Before conjunctions, or prepositions and similes a pause is usually required.

7. There should be a pause before a verb in the infinitive mood, depending upon another verb.

8. Before the relative pronouns, who, which, that, and what, a pause is generally necessary.

9. An adjective placed after its noun, should be separated from it by a short pause.

10. A pause is required after the nominative case, when it is emphatic or consists of more than one word.

The following examples, numbered to correspond with the foregoing rules, will illustrate more fully the effect of appropriate rhetorical pauses :

    1.   Banished | from Rome ! What's banished, but set free ?

           And their young voices rose | A VENGEANCE CRY TO GOD !

           And made | *me* | a poor orphan boy.

    2.   Their palaces were houses not made with hands; their diadems | crowns of glory.

To our faith we should add virtue; and to virtue | knowledge ; and to knowledge | temperance ; and to temperance | patience ; and to patience | godliness ; and to godliness | brotherly kindness ; and to brotherly kindness | charity.

3. The morn | was bright, but the eve | was clouded and dark.
    Some | place the bliss in action | some in ease;
    Those | call it pleasure, and contentment | these.

4. With famine and death | the destroying angel came.
    To whom | the Goblin, full of wrath, replied.
    The pangs of memory are | to madness | wrought.

6. I have watched their pastimes | and their labors.
    We must not yield | to their foolish entreaties.
    He continued steadfast | like the spring-time.

7. He daily strove | to elevate their condition.
    Do not dare | to lay your hands on the constitution.
    I had hoped | to have had an opportunity to oblige so good a friend.

8. Let us look forward to the end of that century | which has commenced.

        Spirit | that breathest through my lattice, thou |
        That cool'st the twilight of the sultry day.
        His natural instinct discovers | what knowledge can perform.

There is not a great author here | who did not write for us; not a man of science | who did not investigate for us. We have received advantages from every hour of toil | that ever made these great and good men weary.

9. He was a man—contented, virtuous, and happy.
    I behold its summit | noble and sublime.

10. A remarkable affair | happened yesterday.
    To be devoid of sense | is a terrible misfortune.
    Industry is the guardian of innocence.

PERSONATION.

We should give especial attention to the change of voice in personation. In public reading and declamation it is of great importance, but is generally overlooked, or but little practiced. The narrative, or descriptive sentences leading to the personation, will depend for *force*, *pitch*, and *time*, upon the character of the ideas in the personation. For instance, if a death scene is being given as in "Poor Little Jim;" the pitch will be low, and diminish until the words, uttered by the dying boy are reached. Then with pure voice, slightly tremor; pitch moderate and time slow, with a pause between the narrative and the quoted words, the speaker will say:

NOTE—The rules for pauses should be applied on the above example, until they are thoroughly understood by the student.

"Tell father when he comes from work, I said good night to him, and mother, now-I'll-go-to-sleep."

The last words very soft and hesitating utterance.

Before this example is another in the same selection, not quite so marked, which we give, from third verse. She gets her answer from the child; soft fall the words from him:

"Mother, the angels do so smile and beckon little Jim;
I have no pain, dear mother, now, but O! I am so dry,
Just moisten poor Jim's lips again, and mother, don't you cry."
With gentle, trembling haste, he held the liquid to his lips, etc.

That which is quoted is supposed to be uttered by the dying child, and cannot be given effectively without the changes in voice, etc., referred to above.

If the climax of the narrative is a battle scene, and the personation represents an officer giving the command to charge, as in "The Light Brigade," then the most marked change will be made in the voice, between the descriptive and the personation.

"Forward the light brigade; take the guns!" demands *full force; quick* time and *high pitch;* compound stress, and the descriptive preceding it will commence with moderate pitch, moderate time (increasing) and medium force, with median stress.

We give a number of examples for the practice of the transitions, necessary in Personation.

(per.)   "Stand to your guns men!" Morris cried.
        Small need to pass the word;
(desc.) Our men at quarters ranged themselves
        Before the drum was heard.

The pitch should fall three notes at least, on the words "Morris cried," and raised but slightly on the remainder of the stanza.

(desc.) And when Peter saw it he answered unto the people: "Ye men
(per.)   of Israel, why marvel ye at this? or, why look ye so earnestly
        on us, as though by our own power or authority we had made
        this man to walk," etc.

To read the Bible acceptably in public, requires the application of every principle in elocution, for nowhere is *expression* so richly rewarded as in the pronunciation of the sacred text. The descriptive and personation should be so distinctly marked that the attention would be at once attracted to the different styles, and the meaning understood.

(desc.) And hark! the deep voices replying
     From the graves where your fathers are lying.

(per.)   "Swear, Oh! swear."

(per.)   "Have you forgotten, General," the battered soldier cried
     "The days of eighteen hundred twelve, when I was at your side.
     Have you forgotten Johnson, that fought at Lundy's Lane;
     It's true I'm old and pensioned, but I want to fight again."

The voice of old age, "piping and whistling in its sound," is easily given if the practice upon the elements has been thorough; even ventriloquism, or ventriloquial power may be acquired by the practice of personation; change of pitch; exploding of elements, etc. The exercise on the elements for this purpose, is what Prof. Bronson calls "swallowing the elements."

And then began the sailors jests:

(per.)   "What thing is that, I say?
    A long-shore meeting-house adrift
    Is standing down the bay!"
    * * * * * * * * * _____

(desc.) We reached the deck.   There Randall stood;

(per.) "Another turn, men, — so!"

(desc.) Calmly he aimed his pivot gun;

(per.) "Now, Tenny, let her go!"

(des.) Brave Randall leaped upon the gun,
    And waved his cap in sport;

(per.) "Well done! Well aimed! I saw that shell
    Go through an open port."

(nar.) I remember once, riding from Buffalo to Niagara Falls, and I said
    to a gentleman: "What river is that sir?"
    "That," *said he*, "is Niagara River." (Give "said he," in a
    whisper at first in the practice, until the pitch can be changed
    naturally.)

(des.) Suddenly some one cries out from the bank,—

(per.) "Young man, ahoy!" (Very loud.)
    "What is it?" (A different voice.)
    "The rapids are below you!" (First voice again.)
    Ha! ha! ha! —————.   We have heard of the rapids, but we
    are not such fools to get into them.
    Young man, ahoy there! (First voice again.)

The selection from which this extract is taken is excellent for the practice of transition and personation, and any one who has heard Mr. Gough, will acknowledge the power of this principle.

In reading a colloquy between two or more persons, recognize the fact that the faces of the speakers must be turned towards each other; and as you change from the utterances of one to the other, turn the face slightly or boldly, as the character of the colloquy may indicate.

These exercises in personation are so frequent in the selections, that further examples do not seem necessary.

The Study of Expression.

The practice of reading or reciting aloud, selections containing different emotions and passions, secures variety of expression. The student should try to personate the passion, or enter so fully into the meaning of the quotation that he will vary the *pitch, force,* and *voice* to correspond with the emotion.

The following extracts from Shakespeare and Milton are so forcible and natural, that the student may succeed in giving them well by practice, without the assistance of the living model.

The organs of speech should be so disciplined as to adapt themselves naturally and easily to all the changes, even the most abrupt and frequent, that are required in continuous reading or speaking. This comprehends the particulars in the above analysis and secures variety of *expression*, which is the great object to be gained by the student of elocution.

LAUGHTER ON SEEING A BUFFOON.

A Fool, a Fool! I met a Fool i' th' forest,
A motley Fool. A miserable world! —
As I do live by food, I met a Fool,
Who laid him down and bask'd him in the sun,
And rail'd on Lady Fortune in good terms,
In good set terms, — and yet a motley Fool.
"Good morrow, Fool," quoth I. "No, sir," quoth he,
"Call me not Fool, till heav'n hath sent me fortune;"
And then he drew a dial from his poke,
And, looking on it with lack-lustre eye,
Says, very wisely, "it is ten o'clock:
Thus we may see," quoth he, "how the world wags:

'Tis but an hour ago since it was nine,
And after one hour more 'twill be eleven ;
And so, from hour to hour, we ripe and ripe,
And then, from hour to hour, we rot and rot ;
And thereby hangs a tale."   When I did hear
The motley Fool thus moral on the time,
My lungs began to crow like chanticleer,
That fools should be so deep-contemplative ;
And I did laugh, sans intermission,
An hour by his dial. —O, noble fool !
A worthy fool !   Motley's the only wear.—*As you Like it.*

INVOCATION OF THE GODDESS OF MIRTH.

But come, thou goddess fair and free,
In heaven yclep'd Euphrosyne,
And by men, heart-easing Mirth ;
Whom lovely Venus at a birth,
With two sister Graces more,
To ivy-crown'd Bacchus bore.
Haste thee, nymph, and bring with thee
Jest, and youthful jollity,
Quips, and cranks, and wanton wiles,
Nods, and becks, and wreathed smiles,
Such as hang on Hebe's cheek,
And love to live in dimples sleek ;
Sport, that wrinkled Care derides,
And Laughter holding both his sides.
Come, and trip it as you go,
On the light fantastic toe ;
And in thy right hand lead with thee
The mountain-nymph, sweet Liberty.—*Milton's L'Allegro.*

JOY EXPECTED.

Ah, Juliet ! if the measure of thy joy
Be heap'd like mine, and that thy skill be more
To blazon it, then sweeten with thy breath
This neighbor air, and let rich music's tongue
Unfold the imagin'd happiness that both
Receive.—*Romeo and Juliet.*

JOY APPROACHING TO TRANSPORT.

Oh! joy, thou welcome stranger, twice three years
I have not felt thy vital beam, but now
It warms my veins, and plays about my heart,
A fiery instinct lifts me from the ground,
And I could mount.— *Dr. Young's Revenge.*

JOY APPROACHING TO FOLLY.

Come, let us to the castle.—
News, friends; our wars are done, the Turks are drown'd.
How does my old acquaintance of this isle?—
Honey, you shall be well desired in Cyprus,
I have found great love amongst them.   O my sweet,
I prattle out of fashion, and I dote
In mine own comforts.—*Othello.*

JOY BORDERING ON SORROW.

O, my soul's joy!
If after every tempest come such calms,
May the winds blow till they have waken'd death;
And let the laboring bark climb hills of seas
Olympus-high, and duck again as low
As hell's from heaven!   If it were now to die,
'Twere now to be most happy; for, I fear,
My soul hath her content so absolute,
That not another comfort like to this
Succeeds in unknown fate.— *Othello.*

DELIGHT ON VIEWING A STATUE.

Leon.—See, my lord,
Would you not deem it breath'd? and that those veins
Did verily bear blood?

Paul.   My lord's almost so far transported that
He'll think anon it lives.

Leon.   O sweet Paulina,
Make me to think so twenty years together;
No settled senses of the world can match
The pleasure of that madness.— *The Winter's Tale.*

DELIGHT IN LOVE

What you do
Still betters what is done. When you speak, sweet,
I'd have you do it ever; When you sing,
I'd have you buy and sell so; so give alms;
Pray so; and, for the ord'ring your affairs,
To sing them too: When you do dance, I wish you
A wave o' th' sea, that you might ever do
Nothing but that; move still, still so,
And own no other function. Each your doing,
So singular in each particular,
Crowns what you are doing in the present deeds,
That all your acts are queens.—*The Winter's Tale.*

PROTESTATION IN LOVE.

O, hear me breathe my life
Before this ancient sir, who, it should seem,
Hath some time loved: I take thy hand; this hand,
As soft as dove's down, and as white as it,
Or Ethiopian's tooth, or the fann'd snow,
That's bolted by the northern blasts twice o'er.—*Winter's Tale.*

PITY FOR A DEPARTED FRIEND.

Alas, poor Yorick!—I knew him, Horatio: a fellow of infinite jest, of
most excellent fancy: He hath borne me on his back a thousand times.
And now, how abhorred my imagination is! my gorge rises at it: Here
hung those lips that I have kissed I know not how oft. Where be your
gibes now? Your gambols? Your songs? Your flashes of merriment,
that were wont to set the table on a roar? Not one now, to mock your own
grinning? Quite chop-fallen? Now, get you to my lady's chamber, and
tell her, let her paint an inch thick, to this favor she must come; make her
laugh at that.—*Hamlet.*

HATRED CURSING THE OBJECT HATED.

Poison be their drink!
Gall, worse than gall, the daintiest that they taste!
Their sweetest shade, a grove of cypress trees!
Their chiefest prospect murthering·basilisks!
Their softest touch, as smart as lizard's stings!

Their music frightful as the serpent's hiss,
And boding screech-owls make the concert full!
All the foul terrors in dark-seated hell!—*Henry VI.*

HOPE OF GOOD TIDINGS.

O Hope! sweet flatterer, whose delusive touch
Sheds on afflicted minds the balm of comfort;
Relieves the load of poverty; sustains
The captive bending with the weight of bonds,
And smooths the pillow of disease and pain;
Send back the exploring messenger with joy,
And let me hail thee from that friendly grove.—*Glover's Boadicea.*

RAGE.

Grace me no grace, nor uncle me no uncle:
I am no traitor's uncle; and that word, grace,
In an ungracious mouth, is but profane.
Why have those banished and forbidden legs
Dared once to touch a dust of England's ground?
But then, more why,—why have they dared to march
So many miles upon her peaceful bosom,
Frighting her pale-faced villages with war,
And ostentation of despised arms?
Coms't thou because th' anointed King is hence?
Why, foolish boy, the King is left behind,
And in my loyal bosom lies his power.
Were I but now the lord of such hot youth,
As when, brave Gaunt, thy father, and myself,
Rescued the Black Prince, that young Mars of men,
From forth the ranks of many thousand French,
O, then, how quickly should this arm of mine,
Now prisoner to the palsy, chastise thee,
And minister correction to thy faults!—*Richard II.*

EAGER REVENGE.

O, I could play the woman with mine eyes,
And braggart with my tongue.—But, gentle Heavens,
Cut short all intermission; front to front,
Bring thou this fiend of Scotland and myself;
Within my sword's length set him; if he 'scape,
Heaven forgive him too!—*Macbeth.*

Unrestrained Fury.

Alive! in triumph! and Mercutio slain!
Away to Heaven, respective lenity,
And fire-ey'd fury be my conduct now! —
Now, Tybalt, take the villain back again,
That late thou gav'st me; for Mercutio's soul
Is but a little way above our heads,
Staying for thine to keep him company:
And thou, or I, or both, must go with him.— *Romeo and Juliet.*

Reproach with Want of Manliness.

O, proper stuff!
This is the very painting of your fear:
This is the air-drawn dagger which, you said,
Led you to Duncan.   O, these flaws and starts
(Impostors to true fear) would well become
A woman's story at a winter's fire,
Authoriz'd by her grandam.   Shame itself!
Why do you make such faces?   When all's done,
You look but on a stool.— *Macbeth.*

Terror before Dreadful Actions Described

Between the acting of a dreadful thing,
And the first motion, all the interim is
Like a phantasma, or a hideous dream:
The Genius, and the mortal instruments,
Are then in council; and the state of man,
Like a little kingdom, suffers then
The nature of an insurrection.— *Julius Cæsar.*

Horror at a Dreadful Apparition.

How ill this taper burns!—Ha! who comes here?
I think it is the weakness of mine eyes
That shapes this monstrous apparition.
It comes upon me.—Art thou any thing?
Art thou some god, some angel, or some devil,
That mak'st my blood cold, and my hair to stare?
Speak to me, what thou art.— *Julius Cæsar.*

Silent Grief.

Seems, madam! nay, it is; I know not seems
'Tis not alone my inky cloak, good mother,
No, nor the fruitful river in the eye,
Nor the dejected 'haviour of the visage,
Together with all forms, modes, shows of grief,
That can denote me truly: these, indeed, seem,
For they are actions that a man might play;
But I have that within, which passeth show;
These but the trappings and suits of wo.— *Hamlet.*

Fear of being Discovered a Murderer.

Alack! I am afraid they have awak'd,
And 'tis not done:—th' attempt, and not the deed,
Confounds us.—Hark!—I laid their daggers ready;
He could not miss 'em.—Had he not resembled
My father as he slept, I had done't.—*Macbeth.*

Grief Choking Expression.

Macd. My children too?
Rosse. Wife, children, servants, all that could be found.
Macd. And I must be from thence! My wife kill'd, too?
Rosse. I have said.
Mal. Be comforted:
Let's make us med'cines of our great revenge,
To cure this deadly grief.
Macd. He has no children.—All my pretty ones?
Did you say all?—O, hell-kite!—All?
What, all my pretty chickens and their dam
At one fell swoop?
Mal. Dispute it like a man.
Macd. I shall do so;
But I must also feel it as a man:
I cannot but remember such things were,
That were most precious to me.—Did Heaven look on,
And would not take their part? Sinful Macduff!
They were all struck for thee. Naught that I am!
Not for their own demerits, but for mine,
Fell slaughter on their souls.— *Macbeth.*
D

BOASTING INDIGNANT CHALLENGE.

'Swounds ! show me what thou'lt do :
Woul't weep ? woul't fight ? woul't fast ? woul't tear thyself ?
I'll do 't. — Dost thou come here to whine ?
To outface me with leaping in her grave ? .
Be buried quick with her, and so will I :
And, if thou prate of mountains, let them throw
Millions of acres on us, till our ground,
Singeing his pate against the burning zone,
Make Ossa like a wart !   Nay, an thou'lt mouth,
I'll rant as well as thou.— *Hamlet.*

VEXATION AT NEGLECTING ONE'S DUTY

O, what a rogue and peasant slave am I !
Is it not monstrous, that this player here,
But in a fiction, in a dream of passion,
Could force his soul so to his own conceit,
That, from her working, all his visage wann'd ;
Tears in his eyes, distraction in 's aspect,
A broken voice, and his whole function suiting
With forms to his conceit ?   And all for nothing !
For Hecuba ?
What's Hecuba to him, or he to Hecuba,
That he should weep for her ? — *Hamlet.*

DESPAIR.

Shakespeare has most exquisitely touched this fearful situation of human
nature, when he draws Cardinal Beaufort, after a wicked life, dying in
despair, and terrified with the murder of Duke Humphrey, to which he was
accessory.

     K. Hen. How fares my lord ? speak, Beaufort, to thy sovereign
     Car. If thou be'st Death, I'll give thee England's treasure,
Enough to purchase such another island,
So thou wilt let me live and feel no pain.
     K. Hen. Ah, what a sign it is of evil life,
Where death's approach is seen so terrible !
     War. Beaufort, it is thy sovereign speaks to thee.
     Car. Bring me unto my trial when you will.
Died he not in his bed ?   Where should he die ?
Can I make men live, whe'r they will or no ? —

O, torture me no more! I will confess.—
Alive again? then show me where he is;
I'll give a thousand pounds to look upon him;
He hath no eyes, the dust hath blinded them.
Comb down his hair : look! look! it stands upright,
Like lime-twigs set to catch my winged soul.—
Give me some drink ; and bid the apothecary
Bring the strong poison that I bought of him.
 K. Hen. O, thou Eternal Mover of the Heavens,
Look with a gentle eye upon this wretch!
O, beat away the busy meddling fiend,
That lays strong siege unto this wretch's soul,
And from his bosom purge this black despair.
 War. See how the pangs of death do make him grin.
 Sal. Disturb him not, let him pass peaceably.
 K. Hen. Peace to his soul, if God's good pleasure be.
Lord Card'nal, if thou think'st on Heaven's bliss,
Hold up thy hand, make signal of thy hope.—
He dies, and makes no sign.   O God, forgive him!
—2d part Henry VI.

The bare situation of the characters, the pause, and the few plain words
of King Henry, "*He dies, and makes no sign!*" have more of the real sublime
in them, than volumes of the labored speeches in most of our modern trag-
edies, which, in the emphatical language of Shakespeare, may be said to
be "full of sound and fury, signifying nothing."

ENVY.

Aside the devil turn'd

For envy, yet, with jealous leer malign,
Eyed them askance, and to himself thus plain'd.
Sight hateful, sight tormenting! thus these two,
Imparadised in one another's arms,
The happier Eden, shall enjoy their fill
Of bliss on bliss; while I to hell am thrust,
Where neither joy nor love, but fierce desire,
Among our other torments not the least,
Still unfulfill'd with pain of longing pines.—*Paradise Lost.*

ENVY AMOUNTING TO HATRED.

How like a fawning publican he looks!

I hate him for he is a Christian;
But more for that, in low symplicity,
He lends out money gratis, and brings down
The rate of usance here with us in Venice.
If I can catch him once upon the hip,
I will feed fat the ancient grudge I bear him.
He hates our sacred nation; and he rails,
Even there where merchants most do congregate,
On me, my bargains, and my well-won thrift,
Which he calls interest. Cursed be my tribe,
If I forgive him.—*Merchant of Venice.*

EXHORTING.

But wherefore do you droop? why look you sad?
Be great in act, as you have been in thought;
Let not the world see fear, and sad distrust
Govern the motion of a kingly eye:
Be stirring as the time; be fire with fire;
Threaten the threatener, and outface the brow
Of bragging horror: so shall inferior eyes,
That borrow their behavior from the great,
Grow great by your example, and put on
The dauntless spirit of resolution.
Away! and glister like the god of war,
When he intendeth to become the field:
Show boldness and aspiring confidence.
What! shall they seek the lion in his den,
And fright him there? and make him tremble there?
O, let it not be said.—Forage, and run
To meet displeasure farther from the doors,
And grapple with him ere he come so nigh.—*King John.*

SURPRISE IN JEALOUSY COMMENCING.

Think, my lord!
By Heaven, he echoes me,
As if there were some monster in his thought
Too hideous to be shown.—Thou dost mean something.
I heard thee say but now,—thou lik'dst not that,
When Cassio left my wife: what did'st not like?
And, when I told thee, he was of my counsel

In my whole course of wooing, thou cried'st, "Indeed!"
And did'st contract and purse thy brow together,
As if thou then had'st shut up in thy brain
Some horrible conceit. If thou dost love me,
Show me thy thought.— *Othello.*

JEALOUSY MIXED WITH RAGE AND REGRET.

The fellow's of exceeding honesty,
And knows all qualities with a learn'd spirit
Of human dealings. If I do prove her haggard,
Though that her jesses were my dear heart-strings,
I'd whistle her off, and let her down the wind,
To prey at fortune. Haply, for I am black,
And have not those soft parts of conversation
That chamberers have ; or, for I am declin'd
Into the vale of years ;—yet, that's not much :—
She's gone ; I am abus'd ; and my relief
Must be to loathe her. O curse of marriage,
That we can call these delicate creatures ours,
And not their appetites ! I had rather be a toad,
And live upon the vapour of a dungeon,
Than keep a corner in the thing I love
For others' uses.— *Othello.*

This collection of extracts is sufficient for our purpose, and will prove a valuable aid to the student in vocalization for the purpose of securing *varied expression.* The best selections in modern speeches have many of the passions combined in them, and, like the voices, they shade into each other so constantly that great care is necessary to observe them, and great practice in order to be able to express them.

The student should not fail to commit to memory the exercise for declamation. This he *can do*, and if he does not, the principles of expression will be of little use to him, as all the energy is directed to the recollection of the words, and he cannot give expression to the ideas. The words should be perfectly familiar, then the soul will cause them to breath and burn with the fire of thought.

SELECTIONS.

EVERETT'S VINDICATION OF AMERICA, — 1863.

In the factories of Europe there is machinery of American invention or improvement; in their observatories, telescopes of American construction, and apparatus of American invention for recording the celestial phenomena. America contests with Europe the introduction into actual use of the electric telegraph, and her mode of operating it is adopted throughout the French empire. American authors in almost every department are found on the shelves of European libraries. It is true no American Homer, Virgil, Dante, Copernicus, Shakespeare, Bacon, Milton, Newton, has risen on the world. These mighty geniuses seem to be exceptions in the history of the human mind. Favorable circumstances do not produce them, nor does the absence of favorable circumstances prevent their appearance. Homer rose in the dawn of Greek culture, Virgil flourished in the court of Augustus, Dante ushered in the birth of the new European civilization, Copernicus was reared in a Polish cloister, Shakespeare was trained in the green room of the theatre, Milton was formed while the elements of English thought and life were fermenting towards a great political and moral revolution, Newton under the profligacy of the restoration. Ages may elapse before any country will produce a man like these, as two centuries have passed since the last mentioned of them were born. But if it is really a matter of reproach to the United States, that in the comparatively short period of their existence as a people, they have not added another name to the illustrious list (which is equally true of all the other nations of the earth,) they may proudly boast of one example of life and character, one career of disinterested service, one model of public virtue, the type of human excellence, of which all the countries and all the ages may be searched in vain for the parallel. I need not—

on this day I need not — speak the peerless name. It is stamped on your hearts, it glistens in your eyes, it is written on every page of your history, on the battle-fields of the Revolution, on the monuments of your fathers, on the portals of your Capitols. It is heard in every breeze that whispers over the fields of independent America. And he was all our own. He grew upon the soil of America; he was nurtured at her bosom. She loved and trusted him in his youth; she honored and revered him in his age; and though she did not wait for death to canonize his name, his precious memory, with each succeeding year, has sunk more deeply into the hearts of his countrymen.

II.

THE TEMPERANCE DRINK.

Water! oh, bright, beautiful water for me. Water! heaven-gifted, earth-blessing, flower-loving water! It was the drink of Adam in the purity of his Eden home — it mirrored back the beauty of Eve in her unblushing toilet — it wakens to life again the crushed and fading flower — it cools, oh, how gratefully! the parched tongue of the feverish invalid — it falls down to us in pleasant showers from its home in the glittering stars — it descends to us in feathery storms of snow — it smiles in shining dew-drops at the glad birth of morning — it clusters in great tear-drops at night over the graves of those we love — its name is wreathed in strange, bright colors by the sunset cloud — its name is breathed by the dying soldier, far away on the torrid field of battle — it paints old forts and turrets, from a gorgeous easel, on your winter window — it clings upon the branches of trees in frost-work of delicate beauty — it dwells in the icicle — it lives in the mountain glacier — it forms the vapory ground-work upon which God paints the rainbow — it gushes in pearly streams from the gentle hillside — it makes glad the sunny vales — it murmurs cheerful songs in the ear of the humble cottager — it answers back the smiles of happy children — it kisses the pure cheek of the water lily — it wanders like a vein of molten silver away, away to the distant sea — oh, bright, beautiful, health-inspiring, heart-gladdening water ! Everywhere around us dwelleth thy meek presence — twin angel sister of all that is good and precious here — in the wild forest — on the grassy plain — slumbering in the bosom of the lonely mountain — sailing with viewless wings through the humid air — floating over us in curtains of more than regal splendor — home of the healing angel when his wings bend to the woes of this fallen world

> " Oh, water, pure water, bright water for me,
> And wine for the trembling debauchee !"

III.

THE OATH.

BY THOMAS BUCHANAN REED.

a Ye freemen, how long will ye stifle
  The vengeance that justice inspires?
With treason how long will ye trifle
  And shame the proud name of your sires?
Out, out with the sword and the rifle
  In defence of your homes and your fires.
The flag of the old Revolution
  Swear firmly to serve and uphold,
That no treasonous breath of pollution,
  Shall tarnish one star of its fold.
          Swear ! *b*
c And hark, the deep voices replying
  From the graves where your fathers are lying,
      d "*Swear, oh, Swear !*"

e In this moment, who hesitates barters
  The rights which his forefathers won;
He forfeits all claim to the charters
  Transmitted from sire to son.
Kneel, kneel at the graves of our martyrs
  And swear on your sword and your gun;
Lay up your great oath on an altar,

As huge and as strong as Stone-henge,
And then, with sword, fire, and halter,
 Sweep down to the field of revenge,
   Swear!
And hark, the deep voices replying
From the graves where your fathers are lying,
  " Swear, oh, Swear ! "

f By the tombs of your sires and brothers,
 The hosts which the traitors have slain,
By the tears of your sisters and mothers,
 In secret concealing their pain,
The grief which the heroine smothers,
 Consuming the heart and the brain—
By the sigh of the penniless widow,
 By the sob of the orphans' despair,
Where they sit in their sorrowful shadow,
g Kneel, kneel every freeman and swear
   Swear !
And hark, the deep voices replying
From the graves where your fathers are lying,
  " Swear, oh, Swear ! "

On mounds which are wet with the weeping,
 Where a Nation has bowed to the sod,
Where the noblest of martyrs are sleeping,
 Let the winds bear your vengeance abroad ;
And your firm oaths be held in the keeping
 Of your patriot hearts and your God.
Over Ellsworth, for whom the first tear rose,
 While to Baker and Lyon you look —
By Winthrop, a star among heroes,
 By the blood of our murdered McCook —
   Swear !
And hark, the deep voices replying
From graves where your fathers are lying,
  " Swear, oh, Swear ! "

---

a Bold address; orotund; with firmness; radical emphasis.   *b* Orotund; full force; with energy.   *c* Aspirate; as if listening.   *d* Very low pitch ; orotund; full force; sepulchral tone.   *e* Same as first stanza; with more feeling; intense force.   *f* Lower pitch ; tremor quality on *sires* and *brothers*.   *g* Moderate pitch; determined utterance; orotund and guttural voice. So vary the reading to the close.

IV.

RESPONSE TO THREATS.

MR. CHAIRMAN: It has been declared here, by some of the ablest speakers from the South, that the success of our party — which seeks to do nothing that may not be clearly done within the protection and under the authority of the Constitution which they profess to admire and venerate — will compel them to withdraw from this Union of sovereign States. I have no desire to discuss a statement which always when made assumes the attitude of a threat. But do you not see, gentlemen, that to make such a threat is to render certain of success, beyond the peradventure of defeat, the party you threaten? The Republican party proposes to ascertain whether the Union is not strong enough to sustain an administration which will rest upon the theory of our Constitution, and upon the foundation which the fathers laid.

You may shatter, if you can, this fair fabric of our freedom; you may make desolate the temple, and strike down the statue; but the terrible responsibility will rest upon yourselves.

In the earlier ages of the world, within one of the old temples of Memnon, a colossal statue had been erected; and it was said that, daily, in the morning, as the rays of the sun fell upon the image, sounds of sweet music went from it to inspirit and encourage the votaries at the shrine. But an Egyptian king caused the statue to be shattered and the music to be hushed, that he might find whence the strains proceeded, and whether the priests within the temple had not deceived the people. Sir, upon this land our fathers reared their temple, and within it the colossal statue of liberty has stood. Not in the morning alone, but at high noon, and at set of sun, day after day, sounds of heavenly harmony have gone from it, calling upon the oppressed and down-trodden to come, and to be free. Rude hands have been laid upon that temple; hard southern blows have fallen upon the statue; but when, if ever, the power shall come that will shatter the edifice and lay the colossal image low, in order that the mystery may be revealed, it will be found, I believe, in the providence of God, that other hands will rebuild and reconsecrate them both; but no Washington, nor Jefferson, nor Madison, nor Hamilton, nor such like artificers, will be commissioned for the work, until that institution, which dishonors man and debases labor, and steals from the stooping brow the sweat which should earn his bread, shall be forever overthrown.—*Hon. Thomas D. Eliot, 1860.*

V.

Twenty Years Ago.

I've wandered to the *village* | Tom; I've sat beneath the *tree*,
Upon the school house *play-ground*, which sheltered you and me ;
But none were there to greet me, Tom, and few were left to know,
That played with us upon the *green*, some twenty years ago.

The *grass* was just as *green*, Tom | bare-footed *boys* at play,
Were sporting just as we did *then*, with spirits *just* as gay ;
But 'Master' sleeps upon the hill, which, coated o'er with snow,
Afforded us a sliding place just twenty years ago.

The school house has *altered* some—the benches are replaced
By *new* ones, very like the same our pen-knives had defaced ;
But the same old *bricks* are in the wall—the *bell* swings to and fro,
Its *music* just the same, dear Tom, 't was twenty years ago.

The boys were playing some old game, beneath that same old tree ;
I do forget the name just now—you've played the same with me—
On that same spot, 't was played with knives, by throwing so and so ;
The leader had a task to do—*there* twenty years ago.

The river's running just as still, the willows on its side,
Are larger than they were, Tom ; the stream appears less wide ;
But the grape-vine swing is ruined now, where once we played the beau,
And swung our sweet-hearts | 'pretty girls ' | just twenty years ago.

The *spring* that bubbled 'neath the *hill*, close by the spreading beech
Is very low—'twas once so high, that we could almost reach ;
And kneeling down to get a *drink*, dear Tom | *I startled so*,
To see how much I've changed | since twenty years ago.

Near by the spring, upon an elm, you know I cut your name,
Your sweet-heart's just beneath it, Tom, and you did mine the same ;

Some heartless wretch has peeled the bark, 't was dying sure but slow,
Just as that one, whose name you *cut* | died twenty years ago.

My *lids* have long been dry, Tom | but *tears* came in my eyes;
I thought of her I loved so well, those early broken ties;
I visited the old church-yard, and took some flowers to strew
Upon the graves of those we *loved* | some *twenty* years ago.

Some are in the church-yard laid — some sleep beneath the sea;
But *few* are left of our old *class*, excepting you and me;
And when our time shall *come*, Tom, and we are called to go,
I hope they'll lay us where we *played* just twenty years ago.

VI.

ENGLAND AGAINST WAR.

H. W. BEECHER, — 1863. — LONDON.

I hear a loud protest against war. Ladies and gentlemen, Mr
Chairman,— there is a small band in our country and in yours — I
wish their number were quadrupled — who have borne a solemn and
painful testimony against all wars, under all circumstances; and
although I differ with them on the subject of defensive warfare
yet when men that rebuked their own land, and all lands, now rebuke
us, though I cannot accept their judgment, I bow with profound
respect to their consistency. But excepting them I regard this
British horror of the American war as something wonderful. Why
it is a phenomenon in itself! On what shore has not the prow of
your ships dashed? What land is there with a name and a people
where your banner has not led your soldiers? And when the great
resurrection reveille shall sound, it will muster British soldiers from
every clime and people under the whole heaven. Ah! but it is
said this is a war against your own blood. How long is it since you
poured soldiers into Canada, and let all your yards work night and
day to avenge the taking of two men out of the Trent? Old England shocked at a war of principle! She gained her glories in such
a war. Old England ashamed of a war of principle! Her national

ensign symbolizes her history—the cross in a field of blood. And will you tell us—who inherit your blood, your ideas, and your pluck —that we must not fight? The child must heed the parents until the parents get old and tell the child not to do the thing that in early life they whipped him for not doing. And then the child says, father and mother are getting too old; they had better be taken away from their present home and come to live with us. Perhaps you think there is coal enough. Perhaps you think the stock is not quite run out yet; but whenever England comes to that state that she does not go to war for principle, she had better emigrate, and we will get room for her.

VII.

THE COLORED SOLDIERS.

H. W. BEECHER,—1863.

I thank God that while we were striving for the rights of manhood in colored men, He by His providence, that is so much wiser than the wisdom of the wisest, has led them to demonstrate what we are trying to prove—and to demonstrate it so as to meet just that apprehension which needs to be met. The colored soldiers that have been regimented and taken to the field, by their courage, by their docility, by their good conduct in the most fiery trials, have shown that they were men. I am sorry that so large a part of human society yet live so low that the capacity of a man to show the courage of an animal is the best test that he is a man; but it is so! There is nothing that will make the common people so sympathize with the black man as to know that he fights well. He *does* fight well, and he *is* a man because he fights well! War is not thought to be a civilizer, yet men may have been held so low that even war is elevation—and so it has been with the colored people. They go up a great way before they have a right to touch the sword; and when they have taken their lives in their hands, and, with enthusiasm inspiring their hearts, have hewn their way on the rocky path to manhood; when this war has ceased, and a hundred thousand colored men can show wounds received in heroic service, or give other evidence that they have bravely fought for our country, I will put these men before the nation, and say, "they have given their blood to your blood; will you let them or their kind be trampled under foot any more?"

VIII.

VERY DARK.

Our boys died game. One was ordered to fall in rank. He answered quietly, "I will if I can." His arm hung shattered by his side, and he was bleeding to death. His last words brought tears to the eyes of all around. He murmured, "It grows very dark, mother—very dark." Poor fellow, his thoughts were far away at his peaceful home in Ohio.—*Cincinnati Gazette.*

The crimson tide was ebbing, and the pulse grew weak and faint,
But the lips of that brave soldier scorned e'en now to make complaint;
"Fall in ranks!" a voice called to him,—calm and low was his reply:
"Yes, if I can, I'll do it—I will do it, though I die,"
And he murmured, when the life-light had died out to just a spark,
"It is growing very dark, mother—growing very dark."

There were tears in manly eyes, then, and manly heads were bowed,
Though the balls flew thick around them, and the cannons thundered loud;
They gathered round the spot where the dying soldier lay,
To catch the broken accents he was struggling then to say;
And a change came o'er the features where death had set his mark,
"It is growing very dark, mother—very, very dark."

Far away his mind had wandered, to Ohio's hills and vales,
Where the loved ones watched and waited with that love that never fails;
He was with them as in childhood, seated in the cottage door,
Where he watched the evening shadows slowly creeping on the floor;
Bend down closely, comrades, closely, he is speaking now, and hark!—
"It is growing very dark, mother—very, very dark."

He was dreaming of his mother, that her loving hand was pressed
On his brow for one short moment, e'er he sank away to rest;

That her lips were now imprinting a kiss upon his cheek,
And a voice he well remembered spoke so soft, and low, and meek.
Her gentle form was near him, her footsteps he could mark,
" But 'tis growing very dark, mother—mother, very dark."

And the eye that once had kindled, flashed forth with patriot light,
Slowly gazing, vainly strove to pierce the gathering gloom of night,
Ah! poor soldier! ah! fond mother! you are severed now for aye,
Cold and pulseless, there he lies now, where he breathed his life away.
Through this heavy cloud of sorrow shines there not one heavenly spark?
Ah! it has grown dark, mother—very, *very* dark.

Gather round him, soldiers, gather, fold his hands and close his eyes,
Near another one is dying, " Rally round our flag! " he cries;
"Heaven protect it—fight on, comrades, speedily avenge our death! "
Then his voice grew low and faltering, slowly came each painful breath.
Two brave forms lay side by side there; death had loved a shining mark,
And two sad mothers say, "It has grown dark, ah! very dark."—*Z. R.*

IX.

THE PLANTING OF THE APPLE-TREE.

BY W. C. BRYANT.

Come, let us plant the apple-tree!
Cleave the tough greensward with the spade;
Wide let its hollow bed be made;
There gently lay the roots, and there
Sift the dark mould with kindly care,
    And press it o'er them tenderly,
As, round the sleeping infant's feet,
We softly fold the cradle-sheet:
    So plant we the apple-tree.

What plant we in the apple-tree?
Buds, which the breath of summer days
Shall lengthen into leafy sprays;
Boughs, where the thrush with crimson breast
Shall haunt and sing and hide her nest.
    We plant upon the sunny lea

A shadow for the noontide hour,
A shelter from the summer shower,
  When we plant the apple-tree.

What plant we in the apple-tree?
Sweets for a hundred flowery springs,
To load the May-wind's restless wings,
When, from the orchard-row, he pours
Its fragrance through our open doors;
  A world of blossoms for the bee;
Flowers for the sick girl's silent room;
For the glad infant sprigs of bloom.
  We plant with the apple-tree.

What plant we in the apple-tree?
Fruits that shall swell in sunny June,
And redden in the August noon,
And drop as gentle airs come by
That fan the blue September sky;
  While children, wild with noisy glee,
Shall scent their fragrance as they pass,
And search for them the tufted grass
  At the foot of the apple-tree.

And when above this apple-tree
The winter stars are quivering bright,
And winds go howling through the night,
Girls, whose young eyes o'erflow with mirth,
Shall peel its fruit by cottage-hearth,
  And guests in prouder homes shall see,
Heaped with the orange and the grape,
As fair as they in tint and shape,
  The fruit of the apple-tree.

The fruitage of this apple-tree
Winds and our flag of stripe and star
Shall bear to coasts that lie afar,
Where men shall wonder at the view,
And ask in what fair groves they grew;
  And they who roam beyond the sea
Shall look, and think of childhood's day,

And long hours passed in summer play
    In the shade of the apple-tree.

Each year shall give this apple-tree
A broader flush of roseate bloom,
A deeper maze of verdurous gloom,
And loosen, when the frost-clouds lower,
The crisp brown leaves in thicker shower,
    The years shall come and pass, but we
Shall hear no longer, where we lie,
The summer's song, the autumn's sigh,
    In the boughs of the apple-tree.

And time shall waste this apple-tree.
Oh, when its aged branches throw
Thin shadows on the sward below,
Shall fraud and force and iron will
Oppress the weak and helpless still?
    What shall the tasks of mercy be,
Amid the toils, the strifes, the tears
Of those who live when length of years
    Is wasting this apple-tree?

" Who planted this old apple-tree?"
The children of that distant day
Thus to some aged man will say;
And, gazing on its mossy stem,
The gray-haired man shall answer them:
    " A poet of the land was he,
Born in the rude, but good old times;
'Tis said he made some quaint old rhymes
    On planting the apple-tree."

X.

THE UNION.

D. S. DICKINSON.— 1861.

Give up the Union? Its name shall be heard with veneration
amid the roar of Pacific's waves, away upon the rivers of the North
and East, where liberty is divided from monarchy, and be wafted in
E

gentle breezes upon the Rio Grande. It shall rustle in the harvest, and wave in the standing corn, on the extended prairies of the West, and be heard in the bleating folds and lowing herds upon a thousand hills. It shall be with those who delve in mines, and shall hum in the manufactories of New England, and in the cotton gins of the South. It shall be proclaimed by the stars and stripes in every sea of earth, as the American Union, one and indivisible; upon the great thoroughfares, wherever steam drives and engines throb and shriek, its greatness and perpetuity shall be hailed with gladness. It shall be lisped in the earliest words, and ring in the merry voices of childhood, and swell to heaven upon the song of maidens. It shall live in the stern resolve of manhood, and rise to the mercy-seat upon woman's gentle prayer. Holy men shall invoke its perpetuity at the altars of religion, and it shall be whispered in the last accents of expiring age. Thus shall survive and be perpetuated the American Union, and when it shall be proclaimed that time shall be no more, and the curtains shall fall, and the good shall be gathered to a more perfect union, still may the destiny of our dear land recognize the conception of the poet of her primitive days:

> " Perfumes as of Eden flowed sweetly along,
> And a voice, as of angels, enchantingly sung,
> Columbia, Columbia, to glory arise,
> The queen of the world and child of the skies."

XI.

A MIRROR FOR TRAITORS.

JOSEPH HOLT. — 1861.

Let no man imagine that, because this rebellion has been made by men renowned in our civil and military history, it is the less guilty or the less courageously to be resisted. It is precisely that class of men who have subverted the best governments that have ever existed. The purest spirits that have lived in the tide of times, the noblest institutions that have arisen to bless our race, have found among those in whom they had most confided, and whom they had most honored, men wicked enough, either secretly to betray them unto death, or openly to seek their overthrow by lawless violence. The Republic of England had its Monk; the Republic of France had its Bonaparte; the Republic of Rome had its Cæsar and its Cataline, and the Saviour of the world had his Judas Iscariot. It cannot be necessary that I should declare to you, for you know them well, who they are whose parricidal swords are now unsheathed against the Republic of the United States. Their names are inscribed upon a roll of infamy that can never perish. The most distinguished of them were educated by the charity of the Government on which they are now making war. For long years they were fed from its table, and clothed from its wardrobe, and had their brows garlanded by its honors. They are the ungrateful sons of a fond mother, who dandled them upon her knee, who lavished upon them the gushing love of her noble and devoted nature, and who nurtured them from the very bosom of her life; and now, in the frenzied excesses of a licentious and baffled ambition, they are stabbing at that bosom with the ferocity with which the tiger springs upon his prey. The President of the United States is heroically and patriotically struggling to baffle the machinations of these most wicked men. I have unbounded gratification in knowing that he has the courage to look traitors in the face, and that, in discharging the duties of his great office, he takes no counsel of his fears. He is entitled to the zealous support of the whole country, and may I not add without offence, that he will receive the support of all who justly appreciate the boundless blessings of our free institutions.

XII.

THE HEART OF THE WAR.

Peace in the clover-scented air,
  And stars within the dome;
And underneath, in dim repose,
  A plain New-England home,
Within, a murmur of low tones
  And sighs from hearts oppressed,

Merging in prayer, at last, that brings
    The balm of silent rest.

I've closed a hard day's work, Marty,—
    The evening chores are done;
And you are weary with the house,
    And with the little one.
But he is sleeping sweetly now,
    With all our pretty brood;
So come and sit upon my knee,
    And it will do me good.

Oh, Marty! I must tell you all
    The trouble in my heart,
And you must do the best you can
    To take and bear your part.
You've seen the shadow on my face,
    You've felt it day and night;
For it has filled our little home,
    And banished all its light.

I did not mean it should be so,
    And yet I might have known
That hearts that live as close as ours
    Can never keep their own.
But we are fallen on evil times,
    And, do whate'er I may,
My heart grows sad about the war,
    And sadder every day.

I think about it when I work,
    And when I try to rest,
And never more than when your head
    Is pillowed on my breast;
For then I see the camp-fires blaze,
    And sleeping men around,
Who turn their faces towards their homes,
    And dream upon the ground.

I think about the dear, brave boys,
    My mates in other years,
Who pine for home and those they love,

Till I am choked with tears.
With shouts and cheers they marched away
  On glory's shining track,
But, ah! how long, how long they stay!
  How few of them come back!

One sleeps beside the Tennessee,
  And one beside the James,
And one fought on a gallant ship
  And perished in its flames.
And some, struck down by fell disease,
  Are breathing out their life;
And others, maimed by cruel wounds,
  Have left the deadly strife.

Ah, Marty! Marty! only think
  Of all the boys have done
And suffered in this weary war!
  Brave heroes, every one!
Oh! often, often in the night,
  I hear their voices call:
" Come on and help us! Is it right
  That we should bear it all ?"

 *   *   *   *   *   *

I feel—I know—I am not mean;
  And though I seem to boast,
I'm sure that I would give my life
  To those who need it most.
Perhaps the Spirit will reveal
  That which is fair and right;
So, Marty, let us humbly kneel
  And pray to heaven for light.

Peace in the clover-scented air,
  And stars within the dome;
And underneath, in dim repose,
  A plain, New-England home.
Within, a widow in her weeds,
  From whom all joy is flown,
Who kneels among her sleeping babes,
  And weeps and prays alone!

XIII.

THE DRUMMER'S BRIDE.

a Hollow-eyed and pale at the window of a jail,
    Thro' her soft disheveled hair, a maniac did stare, *b* stare, stare!
    At a distance, down the street, making music with their feet,
    Came the soldiers from the wars, all embellished with their scars,
c To the tapping of a drum, of a drum;
    To the pounding and the sounding of a drum!
d Of a drum, of a drum, of a drum! drum, drum, drum!

e The woman heaves a sigh, and a fire fills her eye.
    When she hears the distant drum, she cries, *f* 'Here they come! here they come!'
    Then, clutching fast the grating, with eager, nervous waiting,
    See, she looks into the air, through her long and silky hair,
    For the echo of a drum, of a drum;
    For the cheering and the hearing of a drum!
    Of a drum, of a drum, of a drum! drum, drum, drum!

g And nearer, nearer, nearer, comes, more distinct and clearer,
    The rattle of the drumming; shrieks the woman, *h* 'He is coming,
    He is coming *now* to me; quick, drummer, quick, till I see!'
    And her eye is glassy bright, while she beats in mad delight
    To the echo of a drum, of a drum;
    To the rapping, tapping, tapping of a drum!
    Of a drum, of a drum, of a drum! drum, drum, drum!

i Now she sees them, in the street, march along with dusty feet,
    As she looks through the spaces, gazing madly in their faces;
    And she reaches out her hand, *j* screaming wildly to the band;
k But her words, like her lover, are lost beyond recover,
    'Mid the beating of a drum, of a drum;
    'Mid the clanging and the banging of a drum!
    Of a drum, of a drum, of a drum! drum, drum, drum!

    So the pageant passes by, and the woman's flashing eye
l Quickly loses all its stare, and fills with a tear, with a tear;
    As, sinking from her place, with her hands upon her face,
    'Hear!' she weeps and sobs as mild as a disappointed child;
    Sobbing, 'He will never come, never come!
    Now nor ever, never, never, will he come
    With his drum, with his drum, with his drum! drum, drum, drum!'

    Still the drummer, up the street, beats his distant, dying beat,
    And she shouts, within her cell, *m* 'Ha! they're marching down to hell,
    And the devils dance and wait at the open iron gate :
n Hark! it is the dying sound, as they march into the ground,
    To the sighing and the dying of the drum!
    To the throbbing and the sobbing of the drum!
    Of a drum, of a drum, of a drum! drum, drum, drum!'

---

a All the music of the sub-vocal *M*, may be brought out in reading this selection. Begin slow in the narrative voice, with such action as will represent the jail to the audience on the right. *b* Slow and slightly aspirate. *c* Musical and measured. *d* Prolong the *M* sound in imitation of the drum; marching time. *e* Lower pitch; slow movement, with feeling. *f* High pitch; personation, then narrative with gesture. Close the stanza as the first, prolonging the *M* element in the last line. *g* Repetitions require change of pitch. Increase on these words. *h* Shriek this personation; continue little lower pitch, but with animation; close this stanza more rapidly than the others; represent the soldiers marching past. *i* High pitch and animated. *j* Very high. *k* Low pitch; slow, with feeling. *l* Close this line with tremor voice—and personation same—with much emotion. *m* Very loud, with action. *n* Low and slow, with vanishing sound, as if the drum sound was in the distance.

XIV.

THE DUTY OF THE FUTURE.

T. CORWIN — 1860.

Let us, above all, keep our Constitution inviolate, and the Union which it created, unbroken. By the lights that they give us, with the aids of an enlightened religion, and an ever-improving Christian philosophy, let us march onward and onward in the great highway of social progress. Let us always keep in the advancing car of that progress — our book of constitutions and our Bible. Like the Jews of old, let the ark of the covenant be advanced to the front in our march. With these to guide us, I feel the proud assurance that our free principles will take their way through all coming time ; and before them I do believe that the cloven footed altars of oppression, all over the world, will fall down, as Dagon of old fell down, and was shivered to pieces in the presence of the ark of the living God. But if we halt in this great exodus of the nations; if we are broken into inconsiderable fragments, and ultimately dispersed, through our follies of this day, what imagination can compass the enormity of our crime! What would the world say of this unpardonable sin ? Rather than this we would pray the kind Father of all, even his wicked children, to visit us with the last and worst of all the afflictions that fall on sin and sinful man. Better for us would it be that the fruitful earth should be smitten for a season with barrenness and become dry dust and refuse its annual fruits; better that the heavens for a time should become brass, and the ear of God deaf to our prayers; better that famine, with her cold and skinny fingers, should lay hold upon the throats of our wives and children ; better that God should commission the angel of destruction to go forth over the whole land, scattering pestilence and death from his dusky wing, than that we should prove faithless to our trust, and by that means our light should be quenched, our liberties destroyed, and all our bright hopes die out in that night which knows no coming dawn.

XV.

FREE HOMES FOR FREE MEN.

G. A. GROW—1860.

I would provide in our land policy for securing homesteads to actual settlers; and whatever bounties the government should grant to the old soldiers, I would have made in money and not in land warrants, which are bought in most cases by speculators as an easier and cheaper mode of acquiring the public lands. So they only facilitate land monopoly. The men who go forth at the call of their country to uphold its standard and vindicate its honor, are deserving, it is true, of a more substantial reward than tears to the dead and thanks to the living; but there are soldiers of peace as well as of war, and though no waving plume beckons them on to glory or to death, their dying scene is often a crimson one. They fall leading the van of civilization along untrodden paths, and are buried in the dust of its advancing columns. No monument marks the scene of deadly strife; no stone their resting place; the winds sighing through the branches of the forest alone sing their requiem. Yet they are the meritorious men of the Republic—the men who give it strength in war and glory in peace. The achievements of your pioneer army, from the day they first drove back the Indian tribes from the Atlantic seaboard to the present hour, have been the achievements of science and civilization over the elements, the wilderness, and the savage.

If rewards or bounties are to be granted for true heroism in the progress of the race, none is more deserving than the pioneer who expels the savage and the wild beast, and opens in the wilderness a home for science and a pathway for civilization.

XVI.

THE BACHELOR'S CANE-BOTTOMED CHAIR.

In tattered old slippers that toast at the bars,
And a ragged old jacket perfumed with cigars,

Away from the world and its toils and its cares,
I've a snug little kingdom up four pair of stairs.

To mount to this realm is a toil, to be sure,
But the fire there is bright and the air rather pure;
And the view I behold on a sunshiny day
Is grand, through the chimny-pots over the way.

This snug little chamber is crammed in all nooks,
With worthless old knicknacks and silly old books,
And foolish old odds and foolish old ends,
Cracked bargains from brokers, cheap keepsakes from friends

Old armor, prints, pipes, china (all cracked,)
Old rickety tables, and chairs broken-backed;
A twopenny treasury, wondrous to see;
What matter? 'tis pleasant to you, friend, and me.

No better divan need the Sultan require.
Than the creaking old sofa that basks by the fire;
And 'tis wonderful, surely, what music you get
From the rickety, ramshackle, wheezy spinet.

That praying-rug came from the Turcoman's camp;
By Tiber once twinkled that brazen old lamp;
A Mameluke fierce, yonder dagger has drawn:
'Tis a murderous knife to toast muffins upon.

Long, long through the hours, and the night, and the chimes,
Here we talk of old books, and old friends, and old times;
As we sit in a fog made of rich Latakie
This chamber is pleasant to you, friend, and me.

But of all the cheap treasures that garnish my nest,
There's one that I love and cherish the best;
For the finest of couches that's padded with hair,
I never would change thee, my cane-bottomed chair.

'Tis a bandy-legged, high-shouldered, worm-eaten seat,
With a creaking old back, and twisted old feet;
But since the fair morning when FANNY sat there,
I bless thee and love thee, old cane-bottomed chair.

If chairs have but feelings in holding such charms,
A thrill must have passed through your old withered arms.
I looked and I longed, and I wished in despair;
I wished myself turned to a cane-bottomed chair.

It was but a moment she sat in this place,
She'd a scarf on her neck and a smile on her face!
A smile on her face, and a rose in her hair,
And she sat there and bloomed in my cane-bottomed chair.

And so I have valued my chair ever since,
Like the shrine of a saint, or the throne of a prince;
Saint FANNY, my patroness sweet I declare,
The queen of my heart and my cane-bottomed chair.

When the candles burn low, and the company's gone,
In the silence of night as I sit here alone —
I sit here alone, but we yet are a pair —
My FANNY I see in my cane-bottomed chair.

She comes from the past and revisits my room,
She looks as she then did, all beauty and bloom —
So smiling and tender, so fresh and so fair —
And yonder she sits, in my cane-bottomed chair.

XVII.

THE ALARM.

E. J. MORRIS — 1861.

It is time, sir, that we should arouse. Men of America, why
stand ye still? Arouse! Shake off your lethargy! All conside-
rations of party should be lost with us, when our country is in
danger. I am with every man who is for the Union, and against every
man who is against it; and I am ready now to march up to our
national altar, and swear, " The Union, by the Eternal, it must and
shall be preserved!" If its enemies bring war out of it, it must
be so, though none would regret it more than myself. Our national
property, our citizens, public officers, and rights, must be protected

in all the States, and our men-of-war must be stationed off southern ports to collect the revenue; and, if necessary, blockade them.
This may, and I think would, aided by time, and necessity, accomplish all; but unless we mean to give up our Government, and feed
it as carrion to vultures, we ought not to be standing all the day
idle. The enemy is battering at the very doors of the Capitol, and
meditate a seizure of our national records, and the appropriation
of our army and navy. Shall we wait until our flag is no longer
respected, or shall we strike for the Constitution and Union now?
I have but little respect for that patriotism that goes moping about
the streets, wringing its hands, and asking, "What is to be done?"
It was just that kind of patriotism that Patrick Henry rebuked in
the days of the Revolution, when, lifted above ordinary mortals by
the superhuman power of his eloquence, he exclaimed against delay
when the chains of colonial bondage were clanking upon our shores,
and within hearing of the patriots. The cords and sinews of the
Government are snapping around us, and men are boasting that it is
their hands which sever them. And yet there are no arrests for
treason, as there ought to be, and would be, if the laws were
"faithfully executed."

I have said before, and I now repeat again, that my hope is not in
the President, nor in the army or navy, but in the PEOPLE, who are
a power above them all, and who will hold to a fearful accountability
all who are unfaithful to their country. The blessings of this Union
have dropped like the rains from heaven upon them, and they will
see to its protection. It is of more value than all the population it
now contains. Born of the struggles of the Revolution and baptised
in the blood of a noble ancestry, it is committed to them to enjoy
and transmit. My countrymen, you will preserve and guard it
as it is.

XVIII.
THE SLAVE LAWS.
OWEN LOVEJOY—1860.

My honest conviction is, that all these slaveholding laws have the
same moral power and force that rules among pirates have for the

distribution of their booty.   I want to know by what right you can
come and make me a slave?   I want to know by what right you can
say my child shall be your slave?   I want to know by what right
you say that the mother shall not have her child, given to her by
God through the martyrdom of maternity?   Hear that exquisite
warble of a mother's love :

> " Ere last year's sun had left the sky,
>   A birdling sought my Indian nest,
> And folded, ah ! so lovingly,
>   Its tiny wings upon my breast."

Now, where is the wretch that would dare to go up and take that
fluttering and panting bird from the bosom of its mother, and say,
" It is mine; I will sell it like a calf; I will sell it like a pig?"
What right had that mother to her babe?   Was it because she was
Fanny Forrester, the gifted authoress; was it because she was the
wife of a venerable and venerated missionary?   No, it was because
she was its MOTHER; and every slave mother has just as good a right
to *her* babe as Fanny Forrester had to hers.   No laws can make it
right to rob her.   I say in God's name, my child is mine; and yet
I have no right to mine that a slave father has not to his child.
Not a particle.   The same argument that proves my right to my
personal liberty, proves the right of every human being to his.   The
argument that proves my right to my children, gives the same title,
the same sacred claim to every father.   They, as I, get it from their
God, and no human enactment can annul the claim.   No, sir, never !
Therefore, every slave has a right to his freedom, in spite of your
slave laws.   Every slave has a right to run away, in spite of your
slave laws.   I tell you, Mr. Chairman, and I tell you all, that if I
were a slave, and had I the power, and were it necessary to achieve
my freedom, I would not hesitate to fill up and bridge over the chasm
that yawns between the hell of slavery and the heaven of freedom
with the carcasses of the slain.   Give me freedom.   Hands off.
Unthrottle that man.   Give him his liberty.   He is entitled to it
from his God.   With these views, I do not think, of course, it is any

harm to help away a slave. I told you that a year ago. I need not repeat it. A gentleman says I steal them.

Who steals, when a man comes and takes my child from my hearthstone? Who steals, when he comes and takes the babe, flesh of my flesh, bone of my bone? Who steals? I tell you that I have no more hesitation in helping a fugitive slave than I have in snatching a lamb from the jaws of a wolf, or disengaging an infant from the talons of an eagle. Not a bit. Long enough has the nation crouched and cowered in the presence of this stupendous wrong. Here and now I break the spell, and disenchant the Republic from the incantation of this accursed sorceress. It is simply a question whether it will pay to go down into the den where the wolf is. If you would only go into your lair, and crunch the bones and tear the flesh of your victims we might let you alone; but you will not. You claim the right to go with this flesh in your teeth all over our Territories. We deny it.

XIX.

THE BELLS.

E. A. POE.

Hear the sledges with the bells, silver bells—
What a world of merriment their melody fortells!
How they tinkle, tinkle, tinkle, in the icy air of night!
While the stars that oversprinkle all the heavens, seem to twinkle
   With a crystalline delight—
Keeping time, time, time, in a sort of Runic rhyme,
To the tintinnabulation that so musically wells
From the bells, bells, bells, bells, bells, bells, bells—
From the jingling and the tinkling of the bells.

Hear the mellow wedding bells, golden bells,
What a world of happiness their harmony foretells!
Through the balmy air of night how they ring out their delight!
From the molten-golden notes, all in tune,
    What a liquid ditty floats
To the turtle-dove that listens, while she gloats on the moon!

O, from out the sounding cells,
What a gush of euphony voluminously wells!
How it swells, how it dwells
On the Future! how it tells of the rapture that impels
To the swinging and the ringing of the bells, bells, bells,
Of the bells, bells, bells, bells, bells, bells, bells—
To the rhyming and the chiming of the bells.

Hear the loud alarum bells, brazen bells!
What a tale of terror, now, their turbulency tells!
In the startled ear of night how they scream out their affright!
Too much horrified to speak, they can only shriek, shriek,
  Out of tune,
In the clamorous appealing to the mercy of the fire,
In a mad expostulation with the deaf and frantic fire
Leaping higher, higher, higher, with a desperate desire,
And a resolute endeavor, now—now to sit or never,
  By the side of the pale-faced moon.
O, the bells, bells, bells, what a tale their terror tells of Despair!
How they clang, and clash and roar! what a horror they outpour
On the bosom of the palpitating air!
  Yet the ear it fully knows,
By the twanging and the clanging, how the danger ebbs and flows;
  Yet the ear distinctly tells,
In the jangling, and the wrangling, how the danger sinks and swells,
By the sinking or the swelling in the anger of the bells, of the bells,
Of the bells, bells, bells, bells, bells, bells, bells—
In the clamor and the clangor of the bells!

Hear the tolling of the bells, iron bells!
What a world of solemn thought their monody compels!
In the silence of the night, how we shiver with affright
  At the melancholy menace of their tone!
For every sound that floats from the rust within their throats
  Is a groan.
And the people—ah, the people; they that dwell up in the steeple
  All alone,
And who tolling, tolling, tolling, in that muffled monotone,
Feel a glory in so rolling on the human heart a stone—
They are neither man nor woman; they are neither brute nor human,
  They are ghouls:
And their king it is who tolls; and he rolls, rolls, rolls, rolls,

A pæan from the bells! and his merry bosom swells
With the pæan of the bells! and he dances and he yells;
Keeping time, time, time, in a sort of Runic rhyme,
    To the pæan of the bells, of the bells:
Keeping time, time, time, in a sort of Runic rhyme,
To the throbbing of the bells, of the bells, bells, bells—
    To the sobbing of the bells;
Keeping time, time, time, as he knells, knells, knells,
In a happy Runic rhyme, to the rolling of the bells—
Of the bells, bells, bells, to the tolling of the bells,
Of the bells, bells, bells, bells, bells, bells, bells—
To the moaning and the groaning of the bells.

XX.
A CATEGORICAL COURTSHIP.

I sat one night beside a blue-eyed girl—
The fire was out, and so, too, was her mother;
A feeble flame around the lamp did curl,
Making faint shadows, blending in each other;
'Twas nearly twelve o'clock, too, in November,
She had a shawl on, also, I remember.
Well, I had been to see her every night
For thirteen days, and had a sneaking notion
To pop the question, thinking all was right,
And once or twice had made an awkward motion
To take her hand, and stammered, coughed and stuttered,
But somehow nothing to the point had uttered.
I thought this chance too good now to be lost;
I hitched my chair up pretty close beside her,
Drew a long breath, and then my legs I crossed,
Bent over, sighed, and for five minutes eyed her;
She looked as if she knew what next was coming,
And with her foot upon the floor was drumming.
I did'nt know how to begin, or where—
I could'nt speak, the words were always choking;
I scarce could move—I seemed tied in my chair—
I hardly breathed—'t was awfully provoking;
The perspiration from each pore was oozing,
My heart and brain and limbs their power seemed losing.

At length I saw a brindle tabby cat
Walk purring up, inviting me to pat her;
An idea came, electric-like, at that —
My doubts, like summer clouds, began to scatter,
I seized on tabby, though a scratch she gave me,
And said, "Come, Puss, ask Mary if she'll have me?'
'Twas done at once—the murder now was out,
The thing was all explained in half a minute;
She blushed, and turning pussy cat about,
Said, "Pussy, tell him, yes!" Her foot was in it!
The cat had thus saved me my category,
And here's the catastrophe of my story.

XXI.

The Claims of Italy.

I will leave antiquity out of the question, and speak only of modern times. Is it not a striking spectacle to see Italy always give the signal to the world, always open the way to great things? The first modern epic poet is an Italian—Dante; the first lyric poet is an Italian—Petrarch; the first poet of chivalry is an Italian—Boccaccio; the first painter in the world is an Italian—Raffaelle; the first statuary is an Italian—Michael Angelo; the first vigorous statesman and historian of the revival is an Italian—Machiavelli; the first philosophical historian is an Italian—Nico; the discoverer of the New World is an Italian—Christopher Columbus; and the first demonstrator of the laws of the heavenly worlds is an Italian—Galileo. You will find a son of Italy standing on every step of the temple of genius ever since the twelfth century. Then, in times nearer to our own, while all other nations are working at the continuation of this immortal gallery, Italy from time to time collects her strength, and presents to the world a colossus surpassing all. Now, even now, the greatest of living artists—the only one, perhaps, who deserves, solely as an artist, the title of a great man—is he not an Italian—Rossini? And lastly, was he not also a son of Italy— that giant who towered above the whole century, and covered all around him with his light or his shade—Napoleon? In fact, it would seem that when Providence wanted a guide or a leader for humanity, it strikes this favored soil, and a great man springs forth.

———————

XXII.

DRUNKARDS NOT ALL BRUTES.

JOHN B. GOUGH.

I said when I began, that I was a trophy of this movement; and therefore the principal part of my work has been (not ignoring other parts,) in behalf of those who have suffered as I have suffered. You know there is a great deal said about the reckless victims of this foe being " brutes " No, they are not brutes. I have labored for about eighteen years among them and I never have found a brute. I have had men swear at me; I have had a man dance around me as if possessed of a devil, and spit his foam in my face; but he is not a brute. I think it is Charles Dickens who says : " Away up a great many pair of stairs, in a very remote corner, easily passed by, there is a door, and on that door is written 'woman.' " And so in the heart of the vile outcast, away up a great many pair of stairs, in a very remote corner, easily passed by, there is a door on which is written " man." Here is our business to find that door. It may take a time; but begin and knock. Don't get tired; but remember God's long suffering for us and keep knocking a long time if need be. Don't get weary if there is no answer; remember Him whose locks were wet with dew. Knock on—just try it—*you* try it; and just so sure as you do, just so sure, by-and-by, will the quivering lip and starting tear tell you have knocked at the heart of a man, and not of a brute. It is because these poor wretches *are* men, and not brutes that we have hopes of them. They said " he is a brute— let him alone." I took him home with me and kept the " brute " fourteen days and nights, through his delirium; and he nearly frightened Mary out of her wits, once chasing her about the house

F

with a boot in his hand. But she recovered her wits, and he recovered his. He said to me, " You wouldn't think I had a wife and child ? " " Well, I shouldn't." " I have, and—God bless her little heart—my little Mary is as pretty a little thing as ever stepped," said the " brute." I asked, " where do they live ? " " They live two miles away from here." " When did you see them last ? " " About two years ago." Then he told me his story. I said, " you must go back to your home again." " I mus'nt go back—I won't —my wife is better without me than with me ! I will not go back any more ; I have knocked her, and kicked her, and abused her ; do you suppose I will go back again ? " I went to the house with him ; I knocked at the door and his wife opened it. " Is this Mrs. Richardson ? " " Yes, sir." " Well, that is Mr. Richardson. And Mr. Richardson, that is Mrs. Richardson. Now come into the house."

They went in. The wife sat on one side of the room and the " brute " on the other. I waited to see who would speak first ; and it was the woman. But before she spoke she fidgetted a good deal. She pulled her apron till she got hold of the hem, and then she pulled it down again. Then she folded it up closely, and jerked it out through her fingers an inch at a time, and then she spread it all down again ; and then she looked all about the room and said, " Well, William ? " And the " brute " said, " Well, Mary ? " He had a large handkerchief round his neck, and she said, " You had better take the handkerchief off, William ; you'll need it when you go out." He began to fumble about it. The knot was large enough ; he could have untied it if he liked ; but he said, " Will you untie it, Mary ? " and she worked away at it ; but *her* fingers were clumsy, and she couldn't get it off ; their eyes met, and the lovelight was not all quenched ; she opened her arms gently and he fell into them. If you had seen those white arms clasped about his neck, and he sobbing on her breast, and the child looking in wonder first at one and then at the other, you would have said " It is not a brute ; it is a man, with a great, big, warm heart in his breast."

XXIII.

The Admission of California.

W. H. SEWARD.

A year ago, California was a mere military dependency of our own, and we were celebrating with unanimity and enthusiasm its acquisition, with its newly-discovered but yet untold and untouched mineral wealth, as the most auspicious of many and unparalleled achievements.

To-day, California is a State, more populous than the least and richer than several of the greatest of our thirty States. This same California, thus rich and populous, is here asking admission into the Union, and finds us debating the dissolution of the Union itself.

No wonder if we are perplexed with ever-changing embarrassments! No wonder if we are appalled by ever-increasing responsibilities! No wonder if we are bewildered by the ever-augmenting magnitude and rapidity of national vicissitudes!

Shall California be received? For myself, upon my individual judgment and conscience, I answer, Yes. For myself, as an instructed representative of one of the States, of that one even of the States which is soonest and longest to be pressed in commercial and political rivalry by the new commonwealth, I answer, Yes. Let California come in. Every new State, whether she come from the East or from the West, every new State coming from whatever part of the continent she may, is always welcome. But California, that comes from the clime where the west dies away into the rising east; California, which bounds at once the empire and the continent; California, the youthful queen of the Pacific, in her robes of freedom, gorgeously inlaid with gold — is doubly welcome.

Let, then, those who distrust the Union make compromise to save it. I shall not impeach their wisdom, as I certainly cannot their patriotism; but, indulging no such apprehensions myself, I shall vote for the admission of California directly, without conditions, without qualifications, and without compromise.

For the vindication of that vote I look not to the verdict of the passing hour, disturbed as the public mind now is by conflicting interests and passions, but to that period, happily not far distant, when the vast regions over which we are now legislating shall have received their destined inhabitants.

While looking forward to that day, its countless generations seem to me to be rising up and passing in dim and shadowy review before us; and a voice comes forth from their serried ranks, saying, " Waste your treasures and your armies, if you will; raze your fortifications to the ground; sink your navies into the sea; transmit to us even a dishonored name, if you must; but the soil you hold in trust for us —give it to us free.   You found it free, and conquered it to extend a better and surer freedom over it.   Whatever choice you have made for yourselves, let us have no partial freedom; let us all be free; let the reversion of your broad domain descend to us unincumbered, and free from the calamities and the sorrows of human bondage."

XXIV.

POOR LITTLE JIM.

1. The cottage was a thatched one, the outside old and mean,
   But all within that little cot was wondrous neat and clean;
   The night was dark and stormy, the wind was howling wild,
   As a patient mother sat beside the death-bed of her child:
   A little worn-out creature, his once bright eyes grown dim:
   It was a collier's wife and child, they called him little Jim.

2. And oh! to see the briny tears fast hurrying down her cheek,
   As she offered up the prayer, in thought, she was afraid to speak,
   Lest she might waken one she loved far better than her life;
   For she had all a mother's heart, had that poor collier's wife.
   With hands uplifted, see, she kneels beside the sufferer's bed,
   And prays that He would spare her boy, and take herself instead.

3. She gets her answer from the child: soft falls the words from him,
   "Mother, the angels do so smile, and beckon little Jim,
   I have no pain, dear mother, now, but O! I am so dry,
   Just moisten poor Jim's lips again, and, mother, don't you cry."
   With gentle, trembling haste she held the liquid to his lip;
   He smiled to thank her, as he took each little, tiny sip.

4. "Tell father, when he comes from work, I said good-night to him,
And, mother, now I'll go to sleep." Alas! poor little Jim!
She knew that he was dying; that the child she loved so dear,
Had uttered the last words she might ever hope to hear:
The cottage door is opened, the collier's step is heard,
The father and the mother meet, yet neither speak a word.

5. He felt that all was over, he knew his child was dead,
He took the candle in his hand and walked towards the bed;
His quivering lips gave token of the grief he'd fain conceal,
And see, his wife has joined him—the stricken couple kneel:
With hearts bowed down by sadness, they humbly ask of Him,
In heaven, once more, to meet again their own poor little Jim.

XXV.
THE LITTLE ORATOR. *a*

Pray how should I, a little lad,
b In speaking make a figure?
c You're only joking, I'm afraid—
Do wait till I am bigger.

d But, since you wish to hear my part,
And urge me to begin it,
e I'll strive for praise with all my heart,
Though small the hope to win it.

I'll tell a tale, *f* how farmer John
A little roan colt bred, sir,
And every night and every morn,
He watered and he fed, sir.

g Said neighbor Joe to farmer John,
"Ar'n't you a silly dolt, sir,
To spend such time and care upon
A little, useless colt, sir?"

---

a This is the best selection we have ever seen for a child to begin with. He can recite it and retain his childish simplicity, which is much to be desired. *b* Give this line with double gesture, palms up. *c* Right hand extended to the teacher. *d* Return the attention to the audience. *e* Right hand raised to the temples or the region of the heart. *f* Gesticulate to the right or left. *g* Change position; step forward or to one side; raise the voice, and do not fail to be animated in the personation; one voice for Joe, and one for John. It will not be difficult for a child to give these voices, if he will change pitch and force.

Said farmer John to neighbor Joe,
  " I bring my little roan up,
Not for the good he now can do,
  But will do, when he's grown up."

The moral you can well espy,
  To keep the tale from spoiling,
h The little colt, you think, is I—
  I know it by your smiling.

i And now, my friends, please to excuse
  My lisping and my stammers ;
I, for this once, have done my best,
  j And so I'll make my manners.

XXVI.

LIBERTY AND THE LIBERTY OF THE PRESS.

COL. E. D. BAKER—1861.

Sir, the liberty of the press is the highest safeguard to all free government. Ours could not exist without it. It is like a great, exulting and abounding river. It is fed by the dews of heaven, which distil their sweetest drops to form it. It gushes from the rill, as it breaks from the deep caverns of the earth. It is augmented by a thousand affluents, that dash from the mountain top, to separate again into a thousand bounteous and irrigating streams around. On its broad bosom it bears a thousand barks. There genius spreads its purpling sail. There poetry dips its silver oar. There art, invention, discovery, science, morality, religion, may safely and securely float. It wanders through every land. It is a genial, cordial source of thought and inspiration, wherever it touches, whatever it surrounds. Upon its borders, there grows every flower of grace, and every fruit of truth. Sir, I am not here to deny that that river sometimes oversteps its bounds. I am not here to deny

---

h With a smile and gesture to himself; pause after " I." *i* Both hands extended. *j* As the last line is uttered, the lad may step back and with a bow on " manners," retire.

that that stream sometimes becomes a dangerous torrent, and destroys towns and cities upon its bank. But I am here to say that, without it, civilization, humanity, government, all that makes society itself, would disappear, and the world would return to its ancient barbarism. Sir, if that were possible, though but for a moment, civilization would roll the wheels of its car backward for two thousand years, and the fine conception of the poet would be realized :

> " As one by one, in dread Medea's train,
> Star after star fades off the ethereal plain,
> Thus at her fell approach and secret might
> Art after art goes out, and all is night.
> Philosophy, that leaned on heaven before,
> Sinks to her second cause, and is no more.
> Religion, blushing, veils her sacred fires,
> And, unawares, morality expires."

Sir, we will not risk these consequences, even for slavery; we will not risk these consequences even, for union; we will not risk these consequences to avoid that civil war with which you threaten us; that war which you announce as deadly, and which you declare to be inevitable.

XXVII.

THE DRED SCOTT DECISION.

BEN. WADE — 1860.

I believe this is the only nation on God's earth that ever placed any mortal man, or anybody bearing the human form, on so low a level, or any court on so high a one as that. But let this go. Dred Scott brought his suit. The plea in abatement was demurred to; the question arose upon that demurrer, and a majority of the court decided that Dred Scott, being a negro, a descendant of an African, and his ancestors having been slaves, he could not maintain a suit in that court, because he was not a citizen under the law. Now, sir, I ask every lawyer here, was not there an end of the case? In the name of Heaven, Judge Taney, what did you retain it for any longer? You said Dred Scott could not sue; he could not obtain his liberty; he was out of court; and what further had you to do with all the questions that you say were involved in that suit? Upon every principle of adjudication, you ought not to have gone further. No court has ever held more solemnly than the Federal courts that they will not go on to decide any more than is before the court; and every lawyer knows that if they do, all they say more is mere talk, and though said by judges in a court house, has just as much operation and effect as if it had been said by a horse-dealer in a bar-room, and no more. And yet we are told that we must follow the *dicta* of these packed judges—for they were packed, a majority of them interested too, in the very question to be decided. I do not want to go back to see what Jefferson and others said about it. I know the nature of man. I know, as they know, that to arm this judiciary with the power not only to decide questions between private individuals, but to affect the legislation of the nation, to affect the action of your President, to affect the co-ordinate branches of this Government, is a fatal heresy, that, if persisted in by a majority of the people, cannot result in any other than a consolidated despotism; and I am amazed that men who have had their eyes open, and who have held to other doctrines in better days, should, for any temporary purpose, heave overboard, and bury in the deep sea, the sheet-anchor of the liberties of the nation.

XXVIII.

SLAVERY MUST DIE.

OWEN LOVEJOY.

You must sacrifice slavery for the good of your country. Do this, and you will have the sympathy, the prayers, and co-operation of the entire nation.

Refuse or neglect this—refuse to proclaim liberty through all the land, to all the inhabitants thereof—and the exodus of the slaves will be through the Red Sea. It is a well known physiological, as well as psychological fact, that ancestral characteristics reappear after a long interval of years, and even of generations, as streams disappear and gush out at a distant point. It is also well known that the Saxon blood is being infiltrated into the veins of the enslaved. By and by some Marion will be found, calling his guerilla troops from the swamps and everglades of South Carolina; and Patrick Henry will reappear in the Old Dominion, shouting, as of old, " Give me liberty, or give me death ! " Then will transpire those scenes which troubled the prophetic vision of Jefferson, and made him tremble for his country, when he remembered that God was just, and that his justice would not sleep forever, and that every divine attribute would be arrayed upon the side of the struggling bondmen. And he justified the uprising by saying, the little finger of American slavery was thicker than the loins of British despotism.

Sir, Virginia cannot afford, the country cannot afford, to continue a practice fraught with so much peril. It is better to remove the magazine than to be kept evermore in dread of a lighted match. The future glory and usefulness of this nation cannot be sacrificed to this system of crime. The nations of the earth are to be taught by our example. The American Republic must repose queen among the nations of the earth. Slavery must die.

———

XXIX.

BETHEL.

We mustered at midnight,—in darkness we formed,—
And the whisper went round of a fort to be stormed ;
But no drum-beat had called us, no trumpet we heard,
And no voice of command, but our Colonel's low word,—
" Column ! Forward ! "

And out through the mist and the murk of the morn,
From the beaches of Hampton our barges were borne;

And we heard not a sound, save the sweep of the oar,
Till the word of our Colonel came up from the shore,—
"Column! Forward!"

With hearts bounding bravely, and eyes all alight,
As ye dance to soft music, so trod we that night;
Through the aisles of the greenwood, with vines overarched,
Tossing dew-drops, like gems, from our feet, as we marched —
"Column! Forward!"

As ye dance with the damsels, to viol and flute,
So we skipped from the shadows, and mocked their pursuit;
But the soft zephyrs chased us, with scents of the morn,
As we passed through the hay-fields and green waving corn,—
"Column! Forward!"

For the leaves were all laden with fragrance of June,
And the flowers and the foliage with sweets were in tune;
And the air was so calm, and the forest so dumb,
That we heard our own heart-beats, like taps of a drum —
"Column! Forward!"

Till the lull of the lowlands was stirred by a breeze,
And the buskins of Morn brushed the tops of the trees,
And the glintings of glory that slid from her track,
By the sheen of our rifles were gaily flung back,—
"Column! Forward!"

And the woodlands grew purple with sunshiny mist,
And the blue-crested hill-tops with rose-light were kissed,
And the earth gave her prayers to the sun in perfumes,
Till we marched as through gardens, and trampled on blooms,—
"Column! Forward!"

Ay! trampled on blossoms, and seared the sweet breath
Of the greenwood with low-brooding vapors of death;
O'er the flowers and the corn we were borne like a blast,
And away to the fore-front of battle we passed,—
"Column! Forward!"

For the cannon's hoarse thunder roared out from the glades,
And the sun was like lightening on banners and blades,

When the long line of chanting Zouaves, like a flood,
From the green of the woodland rolled, crimson as blood,—
"Column! Forward!"

While the sound of their song, like the surge of the seas,
With the "Star Spangled Banner" swelled over the leas;
And the sword of Duryea, like a torch, led the way,
Bearing down on the batteries of Bethel, that day,—*
"Column! Forward!"

Through green-tasseled cornfields our columns were thrown,
And like corn by the red scythe of fire we were mown;
While the cannon's fierce plowings new furrowed the plain,
That our blood might be planted for Liberty's grain—
"Column! Forward!"

O! the fields of fair June have no lack of sweet flowers,
But the rarest and best breathed no fragrance like ours;
And the sunshine of June sprinkling gold on the corn,
Hath no harvest that ripeneth like Bethel's red morn,—
"Column! Forward!"

When our heroes like bridegrooms, with lips and with breath,
Drank the first kiss of Danger, and clasped her in death;
And the heart of brave Winthrop grew mute with his lyre,
When the plumes of his genius lay moulting in fire,—
"Column! Forward!"

Where he fell shall be sunshine as bright as his name,
And the grass where he slept shall be green as his fame;
For the gold of the Pen and the steel of the Sword
Write his deeds—in his blood—on the land he adored,—
"Column! Forward!"

And the soul of our comrade shall sweeten the air,
And the flowers and the grass-blades his memory upbear;
While the breath of his genius, like music in leaves,
With the corn-tassels whispers, and sing in the sheaves,—
"Column! Forward!"

*The march on Bethel was begun in high spirits at midnight, but it was near noon when the Zouaves in their crimson garments, led by Colonel Duryea, charged the batteries, after singing the "Star Spangled Banner" in chorus. Major Winthrop fell in the storming of the enemy's defences, and was left on the battle-field. Lieut. Greble, the only other officer killed, was shot at his gun soon after. This fatal contest inaugurated the "war of posts," which afterwards raged in V'   .ia.— *Atlantic Monthly.*

XXX.

MISSING.

Not among the suffering wounded!
　Not among the peaceful dead!
Not among the prisoners; —Missing!
　That was *all* the message said.

Yet his mother reads it over,
　Until through the painful tears
Fades the dear name she has called him
　For these two and twenty years.

Round her all is peace and plenty,
　Bright and clean the yellow floor,
While the morning-glories cluster
　All around the kitchen door.

Soberly the sleek old house-cat
　Drowses in his patch of sun;
Neatly shines the oaken dresser;
　All the morning's work is done.

Through the window comes the fragrance
　Of a sunny, harvest morn,
Fragment songs from distant reapers,
　And the rustling of the corn.

And the rich breath of the garden
　Where the golden melons lie,
Where the blushing plums are turning
　All their red cheeks to the sky.

Sitting there within the sunshine,
　Leaning on her easy chair,
With soft lines upon her forehead,
　And the silver in her hair,—

Blind to sunshine, dead to fragrance,
　On that royal harvest morn,
Thinking while her heart is weeping,
　Of her noble-browed first-born.

How he left her in the spring-time,
  With his young heart full of flame,
With his clear and ringing footstep,
  And his light and supple frame.

How with tears his eyes were brimming,
  As he kissed a last "Good Bye,"—
Yet she heard him whistling gaily
  As he went across the rye.

Missing! Still a hope to cheer her;
  Safe, triumphant, he may come,
With the victor army shouting,
  With the clamor of the drum.

So through all the days of autumn,
  In the eve and in the morn,
She will hear his quickening footsteps
  In the rustling of the corn.

Or she will hush the household,
  While the heart goes leaping high,
Thinking that she hears the whistling
  In the pathway through the rye.

Far away, through all the autumn,
  In a lonely, lonely glade,
In a dreary desolation
  That the battle-storm has made,

With the rust upon his musket,
  In the eve and in the morn,
In the rank gloom of the fern-leaves,
  Lies her noble, brave first-born.

XXXI.

WOUNDED.

Let me lie down,
Just here in the shade of this cannon-torn tree,—
Here, low on the trampled grass, where I may see

The surge of the combat, and where I may hear
The glad cry of victory, cheer upon cheer:
      Let me lie down.

      Oh, it was grand!
Like the tempest we charged, in the triumph to share:
The tempest,—its fury and thunder were there;
On, on, o'er intrenchments, o'er living and dead,
With the foe under foot, and our flag overhead:
      Oh, it was grand!

      Weary and faint,
Prone on the soldier's couch, ah, how can I rest
With this shot-shattered head, and sabre-pierced breast?
Comrades, at roll-call, when I shall be sought,
Say I fought till I fell, and fell where I fought,—
      Wounded and faint.

      Oh, that last charge!
Right through the dread hell-fire of shrapnel and shell,
Through without faltering,—clear through with a yell,
Right in their midst, in the turmoil and gloom,
Like heroes we dashed at the mandate of Doom!
      Oh, that last charge!

      It was duty!
Some things are worthless, and some others so good
That nations who buy them pay only in blood;
For Freedom and Union each man owes a part,
And here I pay my share all warm from my heart:
      It is duty!

      Dying at last!
My Mother, dear Mother, with meek, tearful eye,
Farewell! and God bless you, forever and aye!
Oh, that I now lay on your pillowing breast,
To breathe my last sigh on the bosom first prest:
      Dying at last!

      I am no saint;
But, boys, say a prayer. There's one that begins,—
"Our Father;" and then says, "Forgive us our sins,"—

Don't forget that part, say that strongly, and then
I'll try to repeat it, and you'll say, Amen!
   Ah, I'm no saint!

   Hark,— there's a shout!
Raise me up, comrades! We have conquered, I know!
Up, up on my feet, with my face to the foe!
Ah! there flies the Flag, with its star-spangles bright!
The promise of Glory, the symbol of Right!
   Well may they shout.

   I'm mustered out!
O God of our Fathers! our Freedom prolong,
And tread down Rebellion, Oppression, and Wrong!
O Land of Earth's hope! on thy blood-reddened sod,
I die for the Nation, the Union, and God!
   I'm mustered out!

————

XXXII.

BARBARA FRIETCHIE.

Up from the meadows rich with corn,
Clear in the cool September morn,

The clustered spires of Frederick stand
Green-walled by the hills of Maryland.

Round about them orchards sweep,
Apple and peach-tree fruited deep,

Fair as a garden of the Lord
To the eyes of the famished rebel horde,

On that pleasant morn of the early fall,
When Lee marched over the mountain-wall,—

Over the mountains winding down,
Horse and foot, into Frederick town.

Forty flags with their silver stars,
Forty flags with their crimson bars,

Flapped in the morning wind: the sun
Of noon looked down, and saw not one.

Up rose old Barbara Frietchie then,
Bowed with her fourscore years and ten;

Bravest of all in Frederick town,
She took up the flag the men hauled down;

In her attic window the staff she set,
To show that one heart was loyal yet.

Up the street came the rebel tread,
Stonewall Jackson riding ahead.

Under his slouched hat, left and right,
He glanced: the old flag met his sight.

"Halt!"—the dust-brown ranks stood fast.
"Fire!"—out blazed the rifle-blast.

It shivered the window, pane and sash;
It rent the banner with seam and gash.

Quick as it fell from the broken staff,
Dame Barbara snatched the silken scarf;

She leaned far out on the window sill,
And shook it forth with a royal will.

"Shoot, if you must, this old gray head,—
But spare your country's flag!" she said.

A shade of sadness, a blush of shame,
Over the face of the leader came;

The nobler nature within him stirred
To life at that woman's deed and word.

"Who touches a hair of yon gray head,
Dies like a dog! March on!" he said.

All day long through Frederick street
Sounded the tread of marching feet;

All day long that free flag tossed
Over the heads of the rebel host.

Ever its torn folds rose and fell
On the loyal winds that loved it well;

And through the hill-gaps sunset light
Shone over it with a warm good-night.

Barbara Frietchie's work is o'er,
And the Rebel rides on his raids no more.

Honor to her!—and let a tear
Fall, for her sake, on Stonewall's bier.

Over Barbara Frietchie's grave,
Flag of Freedom and Union wave!

Peace, and order, and beauty, draw
Round thy symbol of light and law;

And ever the stars above look down
On thy stars below at Frederick town!

XXXIII.

CAUSE OF REBELLION.

JOSEPH HOLT—1861.

Whence this revolutionary outbreak? Whence the secret spring of this gigantic conspiracy, which, like some huge boa, had completely coiled itself round the limbs and body of the Republic, before a single hand was lifted to resist it? Strange, and indeed startling, as the announcement must appear when it falls on the ears of the next generation, the national tragedy, in whose shadow we stand to-night, has come upon us because, in November last, John C. Breckinridge was not elected President of the United States, and Abraham Lincoln was. This is the whole story. And I would pray to know, on what John C. Breckinridge fed that he has grown so great, that a republic founded by Washington and cemented by the best blood that ever coursed in human veins, is to be overthrown, because forsooth, he cannot be its President? Had he been chosen, we well know that we should not have heard of this rebellion, for

G

the lever with which it is being moved would have been wanting to the hands of the conspirators. Even after his defeat, could it have been guaranteed, beyond all peradventure, that Jeff. Davis or some other kindred spirit, would be the successor of Mr. Lincoln, I presume we hazard nothing in assuming that this atrocious movement against the Government would not have been set on foot. So much for the principle involved in it. This great crime, then, with which we are grappling, sprang from that "sin by which the angels fell" —an unmastered and profligate ambition—an ambition that "would rather reign in hell than serve in heaven"—that would rather rule supremely over a shattered fragment of the Republic than run the chances of sharing with others the honors of the whole.

XXXIV.

MAKING WAR ON REBELS CONSTITUTIONAL.

J. R. DOOLITTLE—1861.

MR. PRESIDENT, I have heard the Senator from Kentucky to-day, and I have heard him again and again, denounce the President of the United States for the usurpation of unconstitutional power. I undertake to say that without any foundation he makes such a charge of usurpation of unconstitutional power, unless it be in a mere form. He has not, in substance; and the case I put to the Senator the other day he has not answered, and I defy him to answer. I undertake to say that, as there are fifty thousand men, perhaps, in arms against the United States, in Virginia, within thirty miles of this capital, I, as an individual, though I am not President, though I am clothed with no official authority, may ask one hundred thousand of my fellow-men to volunteer to go with me, with arms in their hands, to take every one of them, and, if it be necessary, to take their lives. Why do not some of these gentlemen who talk about usurpation and trampling the Constitution under foot, stand up here and answer that position, or forever shut their mouths? I, as an individual, can do all this, though I am not President, and am clothed with no legal authority whatever, simply because I am a loyal citizen of the United States; I have a right to ask one hundred thousand men to volunteer to go with me and capture the whole of the rebels, and if it be necessary to their capture to kill half of them while I am doing it. No man can deny the correctness of the proposition. Away, then, with all this stuff, and this splitting of hairs and pettifogging here, when we are within the very sound of the guns of these traitors and rebels, who threaten to march upon the capital and subjugate the Government.

XXXV.

THE SOUTH MUST BE ANNIHILATED.

WENDELL PHILLIPS—1863.

When England conquered the Highlands, she held them — held them until she educated them; and it took a generation. That is just what we have to do with the South; annihilate the old South, and put a new one there. You do not annihilate a thing by abolishing it. You must supply the vacancy. In the Gospel, when the chambers were swept and garnished, the devils came back, because there were no angels there. And if we should sweep Virginia clean, Jeff. Davis would come back with seven other devils worse than himself, if he could find them, and occupy it, unless you put free institutions there.

Some men say, begin it by exporting the blacks. If you do, you export the very fulcrum of the lever; you export the very best material to begin with. The nation that should shovel down the Alleghanies, and then build them up again, would be a wise nation compared with the one that should export four million blacks, and then import four million of Chinese to take their places. To dig a hole, and then fill it up again, to build a wall for the purpose of beating out your brains against it, would be Shakesperian wisdom compared with such an undertaking. Colonize the blacks ! A man might as well colonize his hands; or, when the robber enters his house, he might as well colonize his revolver. What we want is sympathetic national action. Never until we welcome the negro, the foreigner, all races as equals, and, melted together in a common nationality, hurl them all at despotism, will the North deserve triumph, or earn it at the hands of a just God.

But the North will triumph. I hear it. Do you remember that disastrous siege in India, when the Scotch girl raised her head from the pallet of the hospital, and said to the sickening hearts of the English, " I hear the bagpipes; the Campbells are coming ! " And they said, " Jesse, it is delirium." " No, I know it; I heard it far off." And in an hour the pibroch burst upon their glad ears, and the banner of England floated in triumph over their heads. So I hear in the dim distance the first notes of the jubilee rising from the hearts of the millions. Soon, very soon, you shall hear it at the gates of the citadel, and the stars and stripes shall guarantee liberty forever, from the lakes to the gulf !

XXXVI.

ROLL CALL.

" Corporal Green ! " the Orderly cried;
   " Here ! " was the answer, loud and clear,
   From the lips of the soldier who stood near,—
And " Here ! " was the word the next replied.

" Cyrus Drew ! "—then a silence fell,—
   This time no answer followed the call;
   Only his rear-man had seen him fall,
Killed or wounded, he could not tell.

There they stood in the failing light,
   These men of battle, with grave, dark looks,
   As plain to be read as open books,
While slowly gathered the shades of night.

The fern on the hill-sides was splashed with blood,
   And down in the corn where the poppies grew
   Were redder stains than the poppies knew;
And crimson-dyed was the river's flood.

For the foe had crossed from the other side
　　That day, in the face of a murderous fire
　　That swept them down in its terrible ire;
And their life-blood went to color the tide.

"Herbert Kline!" At the call there came
　　Two stalwart soldiers into the line,
　　Bearing between them this Herbert Kline,
Wounded and bleeding, to answer his name.

"Ezra Kerr!"—and a voice answered, "Here!"
　　"Hiram Kerr!"—but no man replied.
　　They were brothers, these two, the sad winds sighed,
And a shudder crept through the cornfield near.

"Ephraim Deane!"—then a soldier spoke:
　　"Deane carried our Regiment's colors," he said;
　　"Where our Ensign was shot, I left him dead,
Just after the enemy wavered and broke."

"Close to the road-side his body lies;
　　I paused a moment and gave him to drink;
　　He murmured his mother's name, I think,
And Death came with it and closed his eyes."

'T was a victory; yes, but it cost us dear,—
　　For that company's roll, when called at night,
　　Of a *hundred* men who went into the fight,
Numbered but twenty that answered, "Here!"

XXXVII.

THE SMACK IN SCHOOL.

W. P. PALMER.

a A District School, not far away
　　Mid Berkshire hills, one Winter's day,
　　Was humming with its wonted noise
　　Of three score mingled girls and boys—

---

a Narrative; pure voice; unemotional.

Some few upon their tasks intent,
But more on furtive mischief bent;
b The while the Master's downward look
Was fastened on a copy-book—
When suddenly, behind his back,
Rose, loud and clear, a rousing SMACK!
As 't were a battery of bliss
Let off in one tremendous kiss!
c "What's that?" the startled Master cries;
d "That thir," a little imp replies,
"Wath William Willith, if you pleathe—
I thaw him kith Thuthannah Peathe!"
e With frown to make a statue thrill,
The Master thundered, *f* "Hither, Will!"
Like wretch o'ertaken in his track,
With stolen chattels on his back,
Will hung his head in fear and shame,
And to the awful presence came—
A great, green, bashful simpleton,
The butt of all good-natured fun—
With smile suppressed, and birch upraised,
The threatener faltered—*g* "I'm amazed
That you, my biggest pupil, should
Be guilty of an act so rude!
Before the whole set school to boot—
What evil genius put you to 't?"
h "'T was she, herself, sir," sobbed the lad,
"I did'nt mean to be so bad—
But when Susannah shook her curls,
And whispered I was 'feard of girls,
And dass'nt kiss a baby's doll,
I could'nt stand it, sir, at all!
But up and kissed her on the spot,
I know—*boo hoo*—I ought to not,
But, somehow, from her looks, *boo hoo*,
I thought she kind o' wished me to!"

---

b Imitate the teacher. *c* High pitch *d* Low pitch; lisping. *e* Narrative. *f* Personation.
g Personation. *h* Like a bashful booby, crying, talking. Do not be afraid of overdoing it.

XXXVIII.

THE LOST PANTALOONS.

1. It chanced to be on washing day,
   And all our things were drying,
   The storm came roaring through the lines
   And set them all a-flying;
   I saw the shirts and petticoats
   Go riding off like witches,
   I lost—ah! bitterly I wept,—
   I lost my Sunday breeches.

2. I saw them straddling through the air,
   Alas! too late to win them,
   I saw them chase the clouds as if
   The mischief had been in them.
   They were my darlings and my pride,
   My boyhood's only riches;
   Farewell, farewell, I faintly cried,
   My breeches, O, my breeches.

3. That night I saw them in my dreams,
   How changed from what I knew them;
   The dew had steeped their faded seams,
   The wind had whistled through them;
   I saw the wide and ghastly rents
   Where demon claws had torn them:
   A hole was in their hinder parts
   As if an imp had worn them.

4. I have had many happy years
   And tailors kind and clever;
   But those young pantaloons have gone
   For ever and for ever;
   And not till fate has cut the last
   Of all my earthly stitches,
   This aching heart shall cease to mourn
   My loved—my long lost breeches.

XXXIX.

GOTTLIEB'S TOGGY BUP.

SIRIUS.

Vonce I pyed me a toggy bup, vot vas plack all over shust, except his dail, unt dat vas der zame golor, so I call him Shpot. Den I zents him mit tog school unt learns him some liddle dricks. Vcn vas to shtand him town in a blace mit himself unt dell him shtay dere till I gome pack. Den I coes avay shust so a liddle dimes, unt ven I gets pack, I never vints him more ash dree miles vrom der place!—Anoder vas, do blay ted. I lays him town on a dable mit a pox py der site for a goffin; den I says, "ven I vires dish gun you shust go ted in der pox." Den I shoots, unt ven der schmoke glears away, ven I looks in der pox, vot you dinks? Vy, he'd shumped out der vinder unt hided in der shtable mit. Put der pest drick vas dish: I zent mine prudder a den dollar pill in der post office mit a ledder, unt zents Shpot mit it. You pleve dat raskal shlips der monish out, unt teposits mit his own gredit in a putcher's shop? I nefer plays him dat drick put vonce. Afder a vile, Shpot gits der vleas padder as vorse, den I rups him all ofer mit vet cunbowder, unt pids him shtay avay vrom der vire. Burdy soon he shlips unter der shtove, unt so soon he gits try, he plows himzelf up, unt dat vas der last of Shpot unt der vleas doo. I vears grape on my left leg vor dirty years.

XL.

THE ELOCUTION OF THE PULPIT.

REV. JAMES FORDYCE.

I cannot forbear regretting here, that a matter of such vast importance to preaching, as delivery, should be so generally neglected or misunderstood. A common apprehension prevails, indeed, that a strict regard to these rules would be deemed theatrical; and the dread, perhaps, of incurring this imputation, is a restraint upon many. But is it not possible to obtain a just and expressive manner, perfectly consistent with the gravity of the pulpit, and yet quite distinct from the more passionate, strong, and diversified action of the theatre? And is it not possible to hit off this manner so easily and naturally, as to leave no room for just reflection? An affair this, it must be owned, of the utmost delicacy; in which we shall probably often miscarry, *and meet with abundance of censure at first.* But, still, I imagine. that through the regulations of taste, the improvements of experience, the corrections of friendship, the feelings of piety, and the gradual mellowings of time, such an elocution may be acquired, as is above delineated; and such as, *when* acquired, will make its way to the hearts of the hearers, through their ears and eyes, with a delight to both, that is seldom felt; while, contrary to what is now practiced, it will appear to the former the very language of nature, and present to the latter.*the lively image of the preacher's soul.* Were a taste for this kind of elocution to take place, it is difficult to say how much the preaching art would gain by it. Pronunciation would be studied, an ear would be formed, the voice would be modulated, every feature of the face, every motion of the hands, every posture of the body, would be brought under right management. A graceful, and correct, and animated expression in all these would be ambitiously sought after; mutual criticisms and friendly hints would be universally acknowledged; light and direction would be borrowed from every quarter, and from every age. The best models of antiquity would in a particular manner be admired, surveyed, and imitated. The sing-song voice, and the see-saw gestures, if I may be allowed to use those expressions, would, of course, be exploded; and, in time, nothing would be admitted, at least approved, among performers, but what was decent, manly, and truly excellent in kind. Even the people themselves would contract, insensibly, a growing relish for such a manner; and those preachers would at last be in chief repute with all, who followed nature, overlooked themselves, appeared totally absorbed in the subject, and spoke with real propriety and pathos, from the immediate impulse of truth and virtue.

XLI.

THE BLACK REGIMENT.

PORT HUDSON, MAY 27, 1863.

GEO. H. BOKER.

Dark as the clouds of even,
Ranked in the western heaven,
Waiting the breath that lifts
All the dread mass, and drifts
Tempest and falling brand
Over a ruined land ; —
So still and orderly,
Arm to arm, knee to knee,
Waiting the great event,
Stands the black regiment.

Down the long dusky line
Teeth gleam and eyeballs shine ;
And the bright bayonet,
Bristling and firmly set,
Flashed with a purpose grand,
Long ere the sharp command
Of the fierce rolling drum
Told them their time had come,
Told them that work was sent
For the black regiment.

" Now," the flag-sergeant cried,
" Though death and hell betide,
Let the whole nation see
If we are fit to be
Free in this land ; or bound
Down, like the whining hound, —
Bound with red stripes of pain
In our old chains again ! "
O, what a shout there went
From the black regiment !

"Charge ! " Trump and drum awoke,
Onward the bondmen broke ;
Bayonet and sabre-stroke
Vainly opposed their rush.
Through the wild battle's crush,
With but one thought aflush,
Driving their lords like chaff,

In the guns' mouths they laugh ;
Or at the slippery brands
Leaping with open hands,
Down they tear man and horse,
Down in their awful course ;
Trampling with bloody heel
Over the crashing steel,
All their eyes forward bent,
Rushed the black regiment.

" Freedom ! " their battle-cry, —
" Freedom ! or leave to die ! "
Ah ! and they meant the word,
Not as with us 'tis heard,
Not a mere party shout :
They gave their spirits out ;
Trusting the end to God,
And on the gory sod
Rolled in triumphant blood.
Glad to strike one free blow,
Whether for weal or woe ;
Glad to breathe one free breath,
Though on the lips of death.
Praying — alas ! in vain ! —
That they might fall again,
So they could once more see
That burst to liberty !
This was what " freedom " lent
To the black regiment.

Hundreds on hundreds fell ;
But they are resting well ;
Scourges and shackles strong
Never shall do them wrong.
O, to the living few,
Soldiers, be just and true !
Hail them as comrades tried ;
Fight with them side by side ;
Never, in field or tent,
Scorn the black regiment !

XLII.

ON THE SHORES OF TENNESSEE.

a "Move my arm-chair, faithful Pompey,
    In the sunshine bright and strong,
For this world is fading, Pompey —
    Massa won't be with you long;
And I fain would hear the south wind
    Bring once more the sound to me,
Of the wavelets softly breaking
    On the shores of Tennessee.

"Mournful though the ripples murmur,
    As they still the story tell,
How no vessels float the banner
    That I've loved so long and well.
I shall listen to their music,
    Dreaming that again I see
Stars and Stripes on sloop and shallop
    Sailing up the Tennessee.

"And, Pompey, while old Massa's waiting
    For Death's last dispatch to come,
If that exiled starry banner
    Should come proudly sailing home,
You shall greet it, slave no longer—
    Voice and hand shall both be free
That shout and point to Union colors
    On the waves of Tennessee."

b "Massa's berry kind to Pompey;
    But ole darkey's happy here,
Where he's tended corn and cotton
    For dese many a long gone year.
c Over yonder Missis' sleeping—
    No one tends her grave like me.
Mebbe she would miss the flowers
    She used to love in Tennessee.

---

a Slow; voice slightly tremor; with as much variety as would be given by an old man, in the circumstances. *b* Change the voice; endeavor to give the full but subdued voice of a faithful slave. *c* Raise both hands.

d " Pears like she was watching Massa—
    If Pompey should beside him stay,
Mebbe she'd remember better
    How for him she used to pray ;
Telling him that way up yonder
    White as snow his soul would be,
If he served the Lord of Heaven
    While he lived in Tennessee."

e Silently the tears were rolling
    Down the poor old dusky face,
As he stepped behind his master,
    In his long accustomed place.
Then a silence fell around them,
    As they gazed on rock and tree
Pictured in the placid waters
    Of the rolling Tennessee.

Master, dreaming of the battle
    Where he fought by Marion's side,
When he bid the haughty Tarlton
    Stoop his lordly crest of pride.
Man, remembering how yon sleeper
    Once he held upon his knee,
Ere she loved the gallant soldier,
    Ralph Vervair, of Tennessee.

Still the south wind fondly lingers
    'Mid the veteran's silver hair ;
Still the bondman close beside him
    Stands behind the old arm-chair,
f With his dark-hued hand uplifted.
    Shading eyes, he bends to see
Where the woodland boldly jutting
    Turns aside the Tennessee.

Thus he watches cloud-born shadows
    Glide from tree to mountain-crest,

From *d* raise the hands still more and clasping them as you utter the last stanza, raising the eyes to heaven.   *e* Narrative style ; pure voice ; more animated.   *f* Raise one hand above the eyes as if shading them while looking in the distance, step forward.

Softly creeping, aye and ever
  To the river's yielding breast.
g Ha! above the foliage yonder
  Something flutters wild and free!
  " Massa! Massa! Hallelujah!
  The flag's come back to Tennessee!"

h " Pompey, hold me on your shoulder,
  Help me stand on foot once more,
  That I may salute the colors
  As they pass my cabin door.
  Here's the paper signed that frees you,
  Give a freeman's shout with me—
i 'God and Union!' be our watchword
  Evermore in Tennessee!"

j Then the trembling voice grew fainter,
  And the limbs refused to stand;
  One prayer to Jesus—and the soldier
  Glided to the better land.
  When the flag went down the river
  Man and master both were free,
  While the ring-dove's note was mingled
  With the rippling Tennessee.

XLIII.
BEFORE VICKSBURG.
MAY 19, 1863.
GEORGE H. BOKER.

While Sherman stood beneath the hottest fire,
  That from the lines of Vicksburg gleamed,
And bomb-shells tumbled in their smoky gyre,
  And grape-shot hissed, and case-shot screamed;
    Back from the front there came,
    Weeping and sorely lame,
  The merest child, the youngest face
  Man ever saw in such a fearful place.

---

g High pitch, with much animation. *h* Weak voice; low pitch; slow and labored utterance. *i* Raise the pitch; full tone. *j* Narrative style; low and full, with measured utterance; slow time to the close.

Stifling his tears, he limped his chief to meet,
  But when he paused, and tottering stood,
Around the circle of his little feet
   There spread a pool of bright, young blood.
      Shocked at his doleful case,
      Sherman cried, "Halt! front face!"
     Who are you? Speak, my gallant boy!"
    "A drummer, sir: — Fifty-fifth Illinois."

"Are you not hit?" "That' nothing. Only send
  Some cartridges: our men are out;
And the foe press us." "But, my little friend—"
  "Don't mind me! Did you hear that shout?
      What if our men be driven?
      O, for the love of Heaven,
     Send to my Colonel, General, dear!"
    "But you?" "O, I shall easily find the rear."

"I'll see to that," cried Sherman; and a drop,
  Angels might envy, dimmed his eye,
As the boy, toiling towards the hill's hard top,
  Turned round, and with his shrill child's cry
      Shouted, "O, don't forget!
      We'll win the battle yet!
     But let our soldiers have some more,
    More cartridges, sir, — calibre fifty-four!"

XLIV.

PYRAMUS AND THISBE.

JOHN G. SAXE.

This tragical tale, which, they say, is a true one,
Is old; but the manner is wholly a new one.
One *Ovid*, a writer of some reputation,
Has told it before in a tedious narration;
In a style, to be sure, of remarkable fullness,
But which nobody reads on account of its dullness.

Young PETER PYRAMUS—I call him Peter,
Not for the sake of the rhyme of the meter;

But merely to make the name completer—
For Peter lived in the olden times,
And in one of the worst of pagan climes
That flourish now in classical fame,
Long before either noble or boor
Had such a thing as a *Christian* name—
Young Peter, then, was a nice young beau
As any young lady would wish to know;
In years, I ween, he was rather green,
That is to say, he was just eighteen,—
A trifle too short, a shaving too lean,
But "a nice young man" as ever was seen,
And fit to dance with a May-day queen!

Now Peter loved a beautiful girl
As ever ensnared the heart of an earl,
In the magical trap of an auburn curl, —
A little Miss Thisbe, who lived next door,
(They slept, in fact, on the very same floor,
With a wall between them and nothing more, —
Those double dwellings were common of yore,)
And they loved each other, the legends say,
In that very beautiful, bountiful way,
That every young maid and every young blade,
Are wont to do before they grow staid,
And learn to love by the laws of trade.
But (a-lack-a-day, for the girl and boy!)
A little impediment checked their joy,
And gave them awhile, the deepest annoy,
For some good reason, which history cloaks,
The match didn't happen to please the old folks!

So Thisbe's father and Peter's mother
Began the young couple to worry and bother,
And tried their innocent passion to smother,
By keeping the lovers from seeing each other!
But who ever heard of a marriage deterred
Or even deferred
By any contrivance so very absurd
As scolding the boy, and caging the bird?

Now, Peter, who was not discouraged at all
By obstacles such as the timid appall,
Contrived to discover a hole in the wall,
Which wasn't so thick but removing a brick
Made a passage—though rather provokingly small.
Through this little chink the lover could greet her,
And secrecy made their courting the sweeter,
While Peter kissed Thisbe, and Thisbe kissed Peter—
For kisses, like folks with diminutive souls,
Will manage to creep through the smallest of holes!

'T was here that the lovers, intent upon love,
Laid a nice little plot to meet at a spot
Near a mulberry-tree in a neighboring grove;
For the plan was all laid by the youth and the maid,
Whose hearts, it would seem, were uncommonly bold ones,
To run off and get married in spite of the old ones.
In the shadows of evening, as still as a mouse,
The beautiful maiden slipped out of the house,
The mulberry-tree impatient to find;
While Peter, the vigilant matrons to blind,
Strolled leisurely out, some minutes behind.

While waiting alone by the trysting tree,
A terrible lion as e'er you set eye on,
Came roaring along quite horrid to see,
And caused the young maiden in terror to flee,
(A lion's a creature whose regular trade is
Blood—and " a terrible thing among ladies,")
And losing her veil as she ran from the wood,
The monster bedabbled it over with blood.

Now Peter arriving, and seeing the veil
All covered o'er and reeking with gore,
Turned, all of a sudden, exceedingly pale,
And sat himself down to weep and to wail,—
For, soon as he saw the garment, poor Peter,
Made up his mind in very short meter,
That Thisbe was dead, and the lion had eat her!
So breathing a prayer, he determined to share
The fate of his darling, " the loved and the lost,"
And fell on his dagger, and gave up the ghost!

Now Thisbe returning, and viewing her beau,
Lying dead by her vail, (which she happened to know,)
She guessed in a moment the cause of his erring ;
And seizing the knife that had taken his life,
In less than a jiffy was dead as a herring.

MORAL.

Young gentleman ! —pray recollect if you please,
Not to make assignations near mulberry-trees.
Should your mistress be missing, it shows a weak head
To be stabbing yourself, till you know she is dead.
Young ladies ! —you shouldn't go strolling about
When your anxious mammas don't know you are out ;
And remember that accidents often befall
From kissing young fellows through holes in the wall !

XLV.

THE FIREMAN.

F. S. HILL.

a Hark ! that alarm-bell, 'mid the wintry storm !
b Hear the loud shout ! the rattling engines swarm.
Hear that distracted mother's cry to save
Her darling infant from a threatened grave !
That babe who lies in sleep's light pinions bound,
And dreams of heaven, while hell is raging round !
c Forth springs the Fireman—stay ! nor tempt thy fate ! —
He hears not — heeds not, —nay, it is too late !
d See how the timbers crash beneath his feet !
O, which way now is left for his retreat ?
The roaring flames already bar his way,
Like ravenous demons raging for their prey !
He laughs at danger, —pauses not for rest,
Till the sweet charge is folded to his breast.
e Now, quick, brave youth, retrace your path ; —but, lo !
A fiery gulf yawns fearfully below !

---

a Aspirate; long pauses. *b* Bold; high pitched; rapid. *c* Pure; moderate pitch; quick ·
d High pitch; rapid; with much feeling. *e* High; bold; quick.

H

One desperate leap ! —*f* lost ! lost ! — the flames arise,
And paint their triumph on the o'erarching skies !
Not lost ! again his tottering form appears !
The applauding shouts of rapturous friends he hears !
The big drops from his manly forehead roll,
And deep emotions thrill his generous soul.
But struggling nature now reluctant yields ;
Down drops the arm the infant's face that shields,
To bear the precious burthen all too weak ;
When, hark ! —the mother's agonizing shriek !
Once more he's roused, —his eye no longer swims,
And tenfold strength rëanimates his limbs ;
He nerves his faltering frame for one last bound, —
g "Your child ! " he cries, and sinks upon the ground !

h And his reward you ask ; — reward he spurns ;
For him the father's generous bosom burns, —
For him on high the widow's prayer shall go, —
For him the orphan's pearly tear-drop flow.
His boon, —the richest e'er to mortals given, —
Approving conscience, and the smile of Heaven !

XLVI.

THE MERCHANT OF VENICE.

RICHARD GRANT WHITE.

In his introduction to *The Merchant of Venice*, Mr. White, after showing "that the story of this comedy, even to its episodic part and its minutest incidents, had been told again and again long before Shakespeare was born," vindicates him from the charge of plagiarism in the following matchless paragraph : —

What then remains to Shakespeare ? and what is there to show that he is not a plagiarist ? Every thing that makes *The Merchant of Venice* what it is. The people are puppets, and the incidents are all in these old stories. They are mere bundles of barren sticks that the poet's touch causes to bloom like Aaron's rod : they are heaps of dry bones till he clothes them with human flesh and breathes into

---

f High; aspirate; long pauses—Imagine the scene, and adopt such expression and gesture as will portray it to the listener. *g* With much feeling, and as a personation. *h* After a pause, give the closing in pure, narrative style, slow time.

them the breath of life. *Antonio*, grave, pensive, prudent, save in his devotion to his young kinsman, as a Christian hating the Jew, as a loyal merchant despising the usurer; *Bassanio*, lavish yet provident, a generous gentleman although a fortune seeker, wise although a gay gallant, and manly though dependent; *Gratiano*, who unites the not too common virtues of thorough good nature and unselfishness with the sometimes not unserviceable fault of talking for talk's sake; *Shylock*, crafty and cruel, whose revenge is as mean as it is fierce and furious, whose abuse never rises to invective, or his anger into wrath, and who has yet some dignity of port as the avenger of a nation's wrongs, some claim upon our sympathy as a father outraged by his only child; and *Portia*, matchless impersonation of that rare woman who is gifted even more in intellect than in loveliness, and yet who stops gracefully short of the offence of intellectuality;—these, not to notice minor characters no less perfectly arranged or completely developed after their kind,—these, and the poetry which is their atmosphere, and through which they beam upon us, all radiant in its golden light, are Shakespeare's only; and these it is, and not the incidents of old, and, but for these, forgotten tales, that make *The Merchant of Venice* a priceless and imperishable dower to the queenly city that sits enthroned upon the sea;—a dower of romance more bewitching than that of her moonlit waters and beauty-laden balconies, of adornment more splendid than that of her pictured palaces, of human interest more enduring than that of her blood-stained annals, more touching even than the sight of her faded grandeur.

XLVII.

In Memoriam.

A. LINCOLN.

BY. MRS EMILY J. BUGBEE,—APRIL 30, 1865.

There's a burden of grief on the breezes of spring,
And a song of regret from the bird on its wing;

There's a pall on the sunshine and over the flowers,
And a shadow of graves on these spirits of ours;
For a star hath gone out from the night of our sky,
On whose brightness we gazed as the war-cloud rolled by;
So tranquil and steady and clear were its beams,
That they fell like a vision of peace on our dreams.

A heart that we knew had been true to our weal,
And a hand that was steadily guiding the wheel;
A name never tarnished by falsehood or wrong,
That had dwelt in our hearts like a soul-stirring song;
Ah! that pure, noble spirit has gone to its rest,
And the true hand lies nerveless and cold on his breast;
But the name and the memory—*these* never will die,
But grow brighter and dearer as ages go by.

Yet the tears of a nation fall over the dead,
Such tears as a nation before never shed,
For our cherished one fell by a dastardly hand,
A martyr to truth and the cause of the land;
And a sorrow has surged, like the waves to the shore
When the breath of the tempest is sweeping them o'er;
And the heads of the lofty and lowly have bowed,
As the shaft of the lightning sped out from the cloud.

Not gathered, like Washington, home to his rest,
When the sun of his life was far down in the west;
But stricken from earth in the midst of his years,
With the Canaan in view, of his prayers and his tears.
And the people, whose hearts in the wilderness failed,
Sometimes, when the stars of their promise had paled,
Now, stand by his side on the mount of his fame,
And yield him their hearts in a grateful acclaim.

Yet there on the mountain, our Leader must die,
With the fair land of promise spread out to his eye;
His work is accomplished, and what he has done
Will stand as a monument under the sun;
And his name, reaching down through the ages of time,
Will still through the years of eternity shine—

Like a star, sailing on through the depths of the blue,
On whose brightness we gaze every evening anew.

His white tent is pitched on the beautiful plain,
Where the tumult of battle comes never again,
Where the smoke of the war-cloud ne'er darkens the air,
Nor falls on the spirit a shadow of care.
The songs of the ransomed enrapture his ear,
And he heeds not the dirges that roll for him here ;
In the calm of his spirit, so strange and sublime,
He is lifted far over the discords of time.

Then bear him home gently, great son of the West—
'Mid her fair blooming praries lay Lincoln to rest;
From the nation who loved him, she takes to her trust,
And will tenderly garner the consecrate dust.
A Mecca his grave to the people shall be,
And a shrine evermore for the hearts of the free.

XLVIII.

THE ALARM,—APRIL 19, 1776.

GEORGE BANCROFT.

Darkness closed upon the country and upon the town, but it was no night for sleep. Heralds on swift relays of horses transmitted the war-message from hand to hand, till village repeated it to village; the sea to the backwoods; the plains to the highlands; and it was never suffered to droop, till it had been borne North, and South, and East, and West, throughout the land. It spread over the bays that receive the Saco and the Penobscot. Its loud reveille broke the rest of the trappers of New Hampshire, and ringing like bugle-notes from peak to peak, overleapt the Green Mountains, swept onward to Montreal, and descended the ocean river, till the responses were echoed from the cliffs of Quebec. The hills along the Hudson told to one another the tale. As the summons hurried to the South, it was one day at New York; in one more at Philadelphia; the next it lighted a watchfire at Baltimore; thence it waked an answer at Annapolis. Crossing the Potomac near Mount Vernon, it was sent forward without a halt to Williamsburg. It traversed the Dismal Swamp to Nansemond, along the route of the first emigrants to North Carolina. It moved onwards and still onwards through boundless groves of evergreen to Newbern and to Wilmington. "For God's sake, forward it by night and by day," wrote Cornelius Harnett, by the express which sped for Brunswick. Patriots of South Carolina caught up its tones at the border and despatched it to Charleston, and through pines and palmettos and moss-clad live oaks, further to the South, till it resounded among the New England settlements beyond the Savannah. Hillsborough and the Mecklenburg district of North Carolina rose in triumph, now that their wearisome uncertainty had its end. The Blue Ridge took up the voice and made it heard from one end to the other of the valley of Virginia. The Alleghanies, as they listened, opened their barriers that the "loud call" might pass through to the hardy riflemen on the Holston, the Watauga and the French Broad. Ever renewing its strength, powerful enough even to create a commonwealth, it breathed its inspiring word to the first settlers of Kentucky; so that hunters who made their halt in the matchless valley of the Elkhorn, commemorated the nineteenth day of April by naming their encampment LEXINGTON.

With one impulse the colonies sprung to arms; with one spirit they pledged themselves to each other "to be ready for the extreme event." With one heart the continent cried, "Liberty or death."

XLIX.

CHARACTER OF PRESIDENT LINCOLN.

REV. HENRY FOWLER — 1864.

The progress of the President illustrates the progress of the people. Arthur Stanley speaks of Samuel, the prophet, as mediator between the old and new, in Jewish history. His two-sided sympathy enabled him to unite the passing and the coming epoch. Such an epoch of perplexity, transition, change, is not often witnessed. In every such passage of a nation there ought to be a character like that of Samuel. Misunderstood and misrepresented at the time; attacked from both sides; charged with not going far enough and with going too far; charged with saying too much and saying too little; he slowly, conscientiously and honestly worked out the mighty problem. He was not the founder of a new state of things like Moses; he was not a champion of the existing order of things like Elijah. He stood between the two; between the living and the dead; between the past and the present; between the old and the new; with that sympathy for each which, at such a time, is the best hope for any permanent solution of the question that torments it. His duty is carefully to distinguish between that which is temporal and that which is eternal. He has but little praise from partisans; but is the careful healer, binding up the wounds of the age in spite of itself; the good surgeon, knitting together the dislocated bones of the disjointed times.

Such a man was Samuel among the Jews; such a man was Athanasius among the early Christians; such a man is Abraham Lincoln in this day. The explanation for his every act is this: He executes the will of the people. He represents a controlling majority. If he be slow it is because the people are slow. If he has done a foolish act, it was the stupidity of the people which impelled it. His wisdom consists in carrying out the good sense of the nation. His growth in political knowledge, his steady movement towards emancipation, are but the growth and movement of the national mind. Indeed, in character and culture, he is a fair representative of the average American. His awkward speech and yet more awkward silence, his uncouth manners, his grammar self-taught and partly forgotten, his style miscellaneous, concreted from the best authors, like a reading-book, and yet oftimes of Saxon force and classic purity; his humor an argument, and his logic a joke, both unseasonable at times and irresistable always; his questions answers, and his answers questions; his guesses prophesies, and fulfillment even beyond his promise; honest, yet shrewd; simple, yet reticent; heavy, yet energetic; never despairing, and never sanguine; careless in forms; conscientious in essentials; never sacrificing a good servant once trusted, never deserting a good principle once adopted; not afraid of new ideas, nor despising old ones; improving opportunities to confess mistakes, ready to learn, getting at facts, doing nothing when he knows not what to do; hesitating at nothing when he sees the right; lacking the recognized qualification of a party leader, and yet leading his party as no other man can; sustaining his political enemies in Missouri to their defeat, sustaining his political friends in Maryland to their victory; conservative in his sympathies and radical in his acts; Socratic in his style and Baconian in his method; his religion consisting in truthfulness, temperance, asking good people to pray for him, and publicly acknowledging in events the hand of God, he stands before you as the type of "Brother Jonathan," a not perfect man, and yet more precious than fine gold.

L.

THE LOST STEAMSHIP.

FITZ-JAMES O'BRIEN.

"Ho, there! fisherman, hold your hand!
 Tell me what is that far away —
There, where over the Isle of Sand
 Hangs the mist-cloud sullen and gray?
See! it rocks with a ghastly life,
 Raising and rolling through clouds of spray,
Right in the midst of the breakers' strife—
 Tell me, what is it, Fisherman, pray?"

"That, good sir, was a steamer, stout
 As ever paddled around Cape Race,
And many's the wild and stormy bout
 She had with the winds in that self-same place;
But her time had come; and at ten o'clock
 Last night she struck on that lonesome shore,
And her sides were gnawed by the hidden rock,
 And at dawn this morning she was no more."

"Come, as you seem to know, good man,
    The terrible fate of this gallant ship,
Tell me all about her that you can,—
    And here's my flask to moisten your lip.
Tell me how many she had on board—
    Wives and husbands, and lovers true—
How did it fare with her human hoard,
    Lost she many' or lost she few'?"

"Master, I may not drink of your flask,
    Already too moist I feel my lip;
But I'm ready to do what else you ask,
    And spin you my yarn about the ship:
'T was ten o'clock, as I said, last night,
    When she struck the breakers and went ashore,
And scarce had broken the morning's light
    Than she sank in twelve feet of water, or more.

"But long ere this they knew their doom,
    And the Captain called all hands to prayer;
And solemnly over the ocean's boom
    The orisons rose on the troubled air.
And round about the vessel there rose
    Tall plumes of spray as white as snow,
Like angels in their ascension clothes,
    Waiting for those who prayed below.

"So those three hundred people clung
    As well as they could to spar and rope;
With a word of prayer upon every tongue,
    · Nor on any face a glimmer of hope.
But there was no blubbering weak and wild—
    Of tearful faces I saw but one,
A rough old salt, who cried like a child,
    And not for himself, but the Captain's son.

"The Captain stood on the quarter-deck,
    Firm but pale, with trumpet in hand,
Sometimes he looked on the breaking wreck,
    Sometimes he sadly looked on land.

And often he smiled to cheer the crew—
  But, Lord! the smile was terrible grim—
'Till over the quarter a huge sea flew,
  And that was the last they saw of him.

"1 saw one young fellow, with his bride,
  Standing amidship upon the wreck;
His face was white as the boiling tide,
  And *she* was clinging about his neck.
And I saw them try to say good-bye,
  But neither could hear the other speak;
So they floated away through the sea to die—
  Shoulder to shoulder, and cheek to cheek.

"And there was a child, but eight at best,
  Who went his way in a sea we shipped,
All the while holding upon his breast
  A little pet parrot whose wings were clipped.
And as the boy and the bird went by,
  Swinging away on a tall wave's crest,
They were grappled by a man with a drowning cry,
  And together the three went down to rest.

"And so the crew went one by one,
  Some with gladness, and few with fear;
Cold and hardship such work had done
  That few seemed frightened when death was near.
Thus every soul on board went down—
  Sailor and passenger, little and great;
The last that sank was a man of my town,
  A capital swimmer—the second mate."

"Now, lonely Fisherman, who are you,
  That say you saw this terrible wreck?
How do I know what you say is true,
  When every mortal was swept from the deck?
Where were you in that hour of death?
  How do you know what you relate?"
His answer came in an under-breath—
  "Master, I was the second mate!"

LI.

THE SKY-LARK.

JAMES HOGG.

Bird of the wilderness,
Blithesome and cumberless,
Sweet be thy matin o'er moorland and lea !
Emblem of happiness,
Blest is thy dwelling-place,
Oh to abide in the desert with thee !
Wild is thy lay, and loud,
Far in the downy cloud,
Love gives it energy, love gave it birth.
Where, on thy dewy wing,
Where art thou journeying ?
Thy lay is in heaven, thy love is on earth.

O'er fell and fountain sheen,
O'er moor and mountain green,
O'er the red streamers that herald the day,
Over the cloudlet dim,
Over the rainbow's rim,
Musical cherub, soar, singing away !
Then, when the gloaming comes,
Low in the heather blooms,
Sweet will thy welcome and bed of love be !
Emblem of happiness,
Blest is thy dwelling-place—
Oh to abide in the desert with thee !

LII.

FANATICISM.

CHARLES SUMNER — 1856.

The Senator from South Carolina denounces opposition to the usurpation in Kansas as an uncalculating fanaticism. Sir, fanaticism is found in an enthusiasm or exaggeration of opinions, particularly on religious subjects; but there may be a fanaticism for evil as well as for good. Now, I will not deny that there are persons among us loving liberty too well for their personal good, in a selfish generation. Such there may be, and, for the sake of their example, would that there were more! In calling them "fanatics," you would cast contumely upon the noble army of martyrs, from the earliest day down to this hour; upon the great tribunes of human rights, by whom life, liberty, and happiness on earth, have been secured; upon the long line of devoted patriots, who, throughout history, have truly loved their country; and upon all who, in noble aspirations for the general good, and in forgetfulness of self, have stood out before their age, and gathered into their generous bosoms the shafts of tyranny and wrong, in order to make a pathway for truth. You discredit Luther, when alone he nailed his articles to the door of the church at Wittenburg, and then, to the imperial demand that he should retract, firmly replied, "Here I stand; I cannot do otherwise, so help me God!" You discredit Hampden, when alone he refused to pay the few shillings of ship-money, and shook the throne of Charles I.; you discredit Milton, when, amidst the corruptions of a heartless court, he lived on, the lofty friend of liberty, above question or suspicion; you discredit Russell and Sidney, when, for the sake of their country, they calmly turned from family and friends, to tread the narrow steps of the scaffold; you discredit the early founders of American institutions, who preferred the hardships of a wilderness, surrounded by a savage foe, to injustice on beds of ease; you discredit our later fathers, who, few in numbers, and weak in resources, yet strong in their cause, did not hesitate to brave the mighty power of England, already encircling the globe with her morning drum-beats. Yes, sir, of such are the fanatics of history, according to the Senator.*

LIII.
THE GERMAN'S BELL.

Hi up in de shteeble dare hangs de pell, un
Every day tree times comes der schneider man
Un bulls de rope so dat he makes de pell speag,

---

*Butler.

On seven, on zwolf, und at noin o'glock in de
Nite. Den ef dare meetin mit bolitix, oder
Speeches, oder shows, he likewise de rope
Does bull. Ef de breechen time comes, und de
Beeples valk togedder to worship Got,
Und gits der childs baptized, den too
De pig veel fast mit de pell goes rount,
One vay unt todder rich makes ding dong.
Un ef de peebles is glad und comes togedder
Und holler, und say it is de four of Ghuly,
Dat pell do speag loud un make a krat noise.
Yaw, und ef you goes over Chordan it speaks
Shlow und grand, shust like valkin to a barrien.
Ven de chudge comes here und otter beeples
De pell must ring shure.

　Ef it rains, oder snows, oder is hot wedder
As vill burn bowder ; oder ef it is golt as vill
Vreeze wit de mittens off; oder if it pees
Tark as you not can see un inch, oder de glouts
Is pig un dick—no otts—de pell rings.
So Meister Peck, de tailor man, is shust so certain
As de vatch in his bogget.
Oh, if he dies order gits kilt, vot shall ve do !

―――――

LIV.

To the Graduating Class of Columbia College.

CHARLES KING—1861.

My young friends, you enter upon life at the very moment this
great question of secession is under the issue of war. Shrink not
back from it. We must be decided now and forever. The baleful
doctrine of secession must be finally and absolutely renounced. The
poor quibble of double allegiance must be disavowed. An American
—and not a New Yorker, nor a Virginian—is the noble title by
which we are to live, and which you, my young friends, must in your
respective spheres, contribute to make live, whatever it may cost in
blood and money.

Go forth, then, my young friends — go forth as citizens of the great continental American Republic — to which your first, your constant, your latest hopes in life should attach — and abating no jot of obedience to the municipal or State authority within the respective limits of each — bear yourselves always, and every where, as Americans — as fellow-countrymen of Adams, and Ellsworth, and Jay, and Jefferson, and Carroll, and Washington, and Pinckney — as heirs of the glories of Bunker Hill, and Saratoga, and Monmouth, and Yorktown, and Eutaw Springs, and New Orleans, and suffer no traitor hordes to despoil you of so rich an inheritance or so grand and glorious a country.

LV.

SECESSION AND FOREIGN POWERS.

EDWARD EVERETT — 1861.

Let it be remembered that in granting to the seceding States, jointly and severally, the right to leave the Union, we concede to them the right of resuming, if they please, their former allegiance to England, France and Spain. It rests with them, with any one of them, if the right of secession is admitted, again to plant a European government side by side with that of the United States on the soil of America; and it is by no means the most improbable upshot of this ill-starred rebellion, if allowed to prosper. Is this the Monroe doctrine, for which the United States have been contending?

The disunion press in Virginia last year openly encouraged the idea of a French protectorate, and her legislature has, I believe, sold out the James River canal, the darling enterprise of Washington, to a company in France supposed to enjoy the countenance of the Emperor. The seceding patriots of South Carolina were understood by the correspondent of the London "Times" to admit that they would rather be subject to a British prince, than to the Government of the United States. Whether they desire it or not, the moment the seceders lose the protection of the United States, they hold their

independence at the mercy of the powerful governments of Europe
If the navy of the North should withdraw its protection, there is
not a southern State on the Atlantic or the Gulf, which might not
be recolonized by Europe, in six months after the outbreak of *
var.

LVI.

MAN'S NATURAL RIGHT TO THE SOIL.

G. A. GROW—1860.

The associations of an independent freehold is eminently calculated
to ennoble and elevate the possessor. It is the life-spring of a manly
national character, and of a generous patriotism; a patriotism that
rushes to the defence of the country and the vindication of its honor,
with the same zeal and alacrity that it guards the hearthstone and
fireside. Wherever Freedom has unfurled her banner, the men
who have rallied around to sustain and uphold it have come from
the workshop and the field, where, inured to heat and to cold,
and to all the inclemencies of the season, they have acquired
the hardihood necessary to endure the trials and privations of the
camp. An independent yeomanry, scattered over our vast domain,
is the best and surest guarantee for the perpetuity of our liberties;
for their arms are the citadel of a nation's power, their hearts the
bulwarks of liberty. Let the public domain, then, be set apart and
consecrated as a patrimony to the sons of toil; close your land office
forever against the speculator, and thereby prevent the capital of the
country seeking that kind of investment — from absorbing the hard
earnings of labor without rendering an equivalent. While the
laborer is thus crushed by a system established by the Government,
by which so large an amount is abstracted from his earnings for the
benefit of the speculator, in addition to all the other disadvantages
that ever beset the unequal struggle between the bones and sinews
of men and dollars and cents, what wonder is it that misery and

want so often sit at his fireside, and penury and sorrow surround his death bed?

While the pioneer spirit goes forth into the wilderness, snatching new areas from the wild beast and bequeathing them a legacy to civilized man, let not the Government dampen his ardor and palsy his arm by legislation that places him in the power of soulless capital and grasping speculation; for upon his wild battle-field these are the only foes that his own stern heart and right arm cannot vanquish.

LVII.

The Town of Passage — Father Prout.

FRANCIS MAHONY.

The town of Passage
Is both large and spacious,
And situated
　Upon the say:
'Tis nate and dacent
And quite adjacent
To come from Cork
　On a summer's day.
There you may slip in,
To take a dipping
Forenent the shipping
　That at anchor ride;
Or in a wherry
Cross o'er the ferry
To "Carrigaloe,"
　On the other side.

Mud cabins swarm in
This place so charming,
And sailors' garments
　Hung out to dry;
And each abode is
Snug and commodious,
With pigs melodious
　In the straw-built sty.

'T is there the turf is,
And lots of murphies,
Dead sprats and herrings
　And oyster-shells;
Nor any lack, O!
Of good tobacco—
Though what is smuggled
　By far excels.

There are ships from Cadiz,
And from Barbadoes—
But the leading trade is
　In whiskey-punch;
And you may go in
Where one, Molly Bowen,
Keeps a nate hotel,
　For a quiet lunch.
But land or deck on
You may safely reckon,
Whatsoever country
　You come hither from—
On an invitation
To a jollification
With a parish priest
　That's called "Father Tom."

Of ships there's one fixed
For lodging convicts —
A floating "stone jug"
  Of amazing bulk;
The hake and salmon,
Playing at back gammon,
Swim for divarsion
  All round this hulk.

There "Saxon" jailors
Keep brave repailers
Who soon with sailors
  Must anchor weigh —
From th' Em'rald Island
Ne'er to see dry land
Until they spy land
  In sweet Bot'ny Bay.

LVIII.

THE "PROFESSOR OF SIGNS; OR, TWO WAYS OF TELLING A STORY."

When James VI removed to London he was waited on by the Spanish Ambassador who had a *crotchet* in his head that there should be a Professor of Signs in every Kingdom.

He lamented to the King one day that no country in Europe had such a Professor, and that even for himself he was thus deprived of the pleasure of communicating his ideas in that manner. The King replied:

"Why, I have a Professor of Signs in the northernmost College of my dominion, at Aberdeen, but it is a great way off, perhaps six hundred miles."

"Were it ten thousand leagues off, I shall see him, and am determined to set out in two or three days."

The King saw he had committed himself, and wrote to the University of Aberdeen, stating the case, and asking the Professors to put him off in some way, or make the best of him.

The Ambassador arrived — was received with great solemnity and soon inquired which of them had the honor to be Professor of Signs. He was told the Professor was absent in the Highlands, and would return nobody could tell when.

"I will await his return though it be a year."

Seeing that this would not do, as they had to entertain him at great expense, they contrived a strategem.

I

There was one Sandy, a butcher, blind in one eye, a droll fellow, with some wit and roguery about him. They told him the story, instructed him to be a Professor of Signs; but not to speak a word under pain of losing the promised five pounds for his success.

To the great joy of the Ambassador, he was informed that the Professor would be home the next day.

Sandy was dressed in a wig and gown, and placed in a Chair of State in one of the college halls. The Ambassador was conducted to Sandy's door and shown in, while all the Professors waited in another room in suspense and with anxiety for the success of their scheme.

The Ambassador approached Sandy and held up one finger, Sandy held up two; the Ambassador held up three, Sandy clenched his fist and looked stern. The Ambassador then took an orange from his pocket and held it up, Sandy took a barley-cake from his pocket and held that. The Ambassador then bowed and returned to the other Professors, who anxiously inquired the result.

"He is a wonderful man, a perfect miracle of knowledge; he is worth all the wealth of the Indies."

"Well," inquired the Professors, "tell us the particulars."

"Why," the Ambassador replied, "I held up one finger, denoting there is one God; he held up two, signifying that there are Father and Son. I held up three to indicate the Holy Trinity; he clenched his fist to show that these three are one. I then showed him an orange, to illustrate the goodness of God in giving to his creatures the luxuries as well as the necessaries of life; and this most wonderful philosopher presented a piece of bread to show that the staff of life is preferable to every luxury."

The Professors were, of course, highly delighted, and the Ambassador departed for London to thank the King for the honor of knowing a Professor of Signs.

The Professors then called upon Sandy to give his version of the interview.

"The rascal!" said Sandy. "What do you think he did first? He held up one finger, as much as to say, you have only one eye.

Then I held up two, to show that I could see as much with one as he could with two. And then the fellow held up three fingers, to say that we had but three eyes between us. That made me mad, and I doubled up my fist to give him a whack for his impudence, and I would have done it but for my promise to you not to offend him. Yet that was not the end of his provocations; but he showed me an orange, as much as to say, your poor, rocky, beggarly, cold country cannot produce that. I showed him an oat meal bannock that I had in my pocket to let him know that I did na' care a farthing for all his trash, and signs neither, sae lung as I hae this. And, by all that's guid, I'm angry yet that I did not thrash the hide off the scoundrel."

So much for two ways of understanding a thing.

LIX.

THE PICKET GUARD.

a " All quiet along the Potomac, they say,
    Except now and then a stray picket
Shot on his beat as he walks two and fro,
    By a rifleman in the thicket.
'Tis nothing—a private or two now and then
    Will not count in the news of the battle,
Not an officer lost—only one of the men,
b   Moaning out, all alone, the death rattle."

All quiet along the Potomac to-night,
    Where the soldiers lie peacefully dreaming,
Their tents in the rays of the clear Autumn moon,
    Or the light of clear camp-fires gleaming,
A tremulous sigh, as the gentle night wind
    Through the forest leaves softly is creeping.
While stars up above with their glittering eyes,
    Keep guard for our army is sleeping.

There's only the sound of the lone sentry's tread
    As he tramps from the rock to the fountain,

---

a Spoken roughly, like a soldier. *b* Pure Narrative, with expression.

And he thinks of the two in the low trundle bed
   Far away in the cot on the mountain.
His musket falls slack—his face dark and grim,
c   Grows gentle with memories tender,
As he mutters a prayer for the children asleep,
   For their mother—may Heaven defend her!

The moon seems to shine just as brightly as then
   That night, when the love yet unspoken
Leaped up to his lips—when low murmured vows
   Were pledged to be ever unbroken.
Then drawing his sleeves roughly over his eyes
   He dashes off tears that are welling,
And gathers his gun closer up to its place,
   As if to keep down the heart-swelling.

He passes the fountain, the blasted pine-tree,
   The footstep is lagging and weary;
Yet onward he goes through the broad belt of light
   Towards the shades of the forest so dreary.
Hark! was it the night wind that rustled the leaves,
   Was it moonlight so wondrously flashing?
It looked like a rifle—"Ha! Mary, good-bye!"
   And the life-blood is ebbing and plashing.

All quiet along the Potomac to-night,
   No sound save the rush of the river;
   While soft falls the dew on the face of the dead—
     The Picket's off duty forever!

LX.

A PASTORAL.

BY A. J. MUNBY.

I sat with Doris, the Shepherd maiden;
   Her crook was laden with wreathed flowers,
I sat and wooed her, through sunlight wheeling,
   And shadows wheeling for hours and hours.

c Tremor, with feeling.

And she, my Doris, whose lap incloses
  Wild summer roses of faint perfume,
That while I sued her, kept hushed and harkened,
  Till shades had darkened from gloss to gloom.

She touched my shoulder with fearful finger;
  She said, "We linger, we must not stay;
My flock's in danger, my sheep will wander;
  Behold them yonder, how far they stray."

I answered bolder, "Nay, let me hear you,
  And still be near you, and still adore!
Nor wolf, nor stranger will touch one yearling—
  Ah! stay, my darling, a moment more!"

She whispered, sighing, "There will be sorrow
  Beyond to-morrow, if I lose to-day;
My fold unguarded, my flock unfolded—
  I shall be scolded and sent away!"

Said I, replying, "If they do miss you,
  They ought to kiss you when you get home;
And well rewarded by friend and neighbor
  Should be the labor from which you come."

"They might remember," she answered meekly,
  "That lambs are weakly and sheep are wild;
But if they love me, it's none so fervent—
  I am a servant, and not a child."

Then each hot ember glowed quick within me,
  And love did win me to swift reply;
"Ah! do but prove me, and none shall bind you,
  Nor fray nor find you, until I die."

She blushed and started, and stood awaiting,
  As if debating in dreams divine:
But I did brave them—I told her plainly
  She doated vainly, she must be mine.

So we, twin-hearted, from all the valley
  Did rouse and rally her nibbling ewes;
And homeward drove them, we two together,
  Through blooming heather and healing dews.

That simple duty from grace did lend her,
　My Doris tender, my Doris true;
That I, her warder, did always bless her,
　And often press her to take her due.

And now in beauty she fills my dwelling
　With the love excelling, and undefiled;
And love doth guard her, both fast and fervent,
　No more a servant, nor yet a child.

LXI.

PRESIDENT LINCOLN.

GEORGE BANCROFT—APRIL 27TH.

How shall the nation most completely show its sorrow at Mr. Lincoln's death? How shall it best honor his memory? There can be but one answer. He was struck down when he was highest in its service, and, in strict conformity with duty, was engaged in carrying out principles affecting its life, its good name and its relations to the cause of freedom and the progress of mankind. Grief must take the character of action, and breathe itself forth in the assertion of the policy to which he fell a sacrifice. The standard which he held in his hand must be uplifted again, higher and more firmly than before, and must be carried on to triumph. Above everything else, his Proclamation of the first day of January, 1863, declaring throughout the parts of the country in rebellion the freedom of all persons who had been held as slaves, must be affirmed and maintained.

Events, as they rolled onward, have removed every doubt of the legality and binding force of that Proclamation. The country and the Rebel Government have each laid claim to the public service of the slave, and yet but one of the two can have a rightful claim to such service. That rightful claim belongs to the United States, because every one so born on their soil, with the few exceptions of the children of travelers and transient residents, owes them a primary allegiance. Every one so born has been counted among those represented in Congress—imperfectly and wrongly it may be—but still it has been counted and represented. The slave born on our soil always owed allegiance to the General Government. It may in time past have been a qualified allegiance, manifested through his master, as the allegiance of a ward through its guardian, or of an infant through its parent. But when the master became false to his allegiance, the slave stood face to face with his country, and his allegiance, which may before have been a qualified one, became direct and immediate. His chains fell off, and he stood in the presence of the nation, bound, like the rest of us, to its public defense. Mr. Lincoln's proclamation did but take notice of the already existing right of the bondman to freedom. The treason of the master made it a public crime for the slave to continue his obedience; the treason of a State set free the collective bondmen of the State.   *   *   *   *

We owe it to the memory of the dead, we owe it to the cause of popular liberty throughout the world, that the sudden crime which has taken the life of the President of the United States shall not produce the least impediment in the smooth course of public affairs. This great city, in the midst of unexampled emblems of deeply-seated grief, has sustained itself with composure and magnanimity. It has nobly done its part in guarding against the derangement of business or the slightest shock to public credit. The enemies of the Republic put it to the severest trial, but the voice of faction has not been heard — doubt and despondency have been unknown. In serene majesty the country rises in the beauty and strength and hope of youth, and proves to the world the quiet energy and the durability of institutions growing out of the reason and affection of the people.

Heaven has willed it that the United States shall live. The nations of the earth cannot spare them. All the worn-out aristocracies of Europe saw in the spurious feudalism of slaveholding their strongest outpost, and banded themselves together with the deadly enemies of our national life. If the Old World will discuss the respective advantages of oligarchy or equality; of the union of Church and State, or the rightful freedom of religion; of land accessible to the many or of land monopolized by an ever-decreasing number of the few, the United States must live to control the decision by their quiet and unobtrusive example. It has often and truly been observed that the trust and affection of the masses gather naturally round an individual; if the inquiry is made whether the man so trusted and beloved shall elicit from the reason of the people enduring institutions of their own, or shall sequester political power for a superintending dynasty, the United States must live to solve the problem. If a question is raised on the respective merits of Timoleon or Julius Cæsar, of Washington or Napoleon, the United States must be there to call to mind that there were twelve Cæsars, most of them the opprobrium of the human race, and to contrast with them the line of American Presidents.

The duty of the hour is incomplete, our mourning is insincere if, while we express unwavering trust in the great principles that underlie our Government, we do not also give our support to the man to whom the people have intrusted its administration.

LXII.

THE FUGITIVE SLAVE.

CHARLES SUMNER—1852.

Every escape from slavery necessarily and instinctively awakens the regard of all who love freedom. The endeavor, though unsuccessful, reveals courage, manhood, character. No story is read with more interest than that of our own Lafayette, when, aided by a gallant South Carolinian, in defiance of the despotic ordinance of Austria, kindred to our Slave Act, he strove to escape from the bondage of Olmutz. Literature pauses with exultation over the struggles of Cervantes, the great Spaniard, while a slave in Algiers, to regain the liberty for which he says, in his immortal work, "we ought to risk life itself, slavery being the greatest evil that can fall to the lot of man." Science in all her manifold triumphs, throbs with pride and delight that Arago, the astronomer and philosopher — devoted republican also — was redeemed from barbarous slavery to become one of her greatest sons. Religion rejoices serenely, with joy unspeakable, in the final escape of Vincent de Paul. Exposed in the public square of Tunis to the inspection of the trafficers in human flesh, this illustrous Frenchman was subjected to every vileness of treatment; like a horse, compelled to open his mouth, to show his teeth, to trot, to run, to exhibit his strength in lifting burthens, and then, like a horse, legally sold in market overt. Passing from master to master, after a protracted servitude, he achieved his freedom, and regaining France, commenced that resplendent career of charity by which he is placed among the great names of Christendom. Princes and orators have lavished panegyrics upon this fugitive slave; and the Catholic Church, in homage to his extraordinary virtues, has introduced him into the company of saints.

LXIII.

The Jaguar Hunt.

J. T. TROWBRIDGE.

ATLANTIC MONTHLY.

The dark jaguar was abroad in the land;
His strength and his fierceness what foe could withstand?
The breath of his anger was hot in the air,
And the white lamb of Peace he had dragged to his lair.

Then up rose the Farmer; he summoned his sons:
"Now saddle your horses, now look to your guns!"
And he called to his hound, as he sprang from the ground
To the back of his black-pawing steed with a bound.

Oh, their hearts, at the word, how they tingled and stirred!
They followed, all belted and booted and spurred.
"Buckle tight, boys!" said he, "for who gallops with me,
Such a hunt as was never before he shall see!

This traitor, we know him! for when he was younger,
We flattered him, patted him, fed his fierce hunger;
But now far too long we have borne with the wrong,
For each morsel we tossed makes him savage and strong."

Then said one, "He must die!" And they took up the cry.
"For this last crime of his he must die! he must die!"
But the slow eldest-born sauntered sad and forlorn,
For his heart was at home on that fair hunting-morn.

"I remember," he said, "how this fine cub we track
Has carried me many a time on his back!"
And he called to his brothers, "Fight gently! be kind!"
And he kept the dread hound, Retribution, behind.

The dark jaguar on a bough in the brake
Crouched, silent and wily, as lithe as a snake:
They spied not their game, but, as onward they came,
Through the dense leafage gleamed two red eyeballs of flame.

Black-spotted, and mottled, and whiskered, and grim,
White-bellied, and yellow, he lay on the limb,
All so still that you saw but just one tawny paw
Lightly reach through the leaves and as softly withdraw.

Then shrilled his fierce cry, as the riders drew nigh,
And he shot from the bough like a bolt from the sky:
In the foremost he fastened his fangs as he fell,
While all the black jungle reëchoed his yell.

Oh, then there was carnage by field and by flood!
The green sod was crimsoned, the rivers ran blood,
The cornfields were trampled, and all in their track
The beautiful valley lay blasted and black.

Now the din of the conflict swells deadly and loud;
And the dust of the tumult rolls up like a cloud:
Then afar down the slope of the Southland recedes
The wild rapid clatter of galloping steeds.

With wide nostrils smoking, and flanks dripping gore,
The black stallion bore his bold rider before,
As onward they thundered through forest and glen,
A-hunting the dark jaguar to his den.

In April, sweet April, the chase was begun;
It was April again, when the hunting was done:
The snows of four winters and four summers green,
Lay red-streaked and trodden and blighted between.

Then the monster stretched all his grim length on the ground ;
His life-blood was wasting from many a wound ;
Ferocious and gray and snarling he lay,
Amid heaps of the whitening bones of his prey.

Then up spoke the slow eldest son, and he said,
" All he needs now is just to be fostered and fed !
Give over the strife !   Brothers put up the knife !
We will tame him, reclaim him, but take not his life ! "

But the farmer flung back the false words in his face ;
"He is none of my race, who gives counsel so base !
Now let loose the hound ! "   And the hound was unbound,
And like lightning the heart of the traitor he found.

" So rapine and treason forever shall cease ! "
And they washed the stained fleece of the pale lamb of Peace ;
When lo ! a strong angel stands winged and white
In a wonderful raiment of ravishing light !

Peace is raised from the dead !   In the radiance shed
By the halo of glory that shines round her head,
Fair gardens shall bloom where the black jungle grew,
And all the glad valley shall blossom anew !

LXIV.

THE DEMON OF THE FIRE.

E. A. POE.

In the deepest depth of midnight, while the sad and solemn swell
Still was floating, faintly echoed from the forest chapel bell —
Faintly, falteringly floating o'er the sable waves of air
That were thro' the midnight rolling, chafed and billowy with the tolling —
In my chamber I lay dreaming, by the fire-light's fitful gleaming,
And my dreams were dreams foreshadowed on a heart foredoomed to care.

As the last, long, lingering echo of the midnight's mystic chime,
Lifting through the sable billows of the thither shore of Time —
Leaving on the startless silence not a token nor a trace —

In a quivering sigh departed; from my couch in fear I started;
Started to my feet in terror, for my dream's phantasmal error
Painted in the fitful fire a frightful, fiendish flaming face!

On the red hearth's reddest center, from a blazing knot of oak,
Seemed to gibe and grin this phantom when in terror I awoke,
And my slumberous eyelids straining, as I staggered to the floor.
Still in that dread vision seeming, turned my gaze toward the gleaming
Hearth, and there!—oh, God! I saw it; and from its flaming jaw it
Spat a ceaseless, seething, hissing, bubbling, gurgling stream of gore!

Speechless, struck with stony silence, frozen to the floor I stood,
Till methought my brain was hissing with that hissing, bubbling blood;
Till I felt my life-stream oozing from those lambent lips;
Till the demon seemed to name me—then a wondrous calm came o'er me;
And my brow grew cold and dewy, with a death damp stiff and gluey;
And I fell back on my pillow, in apparent soul eclipse.

Then as in death's seeming shadow, in the icy fall of fear
I lay, stricken, came a hoarse and hideous murmur to my ear;
Came a murmer like the murmur of assassins in their sleep—
Muttering, "Higher! higher! higher! I am demon of the Fire!
I am Arch-Fiend of the Fire, and each blazing roof's my pyre,
And my sweetest incense is the blood and tears my victims weep!

"How I revel on the prairie! how I roar among the pines!
How I laugh when from the village o'er the snow the red flame shines,
And I hear the shrieks of terror, with a life in every breath!
How I scream with lambent laughter, as I hurl each crackling rafter
Down the fell abyss of fire—until higher! higher! higher!
Leap the high priests of my altar, in their merry dance of death!

"I am Monarch of the Fire! I am Vassal King of Death!
World enriching, with the shadow of its doom upon my breath!
With the symbol of Hereafter flaming from my fatal face!
I command the Eternal Fire! Higher! higher! higher! higher!
Leap my ministering demons, like phantasamagoric lemans
Hugging Universal Nature in their hideous embrace!"

Then a sombre silence shut me in a solemn, shrouding sleep,
And I slumbered like an infant in the "cradle of the deep,"
Till the belfry in the forest quivered with the matin stroke,

And the martins, from the edges of the lichen-lidded lodges,
Shimmered through the russet arches, where the light in torn files marches
Like a routed army struggling through the serried ranks of oak.

Thro' my ivy-fretted casements, filtered in a tremulous note,
From the tall and stately linden, where the robin swelled his throat—
Querulous quaker-breasted robin, calling quaintly for his mate!
Then I started up unbidden from my slumber, night-mare ridden,
With the memory of that dire demon in my central fire,
On my eye's interior mirror like the shadow of a fate!

Ah! the fiendish fire had smouldered to a white and formless heap,
And no knot of oak was flaming as it flamed upon my sleep;
But around its very center, where the demon face had shone,
Forked shadows seemed to linger, pointing, as with spectral finger,
To a Bible, massive, golden, on a table carved and olden:
And I bowed and said, "All power is of God—of God alone!"

LXV.

LOVE AND LATIN.

"Amo, Amare, Amavi, Amatum."

Dear girls, never marry for knowledge,
 (Though that, of course, should form a part,)
For often the head, while at college,
 Gets wise at the cost of the heart.
Let me tell you a fact that is real—
 I once had a beau in my youth,
My brightest and best "*beau ideal*"
 Of manliness, goodness, and truth.

O, he talked of the Greeks and the Romans,
 Of Normans, and Saxons, and Celt;
And he quoted from Virgil and Homer,
 And Plato, and—somebody else.
And he told his deathless affection,
 By means of a thousand strange herbs,
With numberless words in connection,
 Derived from the roots—of Greek verbs.

One night, as a slight innuendo,
    When Nature was mantled in snow,
He wrote in the frost on the window,
    A sweet word in Latin— " *amo.* "
O, it needed no words for expression,
    For that I had long understood ;
But there was his written confession—
    Present tense and indicative mood.

But O, how man's passion will vary !
    For scarcely a year had passed by,
When he changed the " *amo* " to " *amare,* "
    But instead of an " *e* " was a " *y.* "
Yes, a Mary had certainly taken
    The heart once so fondly my own,
And I, the rejected, forsaken,
    Was left to reflection alone.

Since then I've a horror of Latin,
    And students uncommonly smart ;
True love, one should always put that in,
    To balance the head by the heart.
To be a fine scholar and linguist,
    Is much to one's credit, I know,
But " *I love* " should be said in plain English,
    And not with a Latin " *amo.* "

LXVI.

THE SCULPTOR BOY.

Chisel in hand stood a sculptor boy,
    With his marble block before him ; —
And his face lit up with a smile of joy
    As an angel dream passed o'er him.
He carved that dream on the yielding stone
    With many a sharp incision ;
In Heaven's own light the sculptor shone,
    He had caught that angel vision.

Sculptors of life are *we*, as we stand
  With our lives uncarved before us,
Waiting the hour, when, at God's command,
  Our life dream passes o'er us.
Let us carve it, then, on the yielding stone
  With many a sharp incision ; —
Its heavenly beauty shall be our own,—
  Our lives, that angel vision.

———

LXVII.

"BLESSED IS THE MAN WHOM THOU CHASTENEST."

SIR RICHARD GRANT.

O, Savior, whose mercy, severe in its kindness,
  Has chastened my wanderings and guided my way,
Adored be the power that illumined my blindness,
  And weaned me from phantoms that smiled to betray.

Enchanted with all that was dazzling and fair,
  I followed the rainbow I caught at the toy ;
And still in displeasure Thy goodness was there,
  Disappointing the hope, and defeating the joy.

The blossom blushed bright, but a worm was below ;
  The moonlight shone fair, there was blight in the beam ;
Sweet whispered the breeze, but it whispered of woe,
  And bitterness flowed in the soft flowing stream.

So cured of my folly, yet cured but in part,
  I turned to the refuge Thy pity displayed ;
And still did this eager and credulous heart
  Weave visions of promise that bloomed but to fade.

I thought that the course of the pilgrim to Heaven
  Would be bright as the summer, and glad as the morn ;
Thou show'dst me the path, — it was dark and uneven,
  All rugged with rock and tangled with thorn.

I dreamed of celestial reward and renown,
  I grasped at the triumph that blesses the brave,

I asked for the palm-branch, the robe and the crown,—
    I asked,—and Thou show'dst me a cross and a grave

Subdued and instructed, at length, to Thy will,
    My hopes and my longings I fain would resign;
O, give me the heart that can wait and be still,
    Nor know of a wish or a pleasure but Thine.

There are mansions exempted from sin and from woe,
    But they stand in a region by mortals untrod;
There are rivers of joy, but they flow not below;
    There is rest, but it dwells in the presence of God.

LXVIII.

The Frenchman and the Flea Powder.

ORIGINAL VERSION—BY PROF. RAYMOND.

A Frenchman once—so runs a certain ditty—
Had crossed the Straits to famous London city,
To get a living by the arts of France,
And teach his neighbor, rough John Bull, to dance.
But lacking pupils, vain was all his skill;
His fortunes sank from low to lower still,
Until at last, pathetic to relate,
Poor Monsieur landed at starvation's gate.
Standing, one day, at a cook-shop door,
And gazing in with aggravation sore,
He mused within himself what he should do
To fill his empty maw, and pocket too.
By nature shrewd, he soon contrived a plan,
And thus to execute it straight began:
A piece of common brick he quickly found,
And with a harder stone to powder ground,
Then wrapped the dust in many a dainty piece
Of paper, labled " Poison for de Fleas,"
And sallied forth, his roguish trick to try,
To show his treasures, and see who'd buy.
From street to street he cried, with lusty yell,
" Here's grand and sovereign flea poudare to sell."

And fickle fortune seemed to smile at last,
For soon a woman hailed him as he passed,
Struck a quick bargain with him for the lot,
And made him five crowns richer on the spot.
Our wight, encouraged by this ready sale,
Went into business on a larger scale,
And soon throughout all London scattered he
The " only genuine poudare for de flea."
Engaged one morning in his new vocation
Of mingled boasting and dissimulation,
He thought he heard himself in anger called ;
And sure enough the self-same woman brawled,
In not a very mild or tender mood,
From the same window where before she stood.
" Hey, there ! " said she, " you Monsher Powder-man :
Escape my clutches now, sir, if you can !
I'll let you dirty, thieving Frenchmen know,
That decent people won't be cheated so.
How dare you tell me that your worthless stuff
Would make my bedsteads clean and clear enough
Of bugs ? I've rubbed those bedsteads o'er and o'er,
And now the plagues are thicker than before ! "
Then spoke Monsieur, and heaved a saintly sigh
With humble attitude and tearful eye.
" Ah, madam ! s'il vous plait, attendez-vous —
I vill dis leetle ting explain to you.
My poudare gran' ! magnifique ! why abuse him ?
Aha ! I show you, Madam, *how to use him.*
You must not spread him in large quantité
Upon de bedstead — no ! dat's not de vay.
First, you must wait until you *catch* de flea ;
Den, tickle he on de petite rib, you see ;
And when he laugh — aha ! he ope his throat ;
Den *poke de poudare down !* — Begar ! he choke ! !

LXIX.

DADDY AND SONNY.

Daddy and I is jolly fellows; he, he ! When I laugh, daddy he
laughs ; and when daddy laughs I laugh — he, he, he ! Daddy and

J

me is in company—Daddy and Sonny—he, he, he! Daddy and me has got a couple of very slick dogs, home, he, he. One's name is Towse, and 'tother's name is Bowse—he, he, he! Towse dog is very slick dog; but that Bowse dog is a very lazy dog; he, he, he! I've got a brother Pete, home, too. Pete's a very lazy fellow—just as lazy as the Bowse dog, he, he, he! They ain't neither of them worth their salt, for they don't do nothing in the house, nor out on the house. But that Towse dog is real slick dog, I tell ye; he, he, he, he! Daddy and me has got a couple of very slick tater-patch, too, he, he. That low tater-patch is'nt worth much. We didn't spect to get more than two taters to the hill, out on that lower patch. But that upper tater-patch and that Towse dog is real slick, I tell ye! he, he, he! I've got a sweetheart, too; her name's Sukey Sinder. She and me keeps company together. I tell you what, she's real slick, he, he, he. And Daddy and me's got forty cows: Daddy's got thirty-nine, and I've got one. Mine's an ox. I'll run down and see him; he, he, he!

LXX.

OPPOSITE EXAMPLES.

H. MANN.

I ask the young man who is just forming his habits of life, or just beginning to indulge those habitual trains of thought out of which habits grow, to look around him, and mark the examples whose fortunes he would covet, or whose fate he would abhor. Even as we walk the streets, we meet with examples of each extreme. Here, behold the patriarch, whose stock of vigor three-score years and ten seems scarcely to have impaired. His erect form, his firm step, his elastic limbs, and undimmed senses, are so many certificates of good conduct; or, rather, so many jewels and orders of nobility with which nature has honored him for his fidelity to her laws. His fair complextion shows that his blood has never been corrupted; his pure health that he never yielded his digestive apparatus to abuse; his exact language and keen apprehension, that his brain has never been drugged or stupefied by the poisons of distiller or tobacconist.

Enjoying his appetites to the highest, he has preserved the power of enjoying them. As he drains the cup of life, there are no lees at the bottom. His organs will reach the goal of existence together. Painlessly as the candle burns down in its socket, so will he expire; and a little imagination would convert him into another Enoch, translated from earth to a better world without the sting of death.

But look at an opposite extreme, where an opposite history is recorded. What wreck so shocking to behold as the wreck of a dissolute man;—the vigor of life exhausted, and yet the first steps in an honorable career not taken; in himself a lazar-house of diseases; dead, but, by a heathenish custom of society, not buried! Rogues have had the initial letter of their title burnt into the palms of their hands; even for murder Cain was only branded on the forehead; but over the whole person of the debauchee or the inebriate, the signatures of infamy are written. How nature brands him with stigma and opprobrium! How she hangs labels all over him, to testify her disgust at his existence, and to admonish others to beware of his example? How she loosens all his joints, sends tremors along his muscles, and bends forward his frame, as if to bring him on all fours with kindred brutes, or to degrade him to the reptile's crawling! How she disfigures his countenance, as if intent upon obliterating all traces of her own image, so that she may swear that she never made him! How she pours rheum over his eyes, sends foul spirits to inhabit his breath, and shrieks, as with a trumpet, from every pore of his body, "BEHOLD A BEAST!" Such a man may be seen in the streets of our cities every day; if rich enough, he may be found in the saloons, and at the tables of the "Upper Ten;" but surely, to every man of purity and honor, to every man whose heart is unblemished, the wretch who comes cropped and bleeding from the pillory, and redolent with the appropriate perfumes, would be a guest or a companion far less offensive and disgusting.

Now let the young man, rejoicing in his manly proportions, and in his comeliness, look on *this* picture, and then on *this*, and then say, after the likeness of which model he intends his own erect stature and sublime countenance shall be configured.

LXXI.

THE PERSONAL CHARACTER OF ABRAHAM LINCOLN.

REV. C. H. FOWLER — APRIL, 1865.

I stand to-day in the shadow of the coffin of Abraham Lincoln
What best can I say concerning his character ? The analysis of his
character is difficult on account of its symmetry; its comprehension
is impossible, on account of its greatness. The foundation upon
which this character was built was his moral sense, coming out in
absolute truthfulness. This gave him marvelous moral uprightness,
kept him unseduced by the temptations of his profession, untainted
by the corruptions of politics, and unblamable in public administration. The ruling, all-controlling characteristic of his mind was
his accurate, massive, iron-armed reason. Every element of his being,
even his passion and compassion, and every act of his life was in
most rigid submission to his moral sense and reason. He arrived at
his conclusions not by intuition, but by argument. This made him
appear slow in difficult questions, but it gave him all the certainty
of logic. Once arrived at a decision, he could not be moved from
it. His mental constitution and habits of thought underlaid his felt
consciousness of honor. This made inevitable that firmness which
was more equal to every emergency, and which has so amazed the
world. His imaginative and speculative faculties were of great
native strength; but they were so subjected to his reason that they
only served to suggest causes of action in unprecedented difficulties,
and illustrate by condensed, incarnated argument the correctness of
his position. His caution, that might have been a fault, was bal-
anced by the certainty of his reason and produced only a wise
prudence. His whole character was rounded out into remarkable
practical common sense. Thus his moral sense, his reason, and his
common sense were the three fixed points through which the perfect
circle of his character was drawn, the sacred trinity of his great
manhood. He incarnated the ideal Republic and was the living
personification of the divine idea of free government. No other man
ever so fully realized the people's idea of a ruler. He was our
President — the great Commander. The classics of the schools

might have polished him, but they would have separated him from us. A child of the people, he was as accessible in the splendors of the White House as in the lowly cabin. He stands before us as no man ever stood, the embodiment of the people. Coming among us President in troublous times, the grasp, the accuracy, the activity of his intellect, soon placed him at the head of the world's statesmen. He rallied about him the strong men of the land and showed them he was their master. Everywhere he controlled men according to his purpose. Once arrived at a decision he was there forever. He was firm because he knew he was right. He put men up or down regardless of their popularity. Congress had always referred to his judgment, and the end in every event justified his decisions. As a statesman he was without a peer in the world or in history.

His goodness is said to have made him weak. It was the highest exhibition of his strength. He was mercy, mailed in justice. He was the most magnanimous man of the time. Yesterday he said of inevitable defeat, "I am responsible." To-day he said of triumph, "The glory is not mine." He was the noblest man that ever came in the tide of time.

LXXII.

THE POLISH BOY.

BY MRS. ANN S. STEPHENS.

Whence came those shrieks, so wild and shrill,
    That like an arrow cleave the air,
Causing the blood to creep and thrill
    With such sharp cadence of despair?
Once more they come! as if a heart
    Were cleft in twain by one quick blow,
And every string had voice apart
    To utter its peculiar woe!

Whence came they? From yon temple, where
    An altar raised for private prayer,
Now forms the warrior's marble bed,
    Who Warsaw's gallant armies led.

The dim funereal tapers threw
  A holy lustre o'er his brow,
And burnish with their rays of light
  The mass of curls that gather bright
Above the haughty brow and eye
  Of a young boy that's kneeling by.

What hand is that whose icy press
  Clings to the dead with death's own grasp,
But meets no answering caress—
  No thrilling fingers seek its clasp?
As is the hand of her whose cry
  Rang wildly late upon the air,
When the dead warrior met her eye,
  Outstretched upon the altar there.

Now with white lips and broken moan
She sinks beside the altar stone;
But hark! the heavy tramp of feet,
Is heard along the gloomy street,
Nearer and nearer yet they come,
With clanking arms and noiseless drum.
They leave the pavement. Flowers that spread
Their beauties by the path they tread,
Are crushed and broken. Crimson hands
Rend brutally their blooming bands.
Now whispered curses, low and deep,
Around the holy temple creep.
The gate is burst. A ruffian band
Rush in and savagely demand,
With brutal voice and oath profane,
The startled boy for exile's chain.

The mother sprang with gesture wild,
And to her bosom snatched the child;
Then with pale cheek and flashing eye,
Shouted with fearful energy,—
"Back, ruffians, back! nor dare to tread
Too near the body of my dead!
Nor touch the living boy—I stand
Between him and your lawless band!

No traitor he—But listen! I
Have cursed your master's tyranny.
I cheered my lord to join the band
Of those who swore to free our land,
Or fighting, die; and when he pressed
Me for the last time to his breast,
I knew that soon his form would be
Low as it is, or Poland free.
He went and grappled with the foe,
Laid many a haughty Russian low;
But he is dead—the good—the brave—
And I, his wife, am worse—a slave!
Take me, and bind these arms, these hands,
With Russia's heaviest iron bands,
And drag me to Siberia's wild
To perish, if 'twill save my child!"

"Peace, woman, peace!" the leader cried,
Tearing the pale boy from her side;
And in his ruffian grasp he bore
His victim to the temple door.

"One moment!" shrieked the mother, "one;
Can land or gold redeem my son?
If so, I bend my Polish knee,
And, Russia, ask a boon of thee.
Take palaces, take lands, take all,
But leave him free from Russian thrall.
Take these," and her white arms and hands
She stripped of rings and diamond bands,
And tore from braids of long black hair
The gems that gleamed like star-light there;
Unclasped the brilliant coronal
And carcanet of orient pearl;
Her cross of blazing rubies last
Down to the Russian's feet she cast.

He stooped to seize the glittering store;
Upspringing from the marble floor,
The mother with a cry of joy,
Snatched to her leaping heart the boy!

But no—the Russian's iron grasp
Again undid the mother's clasp.
Forward she fell, with one long cry
Of more than mother's agony.

But the brave child is roused at length,
And breaking from the Russian's hold,
He stands, a giant in the strength
Of his young spirit, fierce and bold.

Proudly he towers, his flashing eye,
So blue and fiercely bright,
Seems lighted from the eternal sky,
So brilliant is its light.
His curling lips and crimson cheeks
Foretell the thought before he speaks.
With a full voice of proud command
He turns upon the wondering band.

"Ye hold me not! no, no, nor can;
This hour has made the boy a man.
The world shall witness that one soul
Fears not to prove itself a Pole.

I knelt beside my slaughtered sire,
Nor felt one throb of vengeful ire;
I wept upon his marble brow—
Yes, wept—I was a child; but now
My noble mother on her knee,
Has done the work of years for me.
Although in this small tenement
My soul is cramped—unbowed, unbent,
I've still within me ample power
To free myself this very hour.
This dagger in my heart! and then,
Where is your boasted power, base men?"

He drew aside his broidered vest,
And there, like slumbering serpent's crest,
The jewelled haft of a poniard bright,
Glittered a moment on the sight.
"Ha! start ye back?   Fool! coward! knav

Think ye my noble father's glave,
Could drink the life blood of a slave?
The pearls that on the handle flame,
Would blush to rubies in their shame!
The blade would quiver in thy breast,
Ashamed of such ignoble rest!
No; thus I rend thy tyrant's chain,
And fling him back a boy's disdain!"

A moment, and the funeral light
Flashed on the jewelled weapon bright;
Another, and his young heart's blood
Leaped to the floor a crimson flood.
Quick to his mother's side he sprang,
And on the air his clear voice rang —
" Up, mother, up! I'm free! I'm free!
The choice was death or slavery;
Up! mother, up! look on my face
I only wait for thy embrace.
One last, last word — a blessing, one,
To prove thou knowest what I have done,
No look! No word! Canst thou not feel
My warm blood o'er thy heart congeal?
Speak, mother, speak — lift up thy head.
What, silent still? Then art thou dead!
Great God, I thank thee! Mother, I
Rejoice with thee, and thus to die."
Slowly he falls. The clustering hair
Rolls back and leaves that forehead bare.
One long, deep breath, and his pale head
Lay on his mother's bosom, dead.

LXXIII.

DARE AND DO.

Upward, — onward! Fellow workmen!
Ours the battle-field of life;
Ne'er a foot to foeman yielding,
Pressing closer midst the strife!

Forward! in the strength of manhood, —
    Forward! in the fire of youth, —
Aim at something; ne'er surrender, —
    Arm thee in the mail of truth!

Though thy way be strewn with dangers,
    Summer rain-drops lay the dust;
Faith and hope are two-edged weapons
    Which will ne'er belie thy trust.
Shrink not, though a host surround thee, —
    Onward! Duty's path pursue;
All who gild the page of story,
    Know the brave words — Dare and do!

Miller was a rough stone-mason;
    Shakespeare, Goldsmith, Keats and Hood,
Franklin, Jerrold, Burns and Gifford,
    Had to toil as we, for food.
Yes: these men with minds majestic,
    Sprang from ranks the rich call poor,
Cast a halo round brown labor, —
    Had to wrestle, fight, endure.

Forward, then! bright eyes are beaming;
    Fight, nor lose the conqueror's crown!
Stretch thy right hand, seize thy birthright,
    Take it, wear it, 'tis thine own!
Slay the giants which beset thee,
    Rise to manhood, glory, fame;
Take thy pen, and in the volume
    Of the gifted write thy name!

LXXIV.

THE AMERICAN UNION.

KOSSUTH

He who sows the wind will reap the storm. History is the revelation of Providence. The Almighty rules, by eternal laws, not
only the material but the moral world; and every law is a principle,
and every principle is a law. Men, as well as nations, are endowed
with free will to choose a principle, but that once chosen, the consequences must be abided. With self-government is freedom, and

with freedom is justice and patriotism. With centralization is ambition, and with ambition dwells despotism. Happy your great country, sir, for being so warmly addicted to that great principle of self-government. Upon this foundation your fathers raised a home to freedom more glorious than the world has ever seen. Upon this foundation you have developed it to a living wonder of the world. Happy your great country, sir, that it was selected, by the blessing of the Lord, to prove the glorious practicability of a federative union of many sovereign states, all conserving their state rights and their self-government, and yet united in one — every star beaming with its own lustre, but altogether one constellation on mankind's canopy.

Upon this foundation your free country has grown to a prodigious power in a surprisingly brief period. You have attracted power, in that your fundamental principles have conquered more in seventy-five years than Rome by arms in centuries. Your principles will conquer the world. By the glorious example of your freedom, welfare and security, mankind is about to become conscious of its aim. The lesson you give to humanity will not be lost; and the respect of the state rights in the federal government of America, and in its several states, will become an instructive example for universal toleration, forbearance, and justice, to the future states and republics of Europe. Upon this basis will be got rid of the mysterious question of language and nationalities, raised by the cunning despotisms in Europe to murder liberty; and the smaller states will find security in the principles of federative union, while they will conserve their national freedom by the principles of sovereign self-government; and while larger states, abdicating the principle of centralization, will cease to be a blood-field to sanguinary usurpation, and a tool to the ambition of wicked men, municipal institutions will insure the developement of local particular elements. Freedom, formerly an abstract political theory, will become the household benefit to municipalities; and out of the welfare and contentment of all parts will flow happiness, peace and security of the whole. That is my confident hope. Then will at once subside the fluctuations of Germany's fate.

LXXV.

Scott and the Veteran.

BAYARD TAYLOR.

An old and crippled veteran to the War Department came,
He sought the Chief who led him, on many a field of fame—
The Chief who shouted "Forward!" where e'er his banner rose,
And bore his stars in triumph behind the flying foes.
"Have you forgotten, General," the battered soldier cried,
"The days of eighteen hundred twelve, when I was at your side?
Have you forgotten Johnson, that fought at Lundy's Lane?
'T is true, I'm old, and pensioned, but I want to fight again."
"Have I forgotten?" said the Chief, "my brave old soldier, No!
And here's the hand I gave you then, and let it tell you so;
But you have done your share, my friend; you're crippled, old, and gray,
And we have need of younger arms and fresher blood to-day."
"But, General!" cried the veteran, a flush upon his brow,
"The very men who fought with us, they say, are traitors, now;
They've torn the flag of Lundy's Lane, our old red, white, and blue,
And while a drop of blood is left, I'll show that drop is true.
I'm not so weak but I can strike, and I've a good old gun
To get the range of traitors' hearts, and pick them one by one.
Your Minie rifles, and such arms, it ain't worth while to try;
I couldn't get the hang o' them, but I'll keep my powder dry!"
"God bless you, comrade!" said the Chief—"God bless your loyal heart!
But younger men are in the field, and claim to have their part.
They'll plant our sacred banner in each rebellious town,
And woe, henceforth, to any hand, that dares to pull it down!"
"But, General,"—still persisting—the weeping veteran cried,
"I am young enough to follow, so long as *you're* my guide;
And some, you know, must bite the dust, and that, at least, can I;
So, give the young ones place to fight, but me a place to die!
If they should fire on Pickens, let the Colonel in command
Put me upon the rampart, with the flag-staff in my hand;
No odds how hot the cannon smoke, or how the shells may fly,
I'll hold the Stars and Stripes aloft, and hold them till I die!
I'm ready, General, so you let a post to me be given,
Where Washington can see me, as he looks from highest Heaven,
And says to Putnam, at his side, or, may be, General Wayne,
'There stands old Billy Johnson, who fought at Lundy's Lane!'
And when the fight is hottest, before the traitors fly,
When shell and ball are screeching, and bursting in the sky,
If any shot should hit me, and lay me on my face,
My soul would go to Washington's, and not to Arnold's place!"

LXXVI.

A VERY IMPORTANT PROCEEDING,—MR. PICKWICK.

DICKENS.

Mr. Pickwick's apartments in Goswell street, although on a limited scale, were not only of a very neat and comfortable description, but peculiarly adapted for the residence of a man of his genius and observation. His sitting-room was the first floor front, his bed-room was the second floor front; and thus, whether he was sitting at his desk in the parlor, or standing before the dressing-glass in his dormitory, he had an equal opportunity of contemplating human nature in all the numerous phases it exhibits, in that not more populous than popular thoroughfare. His landlady, Mrs. Bardell—the relict and sole executrix of a deceased custom-house officer — was a comely woman of bustling manners and agreeable appearance, with a natural genius for cooking, improved by study and long practice into an exquisite talent. There were no children, no servants, no fowls. The only other inmates of the house were a large man and a small boy; the first a lodger, the second a production of Mrs. Bardell's. The large man was always at home precisely at ten o'clock at night, at which hour he regularly condensed himself into the limits of a dwarfish French bedstead in the back parlor; and the infantine sports and gymnastic exercises of Master Bardell were exclusively confined to the neighboring pavements and gutters. Cleanliness and quiet reigned throughout the house; and in it Mr. Pickwick's will was law.

To any one acquainted with these points of the domestic economy of the establishment, and conversant with the admirable regulation of Mr. Pickwick's mind, his appearance and behaviour on the morning previous to that which had been fixed upon for the journey to Eatanswill, would have been most mysterious and unaccountable. He paced the room to and fro with hurried steps, popped his head out of the window at intervals of about three minutes each, constantly referred to his watch, and exhibited many other manifestations of impatience, very unusual with him. It was evident that something of great importance was in contemplation, but what that something was, not even Mrs. Bardell herself had been enabled to discover.

" Mrs. Bardell," said Mr. Pickwick, at last, as that amiable female approached the termination of a prolonged dusting of the apartment.

" Sir," said Mrs. Bardell.

" Your little boy is a very long time gone."

" Why, it is a good long way to the Borough, Sir," remonstrated Mrs. Bardell.

" Ah," said Mr Pickwick, " very true ; so it is."

Mr. Pickwick relapsed into silence, and Mrs. Bardell resumed her dusting.

" Mrs. Bardell," said Mr. Pickwick, at the expiration of a few minutes.

" Sir," said Mrs. Bardell again.

" Do you think it's a much greater expense to keep two people, than to keep one ? "

" La, Mr. Pickwick," said Mrs. Bardell, coloring up to the very border of her cap, as she fancied she observed a species of matrimonial twinkle in the eyes of her lodger ; " La, Mr. Pickwick, what a question ! "

" Well, but *do* you ? " inquired Mr. Pickwick.

" That depends " — said Mrs. Bardell, approaching the duster very near to Mr. Pickwick's elbow, which was planted on the table ; " that depends a good deal upon the person, you know, Mr. Pickwick ; and whether it's a saving and careful person, Sir."

" That's very true," said Mr. Pickwick, " but the person I have in my eye (here he looked very hard at Mrs. Bardell) I think possesses these qualities ; and has, moreover, a considerable knowledge of the world, and a great deal of sharpness, Mrs. Bardell ; which may be of material use to me."

" La, Mr. Pickwick," said Mrs. Bardell, the crimsom rising to her cap-border again.

" I do," said Mr. Pickwick, growing energetic, as was his wont in speaking of a subject which interested him, " I do, indeed ; and to tell you the truth, Mrs. Bardell, I have made up my mind."

" Dear me, Sir," exclaimed Mrs. Bardell.

" You'll think it not very strange now," said the amiable Mr. Pickwick, with a good-humored glance at his companion, " that I never consulted you about this matter, and never mentioned it, till I sent your little boy out this morning—eh ? "

Mrs. Bardell could only reply by a look. She had long worshipped Mr. Pickwick at a distance, but here she was, all at once, raised to a pinnacle to which her wildest and most extravagant hopes had never dared to aspire. Mr. Pickwick was going to propose— a deliberate plan, too—sent her little boy to the Borough, to get him out of the way—how thoughtful—how considerate!

" Well," said Mr. Pickwick, " what do you think ? "

" Oh, Mr. Pickwick," said Mrs. Bardell, trembling with agitation, " you're very kind, Sir."

" It'll save you a good deal of trouble, won't it ? " said Mr. Pickwick.

" Oh, I never thought anything of the trouble, Sir," replied Mrs. Bardell ; " and of course, I should take more trouble to please you then than ever ; but it is so kind of you Mr. Pickwick, to have so much consideration for my loneliness."

" Ah to be sure," said Mr. Pickwick; " I never thought of that. When I am in town, you'll always have somebody to sit with you. To be sure, so you will."

" I'm sure I ought to be a very happy woman," said Mrs. Bardell.

" And your little boy—" said Mr. Pickwick.

" Bless his heart," interposed Mrs. Bardell, with a maternal sob.

" He, too, will have a companion," resumed Mr. Pickwick, " a lively one, who'll teach him, I'll be bound, more tricks in a week, than he would ever learn in a year." And Mr. Pickwick smiled placidly.

" Oh you dear—" said Mrs. Bardell.

Mr. Pickwick started.

" Oh you kind, good, playful dear," said Mrs. Bardell ; and without more ado, she rose from her chair, and flung her arms round Mr. Pickwick's neck, with a cataract of tears, and a chorus of sobs.

"Bless my soul," cried the astonished Mr. Pickwick;—"Mrs. Bardell, my good woman—dear me, what a situation—pray consider Mrs. Bardell, don't—if anybody should come—"

"Oh, let them come," exclaimed Mrs. Bardell, frantically; "I'll never leave you—dear, kind, good, soul;" and, with these words, Mrs. Bardell clung the tighter.

"Mercy upon me," said Mr. Pickwick, struggling violently, "I hear somebody coming up the stairs. Don't, don't, there's a good creature, don't." But entreaty and remonstrance were alike unavailing: for Mrs. Bardell had fainted in Mr. Pickwick's arms; and before he could gain time to deposit her on a chair, Master Bardell entered the room, ushering in Mr. Tupman, Mr. Winkle, and Mr. Snodgrass.

Mr. Pickwick was struck motionless and speechless. He stood with his lovely burden in his arms, gazing vacantly on the countenances of his friends, without the slightest attempt at recognition or explanation. They, in their turn, stared at him; and Master Bardell, in his turn, stared at everybody.

The astonishment of the Pickwickians was so absorbing, and the perplexity of Mr. Pickwick was so extreme, that they might have remained in exactly the same relative situation until the suspended animation of the lady was restored, had it not been for a most beautiful and touching expression of the filial affection on the part of her youthful son. Clad in a tight suit of corduroy, spangled with brass buttons of a very considerable size, he at first stood at the door astounded and uncertain; but by degrees, the impression that his mother must have suffered some personal damage, pervaded his partially developed mind, and considering Mr. Pickwick the aggressor, he set up an appalling and semi-earthly kind of howling, and butting forward with his head, commenced assailing that immortal gentleman about the back and legs, with such blows and pinches as the strength of his arm, and the violence of his excitement allowed.

"Take this little villain away," said the agonised Mr. Pickwick, "he's mad."

"What *is* the matter?" said the three tongue-tied Pickwickians.

"I don't know," replied Mr. Pickwick, pettishly. "Take away the boy—(here Mr. Winkle carried the interesting boy, screaming and struggling, to the farther end of the apartment.) Now help me to lead this woman down stairs."

"Oh, I am better now," said Mrs. Bardell, faintly.

"Let me lead you down stairs," said the ever gallant Mr. Tupman.

"Thank you, Sir—thank you;" exclaimed Mrs. Bardell, hysterically. And down stairs she was led accordingly, accompanied by her affectionate son.

"I cannot conceive"—said Mr. Pickwick, when his friend returned—"I cannot conceive what has been the matter with that woman. I had merely announced to her my intention of keeping a man-servant, when she fell into the extraordinary paroxysm in which you found her. Very extraordinary thing."

"Very," said his three friends.

"Placed me in such an extremely awkward situation," continued Mr. Pickwick.

"Very;" was the reply of his followers, as they coughed slightly, and looked dubiously at each other.

This behavior was not lost upon Mr. Pickwick. He remarked their incredulity. They evidently suspected him.

"There is a man in the passage, now," said Mr. Tupman.

"It's the man that I spoke to you about," said Mr. Pickwick, "I sent for him to the Borough this morning. Have the goodness to call him up, Snodgrass."

LXXVII.

"ETERNAL JUSTICE."

BY CHARLES MACKAY.

"The man is thought a knave or fool
  Or bigot, plotting crime,
Who, for the advancement of his kind,
  Is wiser than his time.
For him the hemlock shall distil;

K

For him the axe be bared;
For him the gibbet shall be built;
  For him the stake prepared:
Him shall the scorn and wrath of men
  Pursue with deadly aim;
And malice, envy, spite, and lies,
  Shall desecrate his name.
But truth shall conquer at the last,
  For round and round we run,
And ever the right comes uppermost,
  And ever is justice done.

"Pace through thy cell, old Socrates,
  Cheerily to and fro;
Trust to the impulse of thy soul
  And let the poison flow.
They may shatter to earth the lamp of clay
  That holds a light divine,
But they cannot quench the fire of thought
  By any such deadly wine;
They cannot blot thy spoken words
  From the memory of man,
By all the poison ever was brewed
  Since time its course began.
To-day abhorred, to-morrow adored,
  So round and round we run,
And ever the truth comes uppermost,
  And ever is justice done.

"Plod in thy cave, gray Anchorite;
  Be wiser than thy peers:
Augment the range of human power
  And trust to coming years.
They may call thee wizard, and monk accursed,
  And load thee with dispraise:
Thou wert born five hundred years too soon
  For the comfort of thy days:
But not too soon for human kind:
  Time hath reward in store;
And the demons of our sires become

The saints that we adore.
The blind can see, the slave is lord ;
  So round and round we run ;
And ever the wrong is proved to be wrong,
  And ever is justice done.

"Keep, Galileo, to thy thought,
  And nerve thy soul to bear ;
They may gloat o'er the senseless words they wring
  From the pangs of thy despair :
They may veil their eyes, but they cannot hide
  The sun's meridian glow ;
The heel of a priest may tread thee down,
  And a tyrant work thee woe;
But never a truth has been destroyed :
  They may curse and call it crime ;
Pervert and betray, or slander and slay
  Its teachers for a time.
But the sunshine aye shall light the sky,
  As round and round we run ;
And the truth shall ever come uppermost,
  And justice shall be done.

"And live there *now* such men as these—
  With thoughts like the great of old ?
Many have died in their misery,
  And left their thought untold ;
And many live and are ranked as mad,
  And placed in the cold world's ban,
For sending their bright far-seeing souls
  Three centuries in the van.
They toil in penury and grief,
  Unknown, if not maligned ;
Forlorn, forlorn, bearing the scorn
  Of the meanest of mankind.
But yet the world goes round and round,
  And the genial seasons run,
And ever the truth comes uppermost,
  And ever is justice done."

LXXVIII.

AGAINST CURTAILING THE RIGHT OF SUFFRAGE.

VICTOR HUGO.

GENTLEMEN : — I address the men who govern us, and say to them,— Go on, cut off three millions of voters ; cut off eight out of nine, and the result will be the same to you, if it be not more decisive. What you do not cut off, is your own fault ; the absurdities of your policy of compression, your fatal incapacity, your ignorance of the present epoch, the antipathy you feel for it, and that it feels for you ; what you will not cut off, is the times which are advancing, the hour now striking, the ascending movement of ideas, the gulf opening broader and deeper between yourself and the age, between the young generation and you, between the spirit of liberty and you, between the spirit of philosophy and you.

What you will not cut off, is this immense fact, that the nation goes to one side, while you go to the other ; that what for you is the sunrise, is for it the sun's setting ; that you turn your backs to the future, while this great people of France, its front all radiant with light from the rising dawn of a new humanity, turns its back to the past.

Gentlemen, this law is invalid ; it is null ; it is dead even before it exists. And do you know what has killed it ? It is that, when it meanly approaches to steal the vote from the pocket of the poor and feeble, it meets the keen, terrible eye of the national probity, a devouring light, in which the work of darkness disappears.

Yes, men who govern us, at the bottom of every citizen's conscience, the most obscure as well as the greatest, at the very depths of the soul, (I use your own expressions,) of the last beggar, the last vagabond, there is a sentiment, sublime, sacred, insurmountable, indestructable, eternal, — the sentiment of right ! This sentiment, which is the very essence of the human conscience, which the Scriptures call the corner-stone of justice, is the rock on which iniquities, hypocrisies, bad laws, evil designs, bad governments, fall, and are shipwrecked. This is the hidden, irresistable obstacle veiled in the recesses of every mind, but ever present, ever active, on which you will always exhaust yourselves; and which, whatever you do, you will never destroy. I warn you, your labor is lost; you will not extinguish it, you will not confuse it. Far easier to drag the rock from the bottom of the sea, than the sentiment of right from the heart of the people!

LXXIX.

IRELAND.

T. F. MEAGHER.

I do not despair of my poor old country, her peace, her liberty, her glory. For that country I can do no more than bid her hope. To lift this island up; to make her a benefactor instead of being the meanest beggar in the world; to restore to her her native powers and her ancient constitution; this has been my ambition, and this ambition has been my crime. Judged by the law of England, I know this crime entails the penalty of death, but the history of Ireland explains this crime, and justifies it. Judged by that history I am no criminal; you are no criminal; I deserve no punishment; we deserve no punishment. Judged by that history, the treason of which I stand convicted loses all its guilt; is sanctified as a duty; will be ennobled as a sacrifice. With these sentiments, my lord, I await the sentence of the court; having done what I felt to be my duty; having spoken what I felt to be the truth, as I have done on every other occasion of my short career. I now bid farewell to the country of my birth, my passion and my death; the country whose misfortunes have invoked my sympathies, whose factions I have sought to still; whose intellect I have prompted to a lofty aim; whose freedom has been my fatal dream. I offer to that country, as a proof of the love I bear her, and the sincerity with which I thought and spoke and struggled for her freedom, the life of a young heart; and with that life all the hopes, the honors, the endearments of an honorable home. Pronounce then, my lords, the sentence which the law directs, and I will be prepared to hear it. I trust I shall be prepared to meet its execution. I hope to be able, with a pure heart and a perfect composure to appear before a higher tribunal — a tribunal where a judge of infinite goodness, as well as of justice, will preside, and where, my lords, many, many of the judgments of this world will be reversed.

LXXX.

PLEA FOR THE UNION.

W. H. SEWARD — 1861.

MR. PRESIDENT: — I have designedly dwelt so long on the probable effects of disunion upon the safety of the American people as to leave me little time to consider the other evils which must follow in its train. But, practically, the loss of safety involves every other form of public calamity. When once the guardian angel has taken flight, everything is lost.

Dissolution would not only arrest, but extinguish the greatness of our country. Even if separate confederacies could exist and endure, they could severally preserve no share of the *prestige* of the Union. If the constellation is to be broken up, the stars, whether scattered widely apart or grouped in smaller clusters, will thenceforth shed feeble, glimmering, and lurid lights. Nor will great achievements be possible for the new confederacies. Dissolution would signalize its triumph by acts of wantonness which would shock and astound the world. It would provincialize Mount Vernon, and give the Capitol over to desolation at the very moment when the dome is rising over our heads that was to be crowned with the statue of Liberty. After this there would remain for disunion no act of stupendous infamy to be committed. No petty confederacy that shall follow the United States can prolong, or even renew, the majestic drama of national progress. Perhaps it is to be arrested because its sublimity is incapable of continuance. Let it be so, if we have indeed become degenerate. After Washington, and the inflexible Adams, Henry, and the peerless Hamilton, Jefferson, and the majestic Clay, Webster, and the acute Calhoun, Jackson, the modest Taylor, and Scott, who rises in greatness under the burden of years, and Franklin, and Fulton, and Whitney, and Morse, have all performed their parts, let the curtain fall.

LXXXI.

THE SCHOOLMASTER.

HENRY W. LONGFELLOW.

Great men stand like solitary towers in the city of God, and secret passages running deep beneath external nature give their thoughts intercourse with higher intelligences, which strengthens and consoles them, and of which the laborers on the surface do not even dream!

Some such thought as this was floating vaguely through the brain of Mr. Churchill as he closed his school-house door behind him; and if in any degree he applied it to himself, it may perhaps be pardoned in a dreamy, poetic man like him; for we judge ourselves by what we feel capable of doing, while others judge us by what we have already done. And, moreover, his wife considered him equal to great things. To the people in the village, he was the schoolmaster, and nothing more. They beheld in his form and countenance no outward sign of the divinity within. They saw him daily moiling and delving in the common path, like a beetle, and little thought that underneath that hard and cold exterior lay folded delicate golden wings, wherewith, when the heat of day was over, he soared and revelled in the pleasant evening air.

To-day he was soaring and reveling before the sun had set; for it was Saturday. With a feeling of infinite relief he left behind him the empty school-house, into which the hot sun of a September afternoon was pouring. All the bright young faces were gone; all the impatient little hearts were gone; all the fresh voices, shrill, but musical with the melody of childhood, were gone; and the lately busy realm was given up to silence, and the dusty sunshine, and the old gray flies that buzzed and bumped their heads against the window panes. The sound of the outer door, creaking on its hebdomadal hinges, was like a sentinel's challenge, to which the key growled responsive in the lock; and the master, casting a furtive glance at the last caricature of himself in red chalk on the wooden fence close by, entered with a light step the solemn avenue of pines that led to the margin of the river.

At first his step was quick and nervous; and he swung his cane as if aiming blows at some invisible enemy. Though a meek man, there were moments when he remembered with bitterness the unjust reproaches of fathers and their insulting words; and then he fought imaginary battles with people out of sight, and struck them to the ground, and trampled upon them; for he was not exempt from the weakness of human nature, nor the customary vexations of a schoolmaster's life.

Unruly sons and unreasonable fathers did sometimes embitter his else sweet days and nights. But as he walked, his step grew slower, and his heart calmer. The coolness and shadows of the great trees comforted and satisfied him, and he heard the voice of the wind as it were the voice of spirits calling around him in the air; so that when he emerged from the black woodlands into the meadows by the river's side, all his cares were forgotten.

LXXXII.

SHERIDAN'S RIDE.

THOMAS BUCHANAN REED.

Up from the South at break of day,
Bringing to Winchester fresh dismay,
The affrighted air with a shudder bore,
Like a herald in haste, to the chieftain's door,
The terrible grumble and rumble and roar,
Telling the battle was on once more,
And Sheridan twenty miles away.

And wilder still those billows of war
Thundered along the horizon's bar,
And louder yet into Winchester rolled
The roar of that red sea uncontrolled,
Making the blood of the listener cold
As he thought of the stake in that fiery fray,
With Sheridan twenty miles away.

But there is a road from Winchester town,
A good, broad highway leading down;
And there through the flash of the morning light,
A steed as black as the steeds of night,
Was seen to pass as with eagle flight —
As if he knew the terrible need,
He stretched away with the utmost speed;
Hills rose and fell—but his heart was gay,
With Sheridan fifteen miles away.

Still sprung from these swift hoofs, thundering South,
The dust, like the smoke from the cannon's mouth,
Or the trail of a comet sweeping faster and faster,
Foreboding to traitors the doom of disaster;
The heart of the steed and the heart of the master
Were beating like prisoners assaulting their walls,
Impatient to be where the battle-field calls;
Every nerve of the charger was strained to full play,
With Sheridan only ten miles away.

Under his spurning feet the road
Like an arrowy Alpine river flowed,
And the landscape sped away behind
Like an ocean flying before the wind;
And the steed, like a bark fed with furnace ire,
Swept on with his wild eyes full of fire,
But, lo! he is nearing his heart's desire—
He is snuffing the smoke of the roaring fray,
With Sheridan only five miles away.

The first that the General saw were the groups
Of stragglers, and then the retreating troops;
What was done—what to do—a glance told him both,
And striking his spurs with a terrible oath,
He dashed down the line 'mid a storm of huzzahs,
And the wave of retreat checked its course there because
The sight of the master compelled it to pause.
With foam and with dust the black charger was gray,
By the flash of his eye, and his red nostril's play,
He seemed to the whole great army to say,
"I have brought you Sheridan all the way
From Winchester down to save the day!"

Hurrah, hurrah for Sheridan!
Hurrah, hurrah for horse and man!
And when their statues are placed on high
Under the dome of the Union sky,—
The American soldier's Temple of Fame,—
There with the glorious General's name
Be it said in letters both bold and bright:
" Here is the steed that saved the day
By carrying Sheridan into the fight,
From Winchester—twenty miles away!"

LXXXIII.

THE RAVEN.

EDGAR A. POE.

Once upon a midnight dreary, while I pondered, weak and weary,
Over many a quaint and curious volume of forgotten lore,—
While I nodded, nearly napping, suddenly there came a tapping,
As of some one gently rapping, rapping at my chamber-door.
"'T is some visitor," I mutter'd, "tapping at my chamber-door—
         Only this, and nothing more."

Ah, distinctly I remember, it was in the bleak December,
And each separate dying ember wrought its ghost upon the floor.
Eagerly I wished the morrow: vainly I had sought to borrow
From my books surcease of sorrow—sorrow for the lost Lenore—
For the rare and radiant maiden whom the angels named Lenore—
         Nameless here forevermore.

And the silken, sad, uncertain rustling of each purple curtain,
Thrill'd me—fill'd me with fantastic terrors never felt before;
So that now, to still the beating of my heart, I stood repeating,
"'T is some visitor entreating entrance at my chamber-door,—
Some late visitor entreating entrance at my chamber-door;
         That it is, and nothing more."

Presently my soul grew stronger: hesitating then no longer,
" Sir," said I, " or Madam, truly your forgiveness I implore;
But the fact is, I was napping, and so gently you came rapping,

And so faintly you came tapping, tapping at my chamber-door,
That I scarce was sure I heard you "—here I open'd wide the door:
      Darkness there, and nothing more.

Deep into that darkness peering, long I stood there, wondering, fearing,
Doubting, dreaming dreams no mortal ever dared to dream before;
But the silence was unbroken, and the darkness gave no token,
And the only word there spoken was the whisper'd word "Lenore!"
This *I* whisper'd, and an echo murmur'd back the word "Lenore!"
      Merely this, and nothing more.

Back into the chamber turning, all my soul within me burning,
Soon again I heard a tapping, something louder than before.
"Surely," said I, "surely that is something at my window-lattice;
Let me see then what thereat is, and this mystery explore,—
Let my heart be still a moment, and this mystery explore;—
      'T is the wind, and nothing more."

Open then I flung the shutter, when, with many a flirt and flutter,
In there stepp'd a stately raven of the saintly days of yore.
Not the least obeisance made he; not an instant stop'd or stay'd he;
But, with mien of lord or lady, perched above my chamber door,—
Perch'd upon a bust of Pallas, just above my chamber door—
      Perch'd, and sat, and nothing more.

Then this ebony bird beguiling my sad fancy into smiling,
By the grave and stern decorum of the countenance it wore,
"Though thy crest be shorn and shaven, thou," I said, "art sure no craven;
Ghastly, grim, and ancient raven, wandering from the nightly shore,
Tell me what thy lordly name is on the Night's Plutonian shore?"
      Quoth the raven, "Nevermore!"

Much I marvl'd this ungainly fowl to hear discourse so plainly,
Though its answer little meaning—little relevancy bore;
For we can not help agreeing that no living human being
Ever yet was bless'd with seeing bird above his chamber door—
Bird or beast upon the sculptured bust above his chamber door,
      With such name as "Nevermore!"

But the raven sitting lonely on the placid bust, spoke only
That one word, as if his soul in that one word he did outpour.
Nothing further then he utter'd—not a feather then he flutter'd—

Till I scarcely more than mutter'd, "Other friends have flown before—
On the morrow *he* will leave me, as my hopes have flown before."
            Then the bird said, "Nevermore!"

Startled at the stillness, broken by reply so aptly spoken,
"Doubtless," said I "what it utters is its only stock and store,
Caught from some unhappy master, whom unmerciful disaster
Follow'd fast and followed faster, till his song one burden bore,—
Till the dirges of his hope that melancholy burden bore,
            Of 'Nevermore—nevermore!'"

But the raven still beguiling all my sad soul into smiling,
Straight I wheel'd a cushion'd seat in front of bird, and bust, and door,
Then, upon the velvet sinking, I betook myself to linking
Fancy unto fancy, thinking what this ominous bird of yore—
What this grim, ungainly, ghastly, gaunt, and ominous bird of yore
            Meant in croaking "Nevermore!"

This I sat engaged in guessing, but no syllable expressing
To the fowl, whose fiery eyes now burned into my bosom's core;
This and more I sat divining, with my head at ease reclining
On the cushion's velvet lining that the lamp-light gloated o'er,
But whose velvet violet lining, with the lamp-light gloating o'er,
            She shall press—ah! nevermore!

Then methought the air grew denser, perfumed from an unseen censer
Swung by seraphim, whose foot-falls tinkled on the tufted floor.
"Wretch," I cried, "thy God hath lent thee—by these angels he hath
      sent thee
Respite—respite and nepenthe from thy memories of Lenore!
Quaff, oh quaff this kind nepenthe, and forget this lost Lenore!"
            Quoth the raven, "Nevermore!"

"Prophet!" said I, "thing of evil!—prophet still, if bird or devil!
Whether tempter sent, or whether tempest toss'd thee here ashore,
Desolate, yet all undaunted, on this desert land enchanted—
On this home by Horror haunted—tell me truly, I implore—
Is there—*is* there balm in Gilead?—tell me—tell me, I implore!"
            Quoth the raven, "Nevermore!"

"Prophet!" said I, "thing of evil!—prophet still, if bird or devil!
By that heaven that bends above us—by that God we both adore,
Tell this soul with sorrow laden, if, within the distant Aidenn,

It shall clasp a sainted maiden, whom the angels name Lenore ;
Clasp a fair and radiant maiden, whom the angels name Lenore ! "
            Quoth the raven, "Nevermore ! "

"Be that word our sign of parting, bird or fiend ! " I shrieked upstarting —
"Get thee back into the tempest and the Night's Plutonian shore !
Leave no black plume as a token of that lie thy soul hath spoken !
Leave my loneliness unbroken ! — quit the bust above my door !
Take thy beak from out my heart, and take thy form from off my door ! "
            Quoth the raven, "Nevermore ! "

And the raven, never flitting, still is sitting, still is sitting
On the pallid bust of Pallas, just above my chamber door ;
And his eyes have all the seeming of a demon that is dreaming,
And the lamp-light o'er him streaming throws his shadow on the floor ;
And my soul from out that shadow that lies floating on the floor,
            Shall be lifted—NEVERMORE !

LXXXIV.

HOME AND SCHOOL INFLUENCE ESPECIALLY NECESSARY IN TIME OF WAR.

J. M. GREGORY—1862.

The grand march of humanity stops not in its course even for war. From the cradle to the coffin, the crowding columns move on with lock-step through the successive stages of life. Childhood cannot halt in its progress for returning peace to afford leisure for education. On into the years — to manhood, to citizenship, to destiny — it rushes, whether learning lights its path and guides its steps, or ignorance involves it in error and conducts it headlong into vice. And if in peace the school is needful to rear our children to an intelligent and virtuous manhood, how much greater the need when war, with its inseparable barbarism, is drifting the nation from its onward course of peaceful civilization, back to the old realms of darkness and brute force.

The high and heroic aims of this conflict will doubtless mitigate the evils which necessarily attend an appeal to arms. To say

nothing of the physical health and prowess that camp life and
military discipline will develop, the love of country and love of
liberty will rise again from mere holiday sentiments to the grandeur
and power of national passions, and the Union, made doubly precious by the blood which its maintenance will cost, will attain a
strength that no mortal force can shake or destroy. History will
grow heroic again, and humanity itself will be inspired and glorified
with this fresh vindication of its God-given rights and duties, in
· this new incarnation and triumph of the principles of Constitutional
and Republican liberty. The too absorbing love of money, which
has hitherto characterized us, has loosened somewhat its clutch, and
been won to acts of genuine benevolence, at the sight of an im-
periled country; and the fiery demon of party spirit slinks away
abashed before the roused patriotism which lays life itself on the
altar of liberty.

But with all this, the barbarisms of war are too palpable and
terrific to be forgotten or disregarded, and the wise and patriotic
statesman will find in them a more urgent reason for fostering those
civilizing agencies which nourish the growing intelligence and virtue of the people. Against the ideas and vices engendered in the
camps, and amidst the battle-fields, we must raise still higher the
bulwarks of virtuous habits and beliefs, in the children yet at home.
We need the utmost stretch of home and school influence to save
society and the State from the terrible domination of military ideas
and military forces, always so dangerous to civil liberty and free
government.

LXXXV.

ABRAHAM LINCOLN.

V. B. DENSLOW—APRIL, 1865.

We have assembled together to unite in national mourning, such
as has never been witnessed by the present generation. A few days
ago every hall was hung with the emblems of victory, and in the
assurance of peace, every heart was filled with gratitude and joy.

Now all is changed; the temples are decked with mourning; the streets of the city are clothed in the weeds of a widowed nation, and only one sentiment pervades the hearts of all — an uncontrollable grief for the loss of one of "the noblest men that ever lived in the tide of times." I believe that the people loved Abraham Lincoln, and leaned upon his strong heart as no nation ever leaned upon the heart of any man. He had slowly, but surely, won his way into their confidence and esteem, by his noble singleness of purpose, honesty and truthfulness. On his first accession to power he was distrusted by the majority of the people because he was unknown to them. He was like a nugget of gold newly dug from the mountain, in which the people could only see the dross; but, having passed through the fiery ordeal of four years, the dross had been separated; he had become stamped with the eagles of the republic and of liberty, and from this time his fame was secure. They loved him because he had stood that ordeal, because he was possessed of a true moral dignity, a courage that was braver than boldness, a firmness that was better than self-will. He was not boastful, but true, and had borne his honors so meekly, and conducted himself so nobly, that the nation at length rose up as one man to vindicate their honor and liberty. He encountered great obstacles in purging the whole country of disloyalty; with what moderation and wisdom he labored to combine what was divided in the nation; he had never sought to be a ruler, but a servant of the people. He forgot all political enmities by calling into important offices men who were his opponents, and thus gathering around him the ablest minds of the nation, who might divide with him, not only the responsibility but the credit. In the selection of his cabinet, and in the moderation of his counsels, were to be seen evidences of that wisdom which endeared him forever to all enlightened men. It is for these great qualities — for his purity, simplicity and patriotism — that the people now mourn for their lamented President with an intelligent mourning, which has an argument for every tear, and a reason for every sigh. Those who thought to end his career and his influence, only succeeded in crowning him with immortal glory, and the people will live long and suffer much before they will see his like again.

LXXXVI.

ON BOARD THE CUMBERLAND.

G. W. BOKER—MARCH 8, 1862.

"Stand by your guns, men!" Morris cried.
　　Small need to pass the word;
　Our men at quarters ranged themselves
　　Before the drum was heard.

And then began the sailors' jests:
　　"What thing is that, I say?"
"A long-shore meeting-house adrift
　Is standing down the bay!"

A frown came over Morris' face;
　　The strange, dark craft he knew.
"That is the iron Merrimac,
　　Manned by a rebel crew.

"So shot your guns, and point them straight;
　　Before this day goes by,
We'll try of what her metal's made."
　　A cheer was our reply.

"Remember, boys, this flag of ours
　　Has seldom left its place;
And when it falls, the deck it strikes
　　Is covered with disgrace.

"I ask but this: or sink or swim,
　　Or live or nobly die,
My last sight upon earth may be
　　To see that ensign fly!"

Meanwhile the shapeless iron mass
　　Came moving o'er the wave,
As gloomy as a passing hearse,
　　As silent as the grave.

Her ports were closed; from stem to stern
　　No sign of life appeared.
We wondered, questioned, strained our eyes,
　　Joked, — everything but feared.

She reached our range. Our broadside rang,
  Our heavy pivots roared ;
And shot and shell, a fire of hell,
  Against her sides we poured.

God's mercy ! from her sloping roof
  The iron tempest glanced,
As hail bounds from a cottage thatch,
  And round her leaped and danced ;

Or when against her dusky hull
  We struck a fair, full blow,
The mighty, solid iron globes
  Were crumbled up like snow.

On, on, with fast increasing speed
  The silent monster came,
Though all our starboard battery
  Was one long line of flame.

She heeded not, no gun she fired,
  Straight on our bow she bore ;
Through riving plank and crashing frame
  Her furious way she tore.

Alas ! our beautiful, keen bow,
  That in the fiercest blast
So gently folded back the seas,
  They hardly felt we passed !

Alas ! alas ! my Cumberland,
  That ne'er knew grief before,
To be so gored, to feel so deep
  The tusk of that sea-boar !

Once more she backward drew a space,
  Once more our side she rent ;
Then, in the wantonness of hate,
  Her broadside through us sent.

The dead and dying round us lay,
  But our foeman lay abeam ;
Her open port-holes maddened us ;
  We fired with shout and scream.

L

We felt our vessel settling fast,
  We knew our time was brief.
"Ho! man the pumps!" But those who worked,
  And fought not, wept with grief.

"O keep us but an hour afloat!
  O, give us only time
To mete unto yon rebel crew
  The measure of their crime!"

From captain down to powder-boy
  No hand was idle then;
Two soldiers, but by chance aboard,
  Fought on like sailor men.

And when a gun's crew lost a hand,
  Some bold marine stepped out,
And jerked his braided jacket off,
  And hauled the gun about.

Our forward magazine was drowned;
  And up from the sick bay
Crawled the wounded, red with blood,
  And round us gasping lay.

Yes, cheering, calling us by name,
  Struggling with failing breath
To keep their shipmates at their post
  Where glory strove with death.

With decks afloat, and powder gone,
  The last broadside we gave
From the guns' heated iron lips
  Burst out beneath the wave.

So sponges, rammers, and handspikes—
  As men-of-war's-men should—
We placed within their proper racks,
  And at our quarters stood.

"Up to the spar-deck! save yourselves!"
  Cried Selfridge. "Up, my men!
God grant that some of us may live
  To fight yon ship again!"

We turned,— we did not like to go;
   Yet staying seemed but vain,
Knee-deep in water; so we left;
   Some swore, some groaned with pain.

We reached the deck.   There Randall stood:
   "Another turn, men,—so!"
Calmly he aimed his pivot gun:
   "Now, Tenny, let her go!"

It did our sore hearts good to hear
   The song our pivot sang,
As, rushing on from wave to wave,
   The whirring bomb-shell sprang.

Brave Randall leaped upon the gun,
   And waved his cap in sport;
"Well done! well aimed! I saw that shell
   Go through an open port."

It was our last, our deadliest shot;
   The deck was overflown;
The poor ship staggered, lurched to port,
   And gave a living groan.

Down, down, as headlong through the waves
   Our gallant vessel rushed,
A thousand gurgling watery sounds
   Around my senses gushed.

Then I remember little more.
   One look to heaven I gave,
Where, like an angel's wing, I saw
   Our spotless ensign wave.

I tried to cheer.   I cannot say
   Whether I swam or sank;
A blue mist closed around my eyes,
   And everything was blank.

When I awoke, a soldier lad,
   All dripping from the sea,
With two great tears upon his cheeks,
   Was bending over me.

I tried to speak. He understood
    The wish I could not speak.
He turned me. There, thank God! the flag
    Still fluttered at the peak!

And there, while thread shall hang to thread,
    O let that ensign fly!
The noblest constellation set
    Against our northern sky.

A sign that we who live may claim
    The peerage of the brave;
A monument, that needs no scroll,
    For those beneath the wave.

LXXXVII.

THE SWORD-BEARER.

G. W. BOKER—MARCH 8, 1862.

Brave Morris saw the day was lost;
    For nothing now remained,
On the wrecked and sinking Cumberland,
    But to save the flag unstained.

So he swore an oath in sight of Heaven,—
    If he kept it the world can tell:—
"Before I strike to a rebel flag,
    I'll sink to the gates of hell!

"Here, take my sword; 't is in my way;
    I shall trip o'er the useless steel;
For I'll meet the lot that falls to all
    With my shoulder at the wheel."

So the little negro took the sword;
    And O with what reverent care,
Following his master step by step,
    He bore it here and there!

A thought had crept through his sluggish brain,
    And shone in his dusky face,

That somehow—he could not tell just how—
    'T was the sword of his trampled race.

And as Morris, great with his lion heart,
    Rushed onward, from gun to gun,
The little negro slid after him,
    Like a shadow in the sun.

But something of pomp and of curious pride
    The sable creature wore,
Which at any time but a time like that
    Would have made the ship's crew roar.

Over the wounded, dying, and dead,
    Like an usher of the rod,
The black page, full of his mighty trust,
    With dainty caution trod.

No heed he gave to the flying ball,
    No heed to the bursting shell;
His duty was something more than life,
    And he strove to do it well.

Down, with our starry flag apeak,
    In the whirling sea we sank,
And captain and crew and the sword-bearer
    Were washed from the bloody plank.

They picked us up from the hungry waves;—
    Alas! not all!—"And where,
Where is the faithful negro lad?"—
    "Back oars! avast! look there!"

We looked; and as heaven may save my soul,
    I pledge you a sailor's word,
There, fathoms deep in the sea, he lay,
    Still grasping his master's sword!

We drew him out; and many an hour
    We wrought with his rigid form,
Ere the almost smothered spark of life
    By slow degrees grew warm.

The first dull glance that his eyeballs rolled
  Was down towards his shrunken hand;
And he smiled, and closed his eyes again
  As they fell on the rescued brand.

And no one touched the sacred sword.
  Till at length, when Morris came,
The little negro stretched it out,
  With his eager eyes aflame.

And if Morris wrung the poor boy's hand,
  And his words seemed hard to speak,
And tears ran down his manly cheeks,
  What tongue shall call him weak?

LXXXVIII.

THE VAGABONDS.

We are two travelers, Roger and I.
  Roger's my dog.—Come here, you scamp!
Jump for the gentlemen,—mind your eye!
  Over the table,—look out for the lamp!—
The rogue is growing a little old;
  Five years we've tramped through wind and weather
And slept out-doors when nights were cold,
  And ate and drank—and starved—together.

We've learned what comfort is, I tell you!
  A bed on the floor, a bit of rosin,
A fire to thaw our thumbs, (poor fellow!
  The paw he holds up there's been frozen,)
Plenty of catgut for my fiddle,
  (This out-door business is bad for strings,)
Then a few nice buckwheats hot from the griddle,
  And Roger and I set up for kings!

No, thank ye, sir,—I never drink;
  Roger and I are exceedingly moral—
Are n't we, Roger?—See him wink!—
  Well, something hot, then,—we won't quarrel.

He's thirsty, too,—see him nod his head?
  What a pity, sir, that dogs can't talk!
He understands every word that's said,—
  And he knows good milk from water-and-chalk.

The truth is, sir, now I reflect,
  I've been so sadly given to grog,
I wonder I've not lost the respect
  (Here's to you, sir!) even of my dog.
But he sticks by, through thick and thin;
  And this old coat, with its empty pockets,
And rags that smell of tobacco and gin,
  He'll follow while he has eyes in his sockets.

There isn't another creature living
  Would do it, and prove, through every disaster,
So fond, so faithful, and so forgiving,
  To such a miserable, thankless master!
No, sir!—see him wag his tail and grin!
  By George! it makes my old eyes water!
That is, there's something in this gin
  That chokes a fellow. But no matter!

We'll have some music, if you're willing,
  And Roger (hem! what a plague a cough is, Sir!)
Shall march a little.—Start, you villain!
  Stand straight! 'Bout face! Salute your officer!
Put up that paw! Dress! Take your rifle!
  (Some dogs have arms, you see!) Now hold your
Cap while the gentlemen give a trifle,
  To aid a poor, old, patriot soldier!

March! Halt! Now show how the rebel shakes,
  When he stands up to hear his sentence.
Now tell us how many drams it takes
  To honor a jolly new acquaintance.
Five yelps,—that's five; he's mighty knowing!
  The night's before us, fill the glasses!—
Quick, Sir! I'm ill,—my brain is going!—
  Some brandy,—thank you,—there!—it passes!

Why not reform ?   That's easily said;
   But I've gone through such wretched treatment,
Sometimes forgetting the taste of bread,
   And scarce remembering what meat meant,
That my poor stomach's past reform ;
   And there are times when, mad with thinking,
I'd sell out heaven for something warm
   To prop a horrible inward sinking.

Is there a way to forget to think ?
   At your age, Sir, home, fortune, friends,
A dear girl's love, — but I took to drink ; —
   The same old story ; you know how it ends.
If you could have seen these classic features, —
   You need n't laugh, sir ; they were not then
Such a burning libel on God's creatures :
   I was one of your handsome men !

If you had seen HER, so fair and young,
   Whose head was happy on this breast !
If you could have heard the song I sung
   When the wine went round, you would n't have guessed
That ever I, sir, should be straying
   From door to door, with fiddle and dog,
Ragged and penniless, and playing
   To you to-night for a glass of grog !

She's married since, — a parson's wife :
   'T was better for her that we should part, —
Better the soberest, prosiest life
   Than a blasted home and a broken heart.
I have seen her ?   Once : I was weak and spent
   On a dusty road : a carriage stopped :
But little she dreamed, as on she went,
   Who kissed the coin that her fingers dropped !

You've set me talking, sir ; I'm sorry ;
   It makes me wild to think of the change !
What do you care for a beggar's story ?
   Is it amusing ? you find it strange ?

I had a mother so proud of me!
  'T was well she died before— Do you know
If the happy spirits in heaven can see
  The ruin and wretchedness here below?

Another glass, and strong, to deaden
  This pain; then Roger and I will start.
I wonder, has he such a lumpish, leaden,
  Aching thing, in place of a heart?
He is sad sometimes, and would weep, if he could,
  No doubt, remembering things that were,—
A virtuous kennel, with plenty of food,
  And himself a sober, respectable cur.

I'm better now; that glass was warming.—
  You rascal! limber your lazy feet!
We must be fiddling and performing
  For supper and bed, or starve in the street.—
Not a very gay life to lead, you think?
  But soon we shall go where lodgings are free,
And the sleepers need neither victuals nor drink;—
  The sooner, the better for Roger and me!

LXXXIX.

CORDIAL SUBMISSION TO LAWFUL AUTHORITY A PRIMARY ATTRIBUTE OF GOOD CITIZENSHIP.

NEWTON BATEMAN.

Obedience is the law of God's universe; the inexorable decree of His providence. And evermore in the back-ground of His love and mercy to the docile and penitent, hangs the cloud of destruction to the incorrigibly guilty. Retribution waits upon invitation. Behind all Jehovah's dealings with angels, men and devils, there lingers an immutable, inexorable, eternal, MUST. Obey and live, refuse and perish, is the epitome of God's natural and spiritual economy. It rules in the moral and material worlds; in the destinies of individuals, of nations, and of the race.

The unsupported body *falls*, is the lesson slowly and gently taught in the nursery, as the little child steps falteringly from father to mother, from chair to chair. Once learned, the law must be obeyed — death lurks at every precipice. Thus one by one, kindly, imperceptibly almost, God teaches us His physical laws, and ever after, by sea and land, through all the realms of nature, the inexorable decree, "*obey or die*," attends our footsteps. It is heard in the howl of the tempest, in the thunders of Niagara — it speaks to us in the earthquake and the avalanche — its fiery letters gleam in the storm-cloud, it sounds forth from the caverns and smoke of Vesuvius.

We cannot escape from this omnipresent, eternal *must*, in the natural world. It is God's tremendous barrier, erected everywhere, to turn us from destruction — erected not in anger, but in love. It is inexorable, because else it would cease to be effective. Some must perish that many may live. We must obey the laws of health ; the penalty of taking poison is *death* — the penalty of breathing foul air, sooner or later is *death* — the penalty of intemperance is misery, decay and *death*.

The same unchangeable decree follows us into the moral world. We must obey the moral law, or *suffer* — physically as well as mentally. Here, too, God has no scruples about enforcing his commands by the ordeal of pain. He does not stop with "moral suasion" merely — He not only *pleads* with divine tenderness, but He *chastises* with divine uncompromising firmness and severity. Sin and suffering are indissoluble. In the cup of every forbidden pleasure there lurks a viper, which sooner or later will sting soul and body to death. No tortures of the body can compare with the agonies of the spirit, but in due time, for every infraction of the moral code, the former are superadded to the latter.

" *Thou shalt not kill*," is the sententious decree which epitomizes the divine regard for human life. Not — "It is not best to be a murderer — it is not right — you will be far happier if you do not — you should respect the rights and happiness of others — do not, I beseech you, do not be a murderer "— but, ringing through the earth, the terse mandate of God falls loud and clear upon the race, "THOU SHALT NOT." And who can depict the terrors that gather about and haunt the guilty wretch who violates the prohibition — goad and haunt him to his dying hour, even if swift destruction does not overtake him at the hands of the law. A fugitive and a vagabond, pursued through the earth by the sleepless and relentless Nemesis of vengeance, scourged by the scorpion lash of conscience, pale and wasted and haggard, he drags himself onward to a premature grave, or invokes the suicide's doom. Thus does the everlasting MUST confront the transgressor at every turn.

And as it is with individuals, so it is with nations. The track of centuries is strewn with the memorials of Jehovah's tremendous judgments upon States and Empires that would not obey his law — "The wicked shall be turned into hell, and all the NATIONS that forget God," is the record which six thousand years have confirmed. "The mills of the gods grind slowly," but sooner or later retribution, resistless and appalling, closes the career of national injustice and wrong. So it has been in the past, so it is now, and so it will ever be. Mercy, forbearance, entreaty, persuasion, are tried first — the light of reason, the warnings of experience, the monitions of Providence are given to avert the impending blow. Truth and virtue, justice and freedom, are inscribed upon the banners beneath which the God of History would lead the nations to the millennial day.

XCI.

MY MOTHER.

BELLE BUSH.

My Mother's a beautiful spirit, and her home is the Holy Evangel's;
There she feels neither sorrow nor pain, and treads not the path of the
  weary.
Years ago, in the bud of my being, I knew her a radiant mortal,
But the house of her soul decayed, and she fled from the crumbling mansion,
And over the sea of eternity, bridged by the hands of angels,

Uniting the links of belief with the golden chain of repentance,
She passed, with the torch of prayer, to the opposite shore in safety,
When, crowned with the garlands of love, she mounted the steps of the city,
And the angels of Mercy and Truth, keeping watch at the heavenly portals,
Beheld her approach from afar, and flung open the pearly partitions;
With song and loud hallelujahs they welcomed the earth-ransomed stranger,
And guided her steps, till she stood on the brink of the Life-giving
      fountain,
Where, tasting its Lethean waters, all the joys of the world were forgotten,
Save the beautiful bloom of the soul—the love in the heart of the mother.
This, the light of her life upon earth, now budded and blossomed in heaven,
Stately and fair it towered, and the hue of its leaves was immortal.
Strong tendrils grew out from each bough, and twined round the chords of
      her spirit.
While the zephyrs of Paradise played and toyed with the delicate branches,
Till each leaf like a harp-string swayed, and murmured in strains Æolian,
And oft with their musical numbers reminded the wondering mother
Of the flowers she had left in the desert,—her weary and sorrowing
      children.
In their half-open leaflets she reads the pledge of her glorious mission,
And rejoiced that her love should gather those earthly buds to her bosom.
The angels beheld her in gladness rise up on those radiant pinions
Which float on the air like a sunbeam, and rival the dove in their fleetness.

Oh, my mother's a beautiful spirit, and her home is the holy Evangel's;
But she comes on her soft-floating pinions to look for her earth-bound
      children.
She comes, and the hearts that were weary no longer remember their
      sorrow
In their joy that the lost is returned, our beloved and radiant mother!
She comes and our spirits rejoice, for we know she's our guardian angel,
O'er our journey in life keeping watch, and giving us gentle caresses.
She comes, she comes with the light when it opens the gates of the morning,
And her voice is our music by night, of perils and storms giving warning.
Her robes are of delicate pink,—sweet emblem of holy affection,—
And twined o'er her radient brow are the amaranth-blossoms of heaven.
She smiles, and the light of her smiles bringeth joy in our seasons of
      darkness;
She whispers, and soft are the zephyrs that echo her musical numbers,
As they waft o'er the chords of our being her thrilling and fervent emotions.
We listen to her in our sorrow, and yield to each gentle impression,

Till pleasant to us is the path leading down to the rushing river ;
O'er the swift-rolling current of death we shall pass to the homes of the
    spirits,
And, waiting beside the still waters, our mother will be there to greet us ;
With songs she will welcome our coming, and fold us to rest on her bosom,
And teach us, like lisping children, to murmur the language of heaven !

Oh, my mother's a beautiful spirit, and her home is the holy Evangel's ;
But she comes on the pinions of love to watch her sorrowing children.
She comes, and the shadows depart, as we thrill to her gentle caresses.
Our Father in Heaven, we bless Thee, that our mother's our Guardian
    Angel !

XCI.

WAITING BY THE GATE.

WILLIAM C. BRYANT.

Beside a massive gateway built up in years gone by,
Upon whose tops the clouds in eternal shadows lie,
While streams the evening sunshine on quiet wood and lea,
I stand and calmly wait till the hinges turn for me.

The tree-tops faintly rustle beneath the breeze's flight
A soft and soothing sound, yet it whispers of the night,
I hear the woodthrush piping one mellow descant more,
And scent the flowers that blow when the heat of day is o'er.

Behold the portals open, and o'er the threshold now,
There steps a weary one with a pale and furrowed brow ;
His count of years is full, his allotted task is wrought ;
He passes to his rest from a place that needs him not.

In sadness then I ponder how quickly fleets the hour
Of human strength and action, man's courage and his power.
I muse while still the woodthrush sings down the golden day,
And as I look and listen the sadness wears away.

Again the hinges turn, and a youth, departing, throws
A look of longing backward, and sorrowfully goes ;
A blooming maid, unbinding the roses from her hair,
Moves mournfully away from amidst the young and fair.

Oh glory of our race that so suddenly decays!
Oh crimson flush of morning that darkens as we gaze!
Oh breath of summer flowers that on the restless air
Scatters a moment's sweetness and flies we know not where!

I grieve for life's bright promise, just shown and then withdrawn;
But still the sun shines round me; the evening birds sing on,
And I again am soothed, and, beside the ancient gate,
In this soft, evening twilight, I calmly stand and wait.

Once more the gates are opened; an infant group goes out,
The sweet smile quenched forever, and stilled the sprightly shout.
Oh frail, frail tree of Life, that upon the greensward strows
Its fair, young buds unopened, with every wind that blows!

So came from every region, so enter, side by side,
The strong and faint of spirit, the meek, and men of pride.
Steps of earth's great and mighty, between those pillows gray,
And prints of little feet, mark the dust along the way.

And some approach the threshold whose looks are blank with fear,
And some whose temples brighten with joy in drawing near,
As if they saw dear faces, and caught the gracious eye
Of Him, the Sinless Teacher, who came for us to die.

I mark the joy, the terror; yet these, within my heart,
Can neither make the dread nor the longing to depart;
And in the sunshine streaming on quiet wood and lea,
I stand and calmly wait till the hinges turn for me.

XCII.

THY WILL BE DONE.

J. G. WHITTIER.

We see not, know not; all our way
Is night, — with Thee alone is day:
From out the torrent's troubled drift,
Above the storm our prayers we lift,
Thy will be done!

The flesh may fail, the heart may faint,
But who are we to make complaint,
Or dare to plead, in times like these,
The weakness of our love of ease ?
  Thy will be done!

We take with solemn thankfulness
Our burden up, nor ask it less,
And count it joy that even we
May suffer, serve, or wait for Thee,
  Whose will be done!

Though dim as yet in tint and line,
We trace Thy picture's wise design,
And thank Thee that our age supplies
Its dark relief of sacrifice.
  Thy will be done!

And if, in our unworthiness,
Thy sacrificial wine we press,
If from Thy ordeal's heated bars
Our feet are seamed with crimson scars,
  Thy will be done!

If, for the age to come, this hour
Of trial hath vicarious power,
And, blest by Thee, our present pain
Be Liberty's eternal gain,
  Thy will be done!

Strike, Thou, the Master, we Thy keys,
The anthem of the destinies:
The minor of Thy loftier strain,
Our hearts shall breathe the old refrain,
  Thy will be done!

XCIII.

TO-DAY AND TO-MORROW.

GERALD MASSEY.

High hopes that burned like stars sublime,
Go down the heavens of Freedom ;

And true hearts perish in the time
    We bitterliest need 'em.
But never sit we down and say
    There is nothing left but sorrow;
We walk the wilderness to-day, —
    The Promised Land to-morrow.

Our birds of song are silent now, —
    There are no flowers blooming;
Yet life beats in the frozen bough,
    And Freedom's Spring is coming!
And Freedom's tide comes up always,
    Though we may strand in sorrow;
And our good bark, aground to-day,
    Shall float again to-morrow!

Through all the long, dark night of years,
    The people's cry ascendeth,
And earth is wet with blood and tears:
    But our meek sufferance endeth!
The few shall not forever sway,
    The many wail in sorrow!
The powers of hell are strong to-day,
    But Christ shall reign to-morrow!

Though hearts brood o'er the past, our eye
    With smiling Futures glisten!
For lo! our day bursts up the skies:
    Lean out your souls, and listen!
The world rolls Freedom's radiant way,
    And ripens with her sorrow:
Keep heart! who bear the cross to-day,
    Shall wear the crown to-morrow!

O Youth, flame-earnest, still aspire
    With energies immortal!
To many a heaven of desire
    Our yearning opes a portal!
And though age wearies by the way,
    And hearts break in the furrow,
We'll sow the golden grain to-day, —
    The harvest comes to-morrow!

Build up heroic lives, and all
    Be like a sheathen sabre,
Ready to flash out at God's call,
    O chivalry of labor ;
Triumph and Toil are twins ; and aye,
    Joy seems the cloud of sorrow ;
And 'tis the martyrdom to-day,
    Brings victory to-morrow !

XCIV.

THE GROVES OF BLARNEY.

R. A. MILLIKIN.

The groves of Blarney they look so charming,
    Down by the purlings of sweet, silent brooks—
All decked by posies, that spontaneous grows there,
    Planted in order in the rocky   nooks.
'T is there the daisy, and the sweet carnation,
    The blooming pink, and the rose so fair ;
Likewise the lily, and the daffodilly—
    All flowers that scent the sweet, open air.

'T is Lady Jeffers owns this plantation,
    Like Alexander, or like Helen fair ;
There 's no commander in all the nation
    For regulation can with her compare.
Such walls surround her, that no nine-pounder
    Could ever plunder her place of strength ;
But Oliver Cromwell, he did her pommel
    And made a breach in her battlement.

There 's gravel walks there for speculation,
    And conversation in sweet solitude ;
'T is there the lover may hear the dove, or
    The gentle plover, in the afternoon.
And if a young lady should be so engaging
    As to walk all alone in those shady bowers,
'T is there the courtier he may transport her
    In some dark fort, or under the ground.

M

For 't is there's the cave where no daylight enters,
  But bats and badgers are forever bred;
Being mossed by natur', that makes it sweeter
  Than a coach and six or a feather bed.
'T is there's the lake that is stored with perches,
  And comely eels in the verdant mud;
Besides the leeches, and the groves of beeches,
  All standing in order for to guard the flood.

'T is there's the kitchen hangs many a flitch in,
  With the maids a stitching upon the stair;
The bread and biske'—the beer and whiskey,
  Would make you frisky if you were there.
'T is there you'd see Peg Murphy's daughter
  A washing praties forenent the door,
With Roger Cleary, and Father Healy,
  All blood relations to my Lord Donoughmore.

There's statues gracing this noble place in,
  All heathen goddesses so fair—
Bold Neptune, Plutarch, and Nicodemus,
  All standing naked in the open air.
So now to finish this brave narration,
  Which my poor geni' could not entwine;
But were I Homer, or Nebuchadnezzar,
  'T is in every feature I would make it shine.

XCV.

OUR SYSTEM OF PUBLIC INSTRUCTION SHOULD DISTINCTIVELY INCULCATE A LOVE OF COUNTRY.

NEWTON BATEMAN.

The true American patriot is ever a *worshipper*. The starry symbol of his country's sovereignty is to *him* radiant with a diviner glory than that which meets his mortal vision. It epitomizes the splendid results of dreary ages of experiments and failures in human government; and, as he gazes upon its starry folds undulating responsive to the whispering winds of the upper air, it sometimes seems to his rapt spirit to recede further and further into the soft blue skies, till the heavens open, and angel hands plant it upon the battlements of Paradise. Wherever that ensign floats, on the sea or on the land, it is to him the very Shekinah of his political love and faith, luminous with the presence of that God who conducted his fathers across the sea and through the fires of the Revolution, to the Pisgah heights of civil and religious liberty. Its stars seem real; its lines of white symbol the purity of his heroic sires; those of red, their patriot blood shed in defense of the right. To defend that flag, is to him something more than a duty, it is a joy, a coveted privilege, akin to that which nerves the arm and directs the blow in defense of wife or child. To insult it, is worse than infamy; to make war upon it, more than treason.

A perfect civil government is the sublimest earthly symbol of Deity—indeed, such a government is a transcript of the divine will; its spirit and principles identical with those with which He governs the universe. Its vigilance, care and protection, are ubiquitous—its strong hand is ever ready to raise the fallen, restrain the violent, and punish the aggressor. Its patient ear is bent to catch alike the complaint of the rich and strong, or the poor and weak, while unerring justice presides at the trial and settlement of every issue between man and man.

Now, our government is not perfect, even in theory, and still less so in practice; but it is good and strong and glorious enough to inspire a loftier patriotism than animates the people of any other nation. What element is wanting to evoke the passionate love and admiration of an American citizen for his country? Is it ancestry? Men of purer lives, sterner principles, or braver hearts than our fathers, never crossed the sea. Is it motives? Not for war or conquest, but for civil and religious liberty, did our fathers approach these shores. Is it perils and obstacles? Wintry storms, and icy coasts, and sterile soils, prowling beasts, and savage men, and hunger, and nakedness, and disease, and death, were the greeting our fathers received. Is it patient endurance? Not till the revelations of the final day, will the dauntless fortitude of our fathers, in the midst of appalling dangers and sufferings, be disclosed. Is it heroic achievement? Again and again has the haughty Lion of St. George been brought to the dust, and the titled chivalry of England overthrown by the resistless onset of the sons of liberty, led by "Mr. Washington!" Is it moral sublimity? Behold Witherspoon in the Continental Congress; Washington at Valley Forge; Clay in the Senate of 1850. Is it that we have no historical Meccas? Where shall a patriot muse and pray, if not by the shades of Vernon or Ashland—at Marshfield or the Hermitage. Have we no great names to go flaming down the ages? When will Henry's clarion voice be hushed, or Warren cease to tell men how to die for liberty—when will Adams, and Franklin, and Jefferson, fade from history? Is it constitutional wisdom, excellence of laws, or incentives to individual exertion? No other land can compare with ours in these respects. Is it grandeur of scenery? God has made but one Niagara, one Missippippi, one Hudson. Is it territorial extent? Our domain stretches from ocean to ocean, and from lake to gulf.

By all these incentives let our school-boys be fired with an enthusiastic love for the dear land of their birth, the precious heritage of their fathers—let them leave the school-room for the arena of active life, feeling that next to God and their parents, their country claims and shall receive their best affections and most uncompromising devotion—let them realize that their conduct will bring honor or dishonor upon their country, as surely as upon their parents and friends—let them learn to identify themselves as citizens with the interests of the commonwealth, blushing at whatever disgraces her, exulting in all that contributes to her glory and renown—let them feel that this great country is *their* country, that they have a personal proprietorship in the lustre of her history, the honor of her name, the magnificence of her commerce, the valor of her fleets and armies, the inviolability of her Constitution and laws, and the magnitude and beneficence of her civil, social and religious institutions.

XCVI.

ADDRESS AT THE DEDICATION OF THE CEMETRY AT GETTYSBURG.

A. LINCOLN — NOV. 1864.

Fourscore and seven years ago our fathers brought forth upon this continent a new nation, conceived in liberty, and dedicated to the proposition that all men are created equal. Now we are engaged in a great civil war, testing whether that nation, or any nation so conceived and so dedicated, can long endure. We are met on a great battle field of that war. We are met to dedicate a portion of it as the final resting-place of those who here gave their lives that that nation might live. It is altogether fitting and proper that we should do this. But in a larger sense we cannot dedicate, we cannot consecrate, we cannot hallow this ground. The brave men, living and dead, who struggled here, have consecrated it far above our power to add or detract. The world will little note, nor long remember what we say here, but it can never forget what they did here. It is for us, the living, rather to be dedicated here to the unfinished work they have thus far so nobly carried on. It is rather for us to be here dedicated to the great task remaining before us that from these honored dead we take increased devotion to the cause for which they gave the last full measure of devotion, that we here highly resolve that these dead shall not have died in vain, that the nation shall, under God, have a new birth of freedom, and that the government of the people, by the people, and for the people, shall not perish from the earth.

XCVII.

NATIONAL LINCOLN MONUMENT.

NEWTON BATEMAN.

The elements of character which most exalted Abraham Lincoln — which earned for him among his friends and neighbors a *soubriquet* more honorable than that awarded to Aristides — which bound him to the good, who knew him, by indissoluble ties of love and confidence—which made him President—which kept him inflexible of purpose and unfailing in faith in the darkest days of the Republic—which caused him in the fullness of time to smite the Pharaohs of Slavery with the flaming breath of his immortal Proclamation, calling a whole race from despair and death up to life and hope—the qualities of head and heart which did these things, and which at last added his name to the Martyrs of Liberty, and shrined his memory in the heart of the nation with a love more tender and reverent than has been given to any other son of the Republic since the death of Washington; are his simple, unswerving truthfulness; his humble trust in God; his inflexible fidelity to his convictions of truth and duty; his unsuspecting frankness and generosity; his quenchless love of liberty, and the unsullied rectitude and purity of his life.

Did not the world seem less bright and beautiful when we heard that Abraham Lincoln was dead? Did not a loving presence seem to have passed from the very atmosphere, leaving a shadow of a vague distress upon our hearts? Was not something wanting to the day—something to the night—when we knew that his loving heart had cease to beat? Did the sun ever look down on such a spectacle as this stricken nation presented, in its voiceless anguish, on the morning of April 15th? Was any man ever borne to the grave so triumphant in death—with a funeral procession fifteen days in duration and over two thousand miles in length, while the air was ever tremulous, day and night, with dirge, and requiem, and minute gun? No dead President alone could evoke such woe. It was dead Abraham Lincoln, the *good and true man*, more than the Chief Magistrate of the nation, that subdued and melted the national heart, and bathed the millions in tears.

Is it not meet that we build a monument to such a man—a monument that shall not only be worthy the immortal dead, but one that shall essay to express the homage of a Christian and educated people for an exalted character whose greatness is made complete by goodness? Will not such a monument teach all future generations, that

"He is not but half great who is not good;" inspiring the young and ardent with a worthy ambition, and that lofty courage which dares to do right for right's sake, while it rebukes and shames the selfish, groveling, politic compromiser? Do we not well, *as educators,* to build a monument to which every parent may point his child and say, " So let it be done to him whom the people delight to honor ? " Will not a new era in our national life be marked by such a monument—will it not still seem grand and worthy, when, in the coming centuries, the nation having consummated the policy for which he died, and become strong and glorious in a Union without a slave, shall appreciate, honor, love and revere, as it cannot now, the sublime character, life and work of her martyred President?

Living as he lived, dying as, and for what, he died, the lapse of time will but render more and more sacred every offering of love which this generation shall lay upon his tomb. Sage and seer, the good and great of every land and clime will come to muse and pray beneath its solemn shade. Let art and genius rear the mighty shaft, and more than classic grace and beauty breathe their inspiration upon it and make it glorious—for while it marks the dust of Lincoln, its nobler mission will be to tell our children and the world, from age to age, HOW WE LOVE THE MARTYRS OF LIBERTY.

XCVIII.

DUTY OF AMERICAN CITIZENS.

STEPHEN A. DOUGLAS—MAY, 1861.

If war must come—if the bayonet must be used to maintain the Constitution—I can say, before God, my conscience is clear. I have struggled long for a peaceful solution of the difficulty. I have not only tendered those States what was theirs of right, but I have gone to the very extreme of magnanimity. The return is War— armies marching upon our Capital; obstructions and dangers to our navigation; letters of marque to invite pirates to prey upon our commerce; a concerted movement to blot out the United States of America from the map of the globe. The question is, are we to maintain the country of our fathers, or allow it to be stricken down by those who, when they can no longer govern, threaten to destroy?   *   *   *   *   *   *

But this is no time for a detail of causes. The conspiracy is now known. Armies have been raised. War is levied to accomplish it. *There are only two sides to the question. Every man must be for the United States or against it. There can be no neutrals in this war* — ONLY PATRIOTS AND TRAITORS!   *   *

We cannot close our eyes to the sad and solemn fact that war does exist. The Government must be maintained; its enemies overthrown; and the more stupendous the preparations, the less bloodshed, and the shorter the struggle.   *   *   *

The Constitution and its guarantees are our birthright; and I am ready to enforce that inalienable right to the last extent. We cannot recognize Secession. Recognize it once, and you have not only dissolved the Government, but you have destroyed civil order, and ruptured the foundations of society; you will have inaugurated anarchy in its worst form, and will shortly experience all the horrors of the French Revolution.

Then we have a solemn duty — to maintain the Government. The greater our unanamity, the speedier the day of peace. We have prejudices to overcome, from the few short months since, of a fierce party contest. These must be allayed. Let us lay aside all criminations and recriminations, as to the origin of these difficulties. When we shall have again a country, with the United States flag floating over it, and respected on every inch of American soil, it will then be time enough to ask who and what brought all this upon us.

It is a sad task to discuss questions so fearful as civil war; but sad as it is, bloody and disastrous as I expect it will be, I express it as my conviction, before God, that it is the duty of every American citizen to rally around the flag of his country.

XCIX.

SOCRATES SNOOKS.

FROM KIDD'S ELOCUTION.

Mister Socrates Snooks, a lord of creation,
A second time entered the marriage relation;
Xantippe Caloric accepted his hand,
And thought him the happiest man in the land.
But scarce had the honeymoon passed o'er his head,
When, one morning, to Xantippe, Socrates said,
"I think, for a man of my standing in life,
This house is too small, as I now have a wife;
So, as early as possible, carpenter Carey
Shall be sent for to widen my house and my dairy."

"Now, Socrates, dearest," Xantippe replied,
"I hate to hear everything vulgarly *my'd*;
Now, whenever you speak of your chattels again,
Say, *our* cow-house, *our* barn-yard, *our* pig-pen."
"By your leave, Mrs. Snooks, I will say what I please
Of *my* houses, *my* lands, *my* gardens, *my* trees."
"Say *Our*," Xantippe exclaimed in a rage.
"I won't, Mrs. Snooks, though you ask it an age!"

Oh, woman! though only a part of man's rib,
If the story in Genesis don't tell a fib,
Should your naughty companion e'er quarrel with you,
You are certain to prove the best man of the two.
In the following case it was certainly true;
For the lovely Xantippe just pulled off her shoe,
And laying about her, all sides at random,
The adage was verified—"*Nil desperandum*."

Mister Socrates Snooks, after trying in vain,
To ward off the blows which descended like rain,—
Concluding that valor's best part was discretion,—
Crept under the bed like a terrified Hessian.
But the dauntless Xantippe, not one whit afraid,
Converted the siege into a blockade.

At last, after reasoning the thing in his pate,
He concluded 't was useless to strive against fate ;
And so, like a tortoise, protruding his head,
Said, "My dear, may we come out from under *our* bed ? "
"Hah ! hah ! " she exclaimed, "Mr. Socrates Snooks,
I perceive you agree to my terms, by your looks :
Now, Socrates,—hear me,—from this happy hour,
If you 'll only obey me, I 'll never look sour."
'T is said the next Sabbath, ere going to church,
He chanced for a clean pair of trowsers to search ;
Having found them, he asked, with a few nervous twitches,
"*My dear, may we put on our new Sunday breeches ? "*

C.

COLLOQUY OF THE NATIONS.

FOR YOUNG LADIES.

ISRAEL,	ITALY,	ENGLAND,
RUSSIA,	GERMANY,	FRANCE,
GREECE,	SWITZERLAND,	UNITED STATES,

ANGLO-AFRICAN, PROPHETESS.

SCENE I.

Israel.—Oh ! that my head were waters, and mine eyes a fountain of tears, that I might weep day and night for the slain of the daughters of my people. Oh ! Jerusalem ! Once the pride of her children and the glory of all lands, now desolated by the Gentile. Even her holy mountains leveled with the plain, and her ancient cedars have been stripped of their glory, which once sheltered the holy prophets, and under whose spreading branches Judea's daughters listened to the sweet songs of Zion, and David tuned his harp and sang the praises of Jehovah.

And where are her children, the chosen people of God?

Ask the four winds of heaven if they visit any land unsought by the Jew. But glory to the Ancient of Days he is still a Jew ; though wandering far from his home, his eyes are ever turned Zionward, and he waits for the Coming of the Lord who shall restore the glory of the Ancient Temple, and gather thither the lost sheep of the House of Israel. The world hates the Jew now, but the time will come when his glory shall again return, and the scoffing Gentile shall acknowledge him the Blessed of the Lord.

But yonder comes the representatives of these proud nations. Let me retire, lest I become the subject of their jeers. [*Exit Jewess.*]

SCENE II.

Russia.—Sisters, we meet. No sound of trump or drum announces to the world our coming. 'T is not that each may prove her strength in arms and claim at last a well fought field. We come in love and each presents her claims to greatness. Let Greece first say what she has done to merit praise, and why she asks her name may stand conspicuous among the nations of the earth.

Greece.—Would you know what ancient Greece can bring in proof of greatness? Ask Platea's well-fought plain, and the narrow pass at Thermopylæ, where the brave three hundred fell, if they belonged to Greece. Or, liking not this bloody picture, gaze upon her classic isles whose shores are washed by Southern seas, and whose beauties fired a Sappho and a Homer's mind with strange, weird fancy. And when you ask for the wise of earth, forget not Plato, nor the mild and gentle Solon; nor Socrates, who taught men how to live and how to meet the gods; nor wise Lycurgus, who gave earth laws that all the world has patterned after.

Italy.—Let not our sister claim too much for Greece; remember Italy has claims. 'T was the " Eternal Rome " that ruled the world for centuries in Church and State. Her warriors brought proud Carthage low, and even Greece acknowledged her dominion. 'T was Cicero who stirred with magic power the hearts of those who listened to his strains of eloquence; and Virgil sang such lays that all the world still listens. Italy has ever claimed the admiration of all lands. Her deep blue sky and southern winds, her very ruins, rich in ancient legends, frescoes, paintings, busts and arabesques, woo the painter and the poet to her shores in reverence. The names of Raphael and Michael Angelo alone make Italy immortal.

Germany. — I am from Germany — a land that boasts not of classic isles or wooing winds, but of stern realities. A land which has given to the world a bold and unrelenting Luther, a mild and gentle Melancthon, and a noble Prince of Orange; men whose names stand foremost as reformers, and to whom all lands will ever owe a debt of gratitude. I do not ask for Germany a place among the classic nations of the earth, for she lives not in the misty past; the present and the future are her portion. But when you ask for those who have done most for the present civilization of mankind, forget not the land which can number among its great men a Humboldt, a Mueller, and a Goethe. Forget not the land whose libraries and public gardens, whose schools and universities, are the wonder and admiration of the world.

Switzerland. — Who has not heard of the gorgeous sunsets of Switzerland; of her cloud-capped mountains and eternal snows; of her dazzling glaciers and beautiful inland lakes. And who does not know that her children are the boldest and the bravest; that for ages, in their mountain fastnesses they have defied the crowned heads of Europe. Inured to hardship, and often to want, they have been content if only they could leap unfettered along the mountain side and breathe its pure air. 'T is Switzerland who has given the world a Tell.

England. — The name of England is enough. I do not need to remind you what she has done to merit greatness. Boundless in wealth and power, she defies the world. To her the sun never rises or sets, and to her the seasons are one. In her manufactories and commerce, in her institutions, both civil and political, she acknowledges no superior. For what can you ask that England does not possess? Does the poet or novelist desire subjects for his pen? Let him visit her ivy-mantled towers and ruined castles rich in legendary lore. Is it the historian who seeks for noble men and daring deeds? Let him read England's record, and he will look no further. Who has made her language immortal but a Milton and a Shakespeare? What other army has been invincible on land and sea but England's? Whether as romantic Crusaders they wrested the Holy Sepulchre from the defiling hands of the Saracen ; or as battlers for the right, they taught proud Spain with her Invincible Armada, and haughty France, at Waterloo, that they were fragile powers. And — and who now keeps the Russian bear from crushing half the world ?

Where do the persecuted of every nation flee, and under the flowing folds of what flag do the chains of the slave fall off ? What other nation, for the last two years, has aided the Southern Confederacy in its noble effort to crush Republicanism and establish a Monarchy ? Surely, in a contest for superiority, no other nation will dare oppose herself to England.

France.—From the vine-clad hills of sunny France I come — the land of mirth and joyous revel. Her very language has caught the rythmic flow of her Rhone and Seine, and falls upon the ear in gentle undulations. Its prose is poetry and music. 'T is France has taught the world to smile and banish gloom. Her children defy cold destiny, and live, if need be, on airy nothings. They see the silver lining to each cloud, and so enjoy its shadow. And yet no land can boast of braver men or nobler deeds. Let haughty England not forget that he who first led forth the bold Crusaders was a hermit and a Frenchman. And while she boasts that England won the bloody field of Waterloo, let her remember that to do it England did her best, while France, by one weak woman, years before — a peasant girl, Joan of Arc — had made the Saxon army seek its island home in terror. She boldly asks who dare contest the right of mastery with England ; I answer, France.

United States.—Sisters, I come not here with mirth and song to urge my claims to greatness, for my heart is sad and desolate. My native land, once the abode of peace and joy, is filled with lamentations,—"Rachels mourning for their children and refusing to be comforted because they are not." Where once was heard the busy hum of industry and the shouts of merry children, now echo the tramp of mighty hosts and clashing arms. 'T is not to oppose a foreign foe, or to repel an invader from her shores, but it is brother against brother, parent against child. When our noble fathers left their English homes, which had justly become hateful to them, and sought for themselves and their children a refuge in the unbroken forests of America, they hoped to form a nation upon the broad basis of equal rights to all; but unfortunately for them, there came a few who still had vivid memories of courts and titles; who loved the pomp of heraldry and knightly honors. And when the brave young colonies stood boldly up and fought for seven long years, they —Arnolds, every one—gave comfort to the enemy; and now their children's children, sighing still for the "Flesh pots of Egypt," have waged this most unholy war.

Encouraged by their English cousins, they had hoped to overthrow the noblest government the world has ever seen, and erect upon its ruins a despotic power. But, glory to the God of battles and the brave thousands who have rallied around their honored flag, the hopes of those base traitors shall be blasted. But oh! the sacrifice! The desolate homes! The orphan children! The widowed wives and lonely maidens!

Anglo-African.—"Ethiopia shall stretch forth her hand," saith the prophet. Hath she not stretched them forth, lo! for ages? But through all the long years of her night there has been no friendly hand thrust through the darkness to aid her. Oppressed by the strong of the earth, trampled upon by the powerful, her children have uttered only this prayer: "How long, oh Lord! how long!" And this prayer, this wail from thousands of breaking hearts, has at last entered the ear of the Lord of Sabbaoth; and glory to His holy name, His arm is laid bare to save.

Already the sound of breaking chains and loosening bolts may be heard. The fiat has gone forth, freedom to all; not from any earthly potentate, but from the great White Throne. All nature proclaims it. The winds whisper it in the ear of the slave as he wanders around his lonely cabin. The quiet rivulet and the dashing mountain torrent bring the same glad news to the bondmen. Finally, it has been written in characters of blood all through the length and breadth of this land. Other nations may boast of hard-earned honors and well-fought fields, but what other nation has so long and so patiently waited as Africa?

Do you say her children possess not the courage to strike ?   Look at their record for the past twelve months; see them, the bravest of the brave, as they have rushed into the very jaws of death; not for honor, for that was denied them; not for country, for they had none. I came uncalled.   You summoned me not; but when next you meet it may be far otherwise.   Remember, when God is for us, who can be against us?   Yes! Glory to God in the highest!   Yes! Glory to Him on the throne!   There's light and there's freedom both dawning, for the east brings the promise of morn.

Russia.— Sisters, I dare not present my country's claim to greatness, for I know that Russia has but just begun to play her noble part in the history of nations.   Take the recent emancipation of her serfs as an earnest of what she will do.   But yonder comes the veiled Prophetess; let us ask her what nation has done the most for the children of men.

France.— Beautiful Prophetess! we appeal to thee.   Draw from the mystic fountain that is veiled from us the knowledge we so much desire.   Tell us which nation has most nobly played her part, and which in the future shall prove the greatest blessing to the world.

Prophetess.— It needs no vision to reveal the past.   History is spread out before you.   Tracing its pages you will find that each nation has done much, that all were necessary to bring about the present state of civilization.   That Italy and Greece, twin maidens of the sea, have given much, whose morning star arose ere the Dryads had been driven from the cool recesses of the forests, and the sea-nymphs frightened from their grottoes and rocky caves.   But the world needed none the less the stern vigor of the Celt and Saxon.   They, too, have brought a noble offering; but in the great drama of nations it would seem some have been allotted a more noble lot than others and in the future — Aye! the future.   'T is the land overshadowed with wings, the latest gift of the ocean. Strong, with the dew of her youth still upon her, struggling now with the giant — Oppression — baptized in blood ; forth from this trial she shall come victorious, bearing the banner of freedom and truth, come with no smell of fire on her garments, pure as the water and snows of her mountains. Then shall the North and the South dwell together, strife and contention shall nowhere be heard, traitors and rebels shall call on the mountains, call on the rocks and the forests to hide them from the holy resentment of those they have wronged; and the glad shout of the ransomed ascending shall swell to a chorus full, deep, and long, rolling over hilltops, through low-lands and valley, and shall sweep through the length and breadth of the land. Thus, coming forth from her great tribulation, all nations shall own her the blessed of the Lord.

CI.

THE COURTIN'.

JAMES RUSSELL LOWELL.

God makes sech nights, all white an' still, furz you can look or listen,
Moonshine an' snow on field an' hill, all silence an' all glisten.
Zekle crep' up, quite unbeknown, an' peeked in thru the winder,
An' there sot Huldy, all alone, with no one nigh to hinder.
A fire-place filled the room's one side with half a cord o' wood in,—
There warn't no stoves till Comfort died, to bake ye to a puddin'.
The wa'nut logs shot sparkles out towárd the pootiest, bless her!
An' leetle flames danced all about the chiny on the dresser.
Agin the chimbley crooknecks hung, and in amongst 'em rusted
The ole queen's-arm that gran'ther Young fetched back from Concord
          busted.
The very room, coz she was in, seemed warm from floor to ceilin',
An' she looked full ez rosy agin ez the apples she was peelin'.
'T was kin' o' kingdom come to look on sech a blessed cretur,
A dogoose blushin' to a brook aint modester nor sweeter.
He was six foot o' man, A 1, clean grit an' human natur,
None couldn't quicker pitch a ton, nor dror a furrer straighter.
He 'd sparked it with full twenty gals, he 'd squired 'em, danced 'em,
          druv 'em,
Fust this one, an' then thet, by spells,—all is, he couldn't love 'em.
But long o' her, his veins 'ould run all crinkly, like curled maple,
The side she breshed felt full o' sun ez a south slope in Ap'il.
She thought no v'ice hed sech a swing as hisn in the choir;

My! when he made Ole Hundred ring, she *knowed* the Lord was nigher.
An' she 'd blush scarlit, right in prayer, when her new meetin-'bunnet
Felt, somehow, thru its crown, a pair o' blue eyes sot upon it.
Thet night, I tell ye, she looked *some!* she seemed to 've gut a new soul,
For she felt sartin-sure he 'd come, down to her very shoe-sole.
She heerd a foot, an' knowed it, tu, a-raspin' on the scraper,—
All ways to once her feelins' flew, like sparks in burnt-up paper.
He kin' o' loitered on the mat, some doubtfle o' the sekle,
His heart kep' goin' pity-pat, but hern went pity-Zckle.
An' yit, she gin her cheer a jerk, ez though she wished him furder,
An' on her apples kep' to work, parin' away like murder.
" You want to see my Pa, I s'pose?" " Wal—no—I come designin' "—
" To see my Ma? She sprinklin' clo'es, agin to-morrer's i'nin. "
To say why gals acts so or so, or don't, would be presumin';
Mebby to mean *yes* an' say *no* comes nateral to women.
He stood a spell on one foot fust, then stood a spell on t' other,
An' on which one he felt the wust, he couldn't ha' told ye, nuther.
Says he, " I 'd better call agin. " Says she, " Think likely, Mister."
That last word pricked him like a pin, an' — wal, he up an' kissed her.
When Ma, bimeby, upon 'em slips, Huldy sot, pale as ashes,
All kin' o' smily roun' the lips, an' teary roun' the lashes.
For she was jest the quiet kind, whose naturs never vary,
Like streams thet keep a summer mind snow-hid in Jenooary.
The blood clost roun' her heart felt glued too tight for all expressin',
Till Mother see how matters stood, an' gin 'em both her blessin'.
Then her red come back, like the tide down to the Bay o' Fundy,
An' all I know is, they was cried in meetin' come nex' Sunday.

CII.

THE INTERESTS OF RICH AND POOR DEMAND UUIVERSAL EDUCATION.

RICHARD EDWARDS.

How stands the account then with the child whom we have allowed to grow up among us in ignorance and vice? On the credit side we have a few dollars—a very few—which we are permitted to hold but a short time, too, and that at a very extravagant interest; on the other, we have the entire loss of all he might and

N

would have done for us, together with an entailment upon us of untold evil, in its worst and most odious forms. How seems it from a business point of view? Does the speculation look inviting? Ye rich men, with no children, do you think it will PAY you to let schools languish and die all about you, because it is nothing to YOU? Is it nothing to you? Which costs the most, a school house or a prison? And be sure that you will have one or the other to pay for.

For the rich, then, there is safety and the highest profit only in universal education. And what shall be said in this respect of the poor? Of the toiling millions who, without figure of speech, earn their bread by the sweat of their brow? How are they affected by the proposition that the property of the State shall educate its children? I tell you that the political and social salvation of these depend upon this principle. We proclaim in our Declaration of Independence that all are born free and equal. We claim to have abolished all artificial and unjust distinctions among men. We point exultingly to our universal suffrage—the right of every man to have a voice in the selection of our rulers—as a proof of sincerity in these professions. But what sort of equality is that which exists between two classes of men, one of whom enjoys the means of education, and the other does not? One of whom is allowed to reach the maximum, while the other is restricted to the minimum of its capacities? Is knowledge power? How, then, can there be any equality between him whose mind has been illumined by her radiance, and him upon whose darkened soul no ray of hers has fallen? To bestow the right of suffrage on ignorant men is no blessing, but a curse to them and all concerned, and least of all is it making them equal to men of culture. As well might you put a sextant into the hands of a child of two years, and say that he has an equal chance with the veteran navigator for finding his longitude, as to claim that the mere right to vote makes men equals in power and influence.

The truth is, that universal education is the greatest equalizer among men. Of all institutions, the public school is the poor man's best and truest friend. It is of all things the most democratic. It has in it more of democracy, ten times over, than free trade, the sub-treasury, the habeas corpus, or the veto of the United States Bank. It is the grand talisman of equality. It puts the child of the poor man on a level, at the threshhold of life, with the heir of thousands, and enables him to maintain the equality, unless nature or his own indolence interfere to prevent. Democracy is impossible without universal intelligence.

CIII.

THE FARMER'S PROFESSION.

ANSON S. MILLER. 1842.

Above all things, farmers, *honor* your vocation. Arise to the nobility of your employment. Occupy that station in society to which the dignity of your calling and the ownership of the soil entitle you. Give your sons as good a *general* education for the farm as for the "learned professions." Banish from your households the false and pernicious sentiment that your sons are too talented to become farmers; and that there are pursuits in our country, other than agriculture, that will open to them a surer way to wealth and honor.

From the beginning, the cultivation of the earth has been the delight of the wise. The great ancestor of our race was ordained a husbandman by the Creator, and placed in a garden,

> "Chosen by the Sovereign Planter, when he framed
> All things to man's delightful use."

Princely patriarchs, prophets, kings, philosophers—the great of all ages—have honored agriculture with their fondest regard. The pursuit is, indeed, laborious. Labor, however, is not an evil except in its excess. Its cheerful performance by man has freed it from the original curse. Work is the gracious ordination of Heaven for human excellence, the parent of value, and the condition of unnumbered blessings.

The farmer's calling is full of moral grandeur. He supports the world, is the partner of Nature, and peculiarly "a co-worker with God." The sun, the atmosphere, the dews, the rains, day and night, the seasons — all the natural agents — are his ministers in the spacious temple of the firmament. Health is the attendant of his toils. The philosophy of Nature exercises and exalts the intellect of the intelligent farmer. His moral powers are ennobled by the manifestations of supreme love and wisdom in everything around him — in the genial air, the opening bud, the delicate flower, the growing and ripening fruit, the stately trees — in vegetable life and beauty, springing out of death and decay; and in the wonderful succession and harmony of the seasons.

> "These, as they change, Almighty Father! these
> Are but the varied God. The rolling year
> Is full of Thee."

We are now beholding a mighty moral revolution. Hitherto, glory has been sought in the *destruction* rather than the *preservation* of man. The history of our race is a history of wars. A better age is rising upon us, in which renown will be found in usefulness. Justice will yet be fully done to the benefactors of mankind. We trust that those who have labored in the cause in which we are now engaged — Young, and Watson, and Clinton, and Buel, and many others, both of the dead and the living, who have laid society under enduring obligations — will receive their share of the public gratitude. How dim, how fleeting, is the fame of the mere warrior, when contrasted with that of the civilian and the philanthropist! What wasting battles, what fields enriched with carnage, what spoils of victory, or what splendid triumphs, could confer the lasting glory of De Witt Clinton!

CIV.

INAUGURAL ADDRESS.

ABRAHAM LINCOLN — MARCH 4, 1865.

FELLOW COUNTRYMEN : — At this second appearing to take the oath of the Presidential office, there is less occasion for an extended address than there was at the first. Then a statement somewhat in detail of a course to be pursued seemed very fitting and proper. Now, at the expiration of four years, during which public declarations have constantly been called forth on every point and phase of the great contest which still absorbs the attention and engrosses the energies of the nation, little that is new could be presented.

The progress of our arms, upon which all else chiefly depends, is as well known to the public as to myself; and it is, I trust, reasonably satisfactory and encouraging to all. With high hope for the future, no prediction in regard to it is ventured. On the occasion corresponding to this, four years ago, all thoughts were anxiously directed to an impending civil war. All dreaded it; all sought to avoid it. While the inaugural address was being delivered from this place, devoted altogether to saving the Union without war, insurgent agents were in the city, seeking to destroy it without war — seeking to dissolve the Union and divide the effects by negotiation.

Both parties deprecated war; but one of them would make war rather than let the nation survive, and the other would accept war rather than let it perish; and the war came.

One-eighth of the whole population were colored slaves — not distributed generally over the Union, but located in the southern part of it. These slaves constituted a peculiar and powerful interest. All knew that this interest was somehow the cause of the war. To strengthen, perpetuate, and extend this interest was the object for which the insurgents would rend the Union by war, while the Government claimed no right to do more than to restrict the territorial enlargement of it. Neither party expected the magnitude or duration which it has already attained. Neither anticipated that the cause of the conflict might cease, even before the conflict itself should cease. Each looked for an easier triumph, and a result less fundamental and astounding. Both read the same Bible and pray to the same God, and each invokes His aid against the other. It may seem strange that any man should dare to ask a just God's assistance in wringing his bread from the sweat of other men's faces. But let us judge not, that we be not judged. The prayer of both should not be answered. That of neither has been answered fully. The Almighty has His own purposes. " Woe unto the world because of offences, for it must needs be that offences come ; but woe to that man by whom the offence cometh." If we shall suppose that American slavery is one of these offences, which, in the providence of God, must needs come, but which, having continued through His appointed time, He now wills to remove, and that He gives to both North and South this terrible war as the woe due to those by whom the offence came, shall we discern therein any departure from those divine attributes which the believers in a living God always ascribe to Him ?

Fondly do we hope, fervently do we pray, that this mighty scourge of war may speedily pass away. Yet, if God wills that it continue until all the wealth piled by the bondman's two hundred and fifty years of unrequited toil shall be sunk, and until every drop of blood drawn with the lash shall be paid by another drawn with the sword, as was said three thousand years ago ; so still it must be said, that the judgments of the Lord are true and righteous altogether.

With malice towards none, with charity for all, with firmness in the right, as God gives us to see the right, let us strive on to finish the work we are in ; to bind up the nation's wound ; to care for him who shall have borne the battle, and for his widow and his orphans ; to do all which may achieve and cherish a just and a lasting peace among ourselves, and with all nations.

CV.

The Old Man Dreams.

OLIVER WENDELL HOLMES.

Oh for one hour of youthful joy !
Give back my twentieth spring !
I 'd rather laugh, a bright-haired boy,
Than reign a gray-beard king !

Off with the wrinkled spoils of age!
Away with learning's crown!
Tear out life's wisdom-written page,
And dash its trophies down!

One moment let my life-blood stream
From boyhood's fount of flame!
Give me one giddy, reeling dream
Of life all love and fame!

My listening angel heard the prayer,
And calmly smiling, said,
" If I but touch thy silvered hair,
Thy hasty wish hath sped.

" But is there nothing in thy track
To bid thee fondly stay,
While the swift seasons hurry back
To find the wished-for day?"

Ah, truest soul of womankind,
Without thee, what were life?
One bliss I cannot leave behind:
I'll take — my — precious — wife!

The angel took a sapphire pen
And wrote in rainbow dew,
" The man would be a boy again,
And be a husband too!"

" And is there nothing yet unsaid
Before the change appears?
Remember, all their gifts have fled
With those dissolving years!"

Why, yes; for memory would recall
My fond paternal joys;
I could not bear to leave them all:
I'll take — my — girl — and — boys!

The smiling angel dropped his pen, —
" Why, this will never do;

The man would be a boy again,
    And be a father, too!'"

And so I laughed, — my laughter woke
    The household with its noise, —
And wrote my dream, when morning broke,
    To please the gray-haired boys.

CVI.

ALL VALUE CENTERS IN MIND.

RICHARD EDWARDS.

Universal education — the culture of every mind born into the world — is necessary: First, because the end of life, and of all things which concern it, is to minister to the needs of mind; and the greatest need that mind has is education. We have said that, as compared with communities, the individual is an end. But a further analysis shows that only the immortal part of him is so. Of all things in any degree entrusted to human management, the human mind is, beyond expression, of most worth, because it is the only thing which is valuable in and of itself. All other forms of existence are only means, to be used and valued so long as they contribute to the development, exaltation, or dignifying of mind, and then to be thrown aside like a worn-out implement, or a cast-off garment. Farms and houses, railroads and shipping, earth and stars, powers and principalities, things present and things to come, have just this one use, or they have none — to minister, in their feeble way, to the illimitable, eternal, infinite necessities of mind. If anything in the range of human knowledge can be pointed to, of which it may be said that it does not contribute to the perfecting, in some way, of mind, then we say that that thing, whatever it may be, has no right to existence, and ought to be abolished.

How shall we test the usefulness of some material interest or possession? As, for an example, of a railroad or a farm? Are we told that a railroad is useful in increasing the facilities for intercourse between different portions of the country, in developing the resources of otherwise inaccessible regions rich in every product that supplies human wants? That it increases the populatian of States, and of the nation, and enhances the value of real estate; and, in short, that it increases the wealth-power, and consequent dignity of the nation? Then, I ask, what is the use of all this? Are these things to be sought for their own sake? If the railroads of our own State have increased her population by numbers that shall soon be counted in millions, yet of what avail is it all if they are millions of knaves and cowards? What is the use of wealth, or civilization, or national greatness, in themselves considered?

No, my friends; if this world was made for any purpose besides the glory of God, (and to contribute to God's glory is to exalt and dignify mind,) unless its creation was an accident or a blunder, it was formed to be the school house of the race—to minister in its various forms of harmony, beauty, and sublimity, to the necessities of the souls that have been placed in it. It is for this that the mountain shoots up from the plain, and stands in majesty against the distant sky; for this the earth puts on her gorgeous robes of spring and summer; for this the sea is spread out in beauty when the winds are hushed, or is roused into terrific sublimity when the tempest is abroad; for this the heavens put on their star-decked mantle, and make the night more glorious than the day; for this planets and suns move with measured and obedient step through an extent of space that appals even the mind to which it ministers; for this all nature, like a grand instrument, with infinite variety of parts and expression, has been uttering her voice, from the time when the morning stars sang together, and all the sons of God shouted for joy. Every tint of the rose, every sigh of the breeze, every glimpse of the sunshine, is laid as an offering upon the shrine of mind; and man, feeble and frail though he be, is admitted to a share of the magnificent homage.

We may depend upon it, there is nothing with which we have to do that is of so much consequence as mind. And, if so, it follows that all mind should be educated. This is the great duty of humanity. Every generation of men owes it to the next succeeding, as a debt before the law of human progress, to give to each INDIVIDUAL of that next, as high and symmetrical a character, one conforming as nearly to the ideal of manly or womanly excellence, as possible. Let the generation now on the stage do all things else, and neglect this duty, and on the grand ledger there will be an infinite balance against it. We may tithe the mint, anise, and cumin, but this, the training of the children entrusted to our care, this is the weightier matter of the everlasting law.

If a skilful lapidary should find, in the possession of some rude savage, a rough, mis-shapen diamond, but of such superior quality as to enable it, when polished, to treasure up the sunlight, and to pour it forth in a glorious flood, would he not be inclined to exclaim, " What a pity that such beauty should be covered up, when a little cutting and polishing might open it in all its wealth to the wondering gaze of men !" If a practical philanthropist should see a province of fertile land lying waste and barren on account of the thriftless indolence of the inhabitants, would not he exclaim, " What a pity that such resources, such capacities for promoting the progress of civilization, should remain dormant and worthless just for the want of a little energy and industry on the part of this people ?" But what are all the diamonds that ever graced the brows of majesty, or gladdened the heart of the miser ? What are all the fertile plains that ever filled the world's granaries, compared to that to which field and gem are but ministers ? And when we contemplate the sad spectacle of a single mind allowed to grow up to the deformities induced by ignorance and vice, transformed by neglect into the likeness of the fiend instead of the divine image, and all for want of that higher industry, that diligence in the performance of duty, which is the prerogative of man alone ; when we think of this we feel that illustration entirely fails; that it is the strongest case that we can conceive — imagination strives in vain to present a spectacle half so sad. Figurative language but dissipates the power of the thought. The plainest statement is the most impressive we can make.

CVII.

MY DARLINGS' SHOES.

God bless the little feet that can never go astray,
For the little shoes are empty in the closet laid away!
Sometimes I take one in my hand, forgetting till I see
It is a little half-worn shoe, not large enough for me;
And all at once I feel a sense of bitter loss and pain,
As sharp as when two years ago it cut my heart in twain.

O, little feet that wearied not, I wait for them no more,
For I am drifting with the tide, but *they* have reached the shore;
And while the blinding tear-drops wet those little shoes so old, .
I put on them a value high above their price in gold;
And so I lay them down again, but always turn to say—
God bless the little feet that *now so surely* cannot stray.

And while I thus am standing, I almost seem to see
Two little forms beside me, just as they used to be!
Two little faces lifted with their sweet and tender eyes!
Ah, me! I might have known that look was born of Paradise.
I reach my arms out fondly, but they clasp the empty air!
There is nothing of my darlings but the shoes they used to wear.

O, the bitterness of parting cannot be done away
Till I see my darlings walking where the feet can never stray;
When I no more am drifted here upon the surging tide,
But *with them safely* landed there upon the river side;
Be patient, heart! while waiting to see *their* shining way,
For the little feet in the golden street can never go astray.

CVIII.

UNIVERSAL SUFFRAGE.

RICHARD YATES—1865.

We are making the experiment of self-government, and that test can never be properly made except by allowing all to vote, and giving the majority the right to rule. This is the genius of our government. I am willing to trust it, and believe that with these principles our glorious government, founded on the will of all, protected by the power of all, and protecting the rights of all, will survive all the storms of internal convulsions, defy the world combined, and rising higher and higher in grandeur and in glory, will be the happiest, freest, and most honored nation among the nations of the world.   *   *   *   *   *   *   *

I am here to-day fearlessly to proclaim my creed, and to stand or fall by it. I am for the abolition of slavery, not because I am for the white man or the red man or the black man, but because I am for *man*, for God's humanity. And I here declare that no earthly motive, no lofty summit of human ambition, no proud pinnacle of human power, no loud acclaims of the multitude shall ever seduce me from the God-given sentiments of my heart in favor of liberty and humanity.

Now, here, elsewhere, always, I am *against* secession and slavery, *for* an undivided Union, *for* universal freedom, and universal suffrage.

If slavery had any lease for longer life when it laid its assassin hand upon the life of the noble Lincoln, for that fearful crime its last lingering breath would be driven from its accursed body. Abraham Lincoln lived long enough to lead us through the Red Sea of this terrible war; he laid down the true policy upon which this nation is to live; and in his speeches, letters, messages, proclamations and great acts, he has left us lessons enough to guide us in all our duties as citizens, and in all our public affairs.

Hundreds of books will be written; but were it my object simply to make him immortal through all time, it would be enough—all else would be waste of paper—to say that on the first of January, 1863, Abraham Lincoln, the great emancipator, issued his proclamation of emancipation, and gave freedom to his country and a long oppressed race.

But though Slavery and Treason assassinated our President, the Government still lives. The assassin may slay an hundred Presidents, but thank God the great government of the United States shall stand, and the gates of hell and death shall not prevail against it. Our Government, by reason of the fiery ordeal through which it has passed, will be more honored, respected and feared throughout the world than ever before; and standing over the grave of Treason with the eyes of the good God beaming upon us, and with new and and increasing faith in the capacity of man for self-government, like Miriam the prophetess, we will raise our songs of triumph on the banks of our deliverance, and joyfully exclaim: "Sing ye to the Lord, for He hath triumphed gloriously; the horse and his rider hath He thrown into the sea!"

CIX.

The Rival Orators.

AIMWELL STORIES.

SCENE—The platform of a School-room.

THOMAS TROTTER, a large boy, with a "big voice," and SAMUEL SLY, a small boy, whose vocal organ is pitched on a high key.

[Thomas enters and makes his bow to the audience, followed by Samuel, who goes through the same ceremony a little in his rear.]

Tom. (*Turning partially round.*) What do you want here?

Sam. I want to speak my piece, to be sure.

T. Well, you will please to wait until *I* get through; it's my turn now.

S. No, 't ain't your turn, either, my learned friend; excuse me for contradicting, but if I don't stick out for my rights, nobody else will. My turn came before that fellow's who said "his voice was still for war;" but I couldn't think how my speech began then, and he got the start of me.

T. Very well; if you were not ready when your turn came, that's your fault, and not mine. Go to your seat, and don't bother me any more.

S. Well, that's cool, I declare—as cool as a load of ice in February. Can't you ask some other favor, Mr. Trotter?

T. Yes; hold your tongue.

S. Can't do that; I'm bound to get off my speech first. You see it's running over like a bottle of beer, and I can't keep it in. So here goes:

"My name is Norval; on the Grampian Hills

My father feeds—"

T. (*interrupting him, commences his piece in a loud tone.*) "Friends, Romans, countrymen!"

S. Greeks, Irishmen, and fellow-sojers!

T. "Lend me your ears."

S. Don't you do it; he's got ears enough of his own.

T. "I come to bury Cæsar, not to praise him."

S. (*mimicing his gestures.*) I come to speak my piece, and I'll do it, Cæsar or no Cæsar. "My name is Norval—"

T. (*advancing towards him in a threatening attitude.*) Sam Sly, if you don't stop your fooling I'll put you off the stage.

S. (*retreating.*) Don't, don't you touch me, Tom; you'll joggle my piece all out of me again.

T. Well, then, keep still until I get through. (*Turns to the audience.*)

"Friends, Romans, countrymen! lend me your ears;

I come to bury Cæsar, not to praise him."

S. I say, Tommy, what are you bla-a-a-r-ting about; have you lost your calf?

T. "The evil that men do lives after them,

The good is oft interred with their bones.

So let it be with Cæsar."

(*He is again brought to a stand by Sam, who is standing behind him, mimicing his gesturcs in a ludicrous manner.*)

Now, Sam, I tell you to stop your monkey shines; if you don't, I'll make you!

S. You stop spouting about Cæsar, then, and let me have my say. You needn't think you can cheat me out of my rights because you wear higher heeled shoes than I do.

T. I can tell you one thing, sir — nothing but your size saves you from a good flogging.

S. Well, that *is* a queer coincidence, for I can tell you that nothing but *your* size saves *you* from a good dose of Solomon's grand panacea. (*To the audience.*) I do n't know what can be done with such a long-legged fellow — he 's too big to be whipped, and he is 't big enough to behave himself. Now, all keep still, and let me begin again : " My name is Norval — "

T. " I come to bury Cæsar — "

S. I thought you 'd buried him once, good deeds, bones and all ; how many more times are you going to do it ?

T. Sam, I 'm a peaceable fellow ; but if you go much further I won't be responsible for the consequences.

S. I 'm for *piece*, too, but it 's *my* piece, and not your long rigmarole about Cæsar, that I go in for. As I said before, " My name is — "

T. " The noble Brutus

Hath told you Cæsar was ambitious ;

If it were so, it were a grevious fault,

And grievously hath Cæsar answered it."

S. (*in a low whisper.*) I say, Tom, did you know you had got a hole in your unwhisperables ?

T. " Here, under leave of Brutus, and the rest,

(For Brutus is an honorable man —

So are they all, all honorable men,)

Come I to speak at Cæsar's funeral."

S. This is n't Cæsar's funeral — it 's the exhibition of the Spankertown Academy, and it 's my turn to officiate, so get out with Cæsar — " My name is Nor — "

T. " He was my friend, faithful and just to me ;

But Brutus says he was ambitious ;

And Brutus is an honorable man."

S. Brutus be hanged ; who cares for what he said ? Come, you 've sputtered enough ; now give me a chance to say something." " My name is — "

T. Come, Sammy, *do n't* interrupt me again, that's a clever fellow. Let me finish my piece, and then you shall have the whole platform to yourself.

S. You 're very kind, Mr. Trotter—altogether too kind! Your generosity reminds me òf an Irish gentleman, who could n't live peaceably with his wife, and so they agreed to divide the house between them. "Biddy," says he, " ye 'll jist be afther taking the outside of the house, and I 'll kape the inside."

T. (*To the audience.*) Ladies and gentlemen, you see it is useless for me to attempt to proceed, and I trust you will excuse me from performing my part. (*Bows, and withdraws.*)

S. Yes, I hope you will excuse him, ladies and gentlemen. The fact is, he means well enough ; but between you and me, he does n't know a wheelwright from a right wheel. I 'm sorry to say his education has been sadly neglected, as you all perceive. He has n't enjoyed the advantages that I have for learning good manners. And, then, did you ever hear such a ridiculous spouter ! He might make a very decent town crier, or auctioneer, or something of that sort—but to think of Tommy Trotter pretending to be an orator, and delivering a 'funeral oration over Cæsar ! O my ! it 's enough to make a cat laugh! And, now, ladies and gentlemen, as the interruption has ceased, I will proceed with my part :

" My name is Norval ; on the Grampian Hills

My father feeds his flocks —— "

And — and — and — (*aside, to a boy near him*) — what is it ? (*To the audience*) — " feeds his flocks"—and — and — and —there ! I 'll be blowed if I hav n't got dead stuck a'ready ! Just as I expected ; that lubber that came to bury Cæsar has bullied all the ideas out of my head ! (*Beats an inglorious retreat, with his hands over his face.*)

THE END.

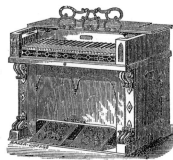

STANDARD EDUCATIONAL WORKS,

EMBRACING THE

History, Systems, Philosophy and Methods of Education, by the best Teachers and in the best Schools of Europe and America, with Biographical Sketches of Eminent Teachers, Promoters and Benefactors of Education.

BY HENRY BARNARD, L. L. D.,

Late Superintendent of Common Schools in Connecticut, Commissioner of Public Schools in Rhode Island, and Chancellor of the University of Wisconsin.

National Education in Europe,.. ....$3 50
School Architecture,............................... 2 00
American Pedagogy,................................ 2 00
Primary and Common School Teaching in Great Britain,................................ 2 50
German Schools and Pedagogy,.............. 2 50
Aphorisms on Education,........................ 1 50
Pestalozzi and Pestalozzianism,.............. 2 50
English Pedagogy,................................. 2 50
Ascham, Bacon, Wotton, Milton, Locke, Spencer, &c., on Education,.................. 1 50
Normal Schools and Institutes,.............. 2 50
Reformatory Education and Schools,...... 2 00
Military Schools and Education in France and Prussia,............................ 3 00
Polytechnic School of France,................ 1 00
Tribute to T. H. Gallaudet, and Deaf Mute Instruction,............................... 1 50
Raumer's German Universities,.............. 2 00
Ezekiel Cheever, and the Original Free School of New England,...................... 50
Russell's Normal Training, Part I,......... 1 25
Hill's True Order of Studies,.................. 25
Thayer's Letters to a Young Teacher,......... 50
Huntington's Unconscious Tuition,......... 25
Benefactors of American Education,...... 3 50

Mansfield's History of the United States Military Academy,............................$ .10
American Teachers and Educators, with 20 Portraits,............................ .... 3 50
German Educational Reformers — Sturm, Luther, Melancthon, Ratitch, Comenius, Basedow, Francke and Herder....... 3 50
Military Schools in Austria, Sardinia, Russia, Switzerland and England,........ 2 50
French Schools and Educators — Fenelon, Montaigne, Rousseau, Guizot, Cousin, Wilm, Marcel and others,.................. 3 00
Amer. Journal of Education, Single No.. 1 50
Do. do. Single Vol. in Cloth,..... 4 25
Do. do. Vols. I to XIV., Cloth...50 00
Do. do. " " Half Goat.63 00
Mann's Lecture on the Teacher's Motives. 25
Everett, Stowe, Mann, Gallaudet and Carter on Normal Schools, and the Professional Training of Teachers,............ 50
Raumer on the Education of Girls,......... 50
The United States Naval Academy and Competitive Examination,.................. 50
National and State Associations for Educational Purposes, with over 50 Portraits, (in two parts, each,).................. 3 00

AMERICAN LIBRARY OF EDUCATION,

Including (1,) American Pedagogy; (2,) Object Teaching and Methods of Primary Instruction in Great Britain; (3,) German Schools and Pedagogy; (4,) Educational Aphorisms; (5,) English Pedagogy; (6,) Pestalozzi and Pestalozzianism; (7,) German Educational Reformers — 7 volumes, in cloth binding, $14 cash.

The American Journal of Education, for 1865, issued on the 15th March, June, September and December, making one volume of 824 pages octavo, with 15 portraits of Eminent American Teachers. Among the Portraits of this volume will be found *S. R. Hall,* Principal of the first Normal School in the United States; *Theron Baldwin,* Secretary of the Western College Society; *Newton Bateman, O. Faville, J. M. Gregory, P. Coburn, E. E. White, D. N. Camp,* State Superintendents of Public Schools in Illinois, Iowa, Michigan, Pennsylvania, Ohio and Connecticut; *R. Edwards, J. P. Wickersham, D. P. Hagar, A. P. Stone, C. Northend, C. Davies. S. P. Bates, L Andrews,* and other prominent teachers in different States. Terms, $4. Single number, $1.25.

A Classified Index to the Contents of *Barnard's American Journal of Education,* (Vols. I. — xv.,) with an Index to each Volume, together with the Contents of other publications by the same author, $3.

School Economy — A Treatise on the Preparation, Organization, Employment, Government and Authorities of Schools. By *James Pyle Wickersham, A. M., Prin.* Pennsylvania State Normal School. 12 mo. Price, $1.

Methods of Instruction — That part of the Philosophy of Education which treats of the Nature of the several Branches of Knowledge, and the Methods of Teaching them. By *James Pyle Wickersham, A. M., Prin.* of Pennsylvania State Normal School. 12 mo. Price, $1.75.

We are prepared to furnish any of the above valuable works, and copies will be forwarded by mail on receipt of the price.

ADAMS BLACKMER, & LYON,

Chicago.

VALUABLE EDUCATIONAL WORKS

Just Published by J. P. LIPPINCOTT & CO., Philadelphia.

Methods of Instruction;

Or, that part of the Philosophy of Education which treats of the Nature of the several branches of Knowledge and the methods of teaching them according to that Nature. By JAMES PYLE WICKERSHAM, A. M., Principal Pennsylvania State Normal School at Millersville. 12mo. $1.75.

Ritter's Comparative Geography.

Lectures on Comparative Geography. By CARL RITTER, late Professor of Geography in the University of Berlin. Translated for the use of Seminaries and Colleges by Rev. WILLIAM L. GAGE. One vol. 12mo. $1.50.

STATE NORMAL SCHOOL,
MILLERSVILLE, PA. April 27th, 1865.

I have read Ritter's "Comparative Geography," as translated by William L. Gage, with very great satisfaction. It is a comprehensive, compact, and clear statement of the great principles of Geographical Science. Geography, as presented in our ordinary treatises, is not at all a science, but merely a collection of facts and fragments; in this book, however, all details find their proper place in a philosophical system. No teacher of Geography should be without the book. J. P. WICKERSHAM.

School Economy:

A Treatise on the Preparation, Organization, Employment, Government, and Authorities of Schools. By JAMES PYLE WICKERMAN, A. M., Principal of the Pennsylvania State Normal School at Millersville. 12mo. $1.50.

FROM THE MASSACHUSETTS TEACHER.

We heartily invite the readers of the TEACHER to examine this excellent volume, believing that it will tend to hasten the time when teaching will be recognized as a profession, and the teacher be so fitted for his work as to command the respect of the wise and good.

Lincoln's Botanies.

I. BOTANY FOR BEGINNERS. A New Edition. An introduction to Mrs. Lincoln's "Lectures on Botan ." For the use of Public Schools, and the younger pupils of higher Schools and Academies. By MRS. ALMIRA LINCOLN PHELPS, author of "Lincoln's Botany," "Phelps's Chemistry, Philosophy," etc. 12mo. 60c.

II. LINCOLN'S LECTURES ON BOTANY. Revised and enlarged. Familiar Lectures on Botany, explaining the Structure, Classification, and Use of Plants, illustrated upon the Linnæan and Natural Methods; with a Flora for Practical Botanists, for Colleges, Schools, and Private Students. By MRS. ALMIRA H. LINCOLN, (now Mrs. Lincoln Phelps,) late Principal of the Patapsco Institute of Maryland, author of a series of works on Botany, Chemistry, Natural Philosophy, etc. etc. New edition, revised and enlarged, and illustrated by many additional Engravings. With a Supplement containing a Familiar Introduction to the Natural Orders, and an Artificial Key for Analysis to the same. 12mo. $2.

A Guide to Experiments in Philosophy.

FRICK'S PHYSICAL TECHNICS; or, Practical Instructions for making experiments in Physics and the construction of Physical Apparatus with the most limited means. By Dr. I. FRICK, Director of the High School at Freiburg, and Professor of Physics in the Lyceum. Translated by PROF. JOHN D. EASTER, D. D. 1 vol. 8 vo. Amply Illustrated. $3.

FROM SILLIMAN'S JOURNAL.

We cordially commend this work to all teachers of Physics, and especially to those whose situations or circumstances cut them off from access to a good collection of Physical In- struments. * * * * While the most expert demonstrator may gain some useful hints from Dr. Frick's book, the less experienced teacher and student will find it an available vade mecum in the Physical Laboratory.

Crooks and Schem's New Latin-English School Lexicon.

On the basis of the Latin-German Lexicon of Dr. C. F. Ingerslev. By G. R. CROOKS, D. D. and A. J. SCHEM, A. M. One vol. 8 vo. $3.50.

FROM PROF. H. B. SMITH, Union Theological Seminary.

It seems to me to be admirably adapted to its object—erring neither on the score of redun- dancy nor deficiency· * * * * The introduction of synonyms, of etymologies, and of proper names adds much to its value. Clearness, conciseness, and remarkable adapta- tion to use are among the valuable qualities of your work. * * * I trust this volume may have the success it so richly deserves.

Will be sent by mail on receipt of the price by the publishers.

1865. THIRD EDITION. 1865.

REVISED, ENLARGED AND IMPROVED.

WILBER'S

NEW SURVEY OF ILLINOIS

SHOWING ALL THE TOWNSHIPS, SECTIONS, RAILROADS, STATIONS, CITIES
AND TOWNS, AND EXHIBITING IN COLORS THE

GEOLOGICAL FEATURES OF THE STATE.

ALSO, ITS CLIMATOLOGY AND BOTANY, TOGETHER WITH TOPOGRAPHICAL
AND STATISTICAL TABLES, ETC., FROM RECENT SURVEYS.

BY C. D. WILBER, M. A.,

SECRETARY OF THE ILLINOIS NATURAL HISTORY SOCIETY.

Size 50 by 50 Inches, on Rollers, Muslin Backs.

PRICE $5 PER COPY.

ADDRESS **C. D. WILBER, Care Adams, Blackmer, & Lyon,**

Lombard Block, Chicago.

AGENTS WANTED IN EVERY COUNTY.

BATAVIA INSTITUTE

AND

𝔓𝔯𝔢𝔭𝔞𝔯𝔞𝔱𝔬𝔯𝔶 𝔖𝔠𝔥𝔬𝔬𝔩, 𝔣𝔬𝔯 𝔅𝔬𝔱𝔥 𝔖𝔢𝔵𝔢𝔰,

LOCATED AT

BATAVIA, ILLINOIS.

ALLEN A. GRIFFITH, - - Principal and Proprietor.

A FULL CORPS OF TEACHERS EMPLOYED.

Students are Boarded in the Institution—a limited number rooming with a Teacher, who will have especial care of their instruction and discipline; or good boarding places may be had in private families.

☞ This Institution is intended to be a *Home* for Students while getting their education, and to supply the advantages of a well regulated family.

Fall Term begins September 4th.

For Terms, address the Principal, and receive a Catalogue.

CATALOGUE

OF

BOOKS AND BLANKS,

PUBLISHED AND SOLD BY US AND OUR AGENTS,

IN THE

STATES OF ILLINOIS, IOWA, AND MICHIGAN.

————•◆•————

BOOKS AND BLANKS FOR ILLINOIS.

Teachers' Daily Register — Designed to record, *even to a minute*, the attendance of pupils.. It is easily understood and easily kept. There are two sizes, made of firm, heavy linen paper, put up in strong half cloth and muslin binding. 1st size, $2. 2d size, $4.

School Tablet — Designed for marking the tardiness or irregularity of teachers and pupils, and used in connection with the Daily Register. $1.

Class Book — Designed for marking the character of each pupil's recitations, and also his deportment. 75 cents.

School Ledger — This sustains the same relation to the Register and Class Book that a merchant's Ledger does to his Day Book and Journal. It contains a summary of the pupil's marking in each study, his punctuality and deportment, and his average standing. In fact, it is the crowning Book of the series, and makes the system complete. $3.

Report Card — Designed to report monthly to parents and patrons the average and relative standing of the pupils. $2 per 100.

Special Report Card — Designed to inform the parents, in special cases, of the tardiness and absence of pupils, and number of recitations lost thereby. $1 per 100.

Teachers' Schedules — The best ever published. They are put up in packages of three quires each, strongly sealed in heavy wrappers, expressly for the trade. Merchants should not fail to send for our Schedules. They are arranged according to the late law and under the supervision of the State Department, and are sold lower than those of any other House in the State. $1.50 per quire.

School District Record — For Clerk of the Board, containing ten different forms, with printed headings. $5.

Directors' Order Book — Neatly bound in half cloth. Filing and receipt on the back of each order. $1 per book of 100 orders.

School District Bond for use of Directors. $1 per quire.

School District Blanks — Consisting of Election Notices, Poll Books, Tally Lists, Certificates of Election, Tax Certificates, Census Reports and Teachers' Contracts. 1 set — enough for one year — 30 cents. 1 package — 4 sets — $1.

Township Treasurers' Books — 3 volumes, Journal and Record, Cash Book, Ledger and Loan Book. Bound in half sheep, spring back, and in half Russia, spring back. 1st size, $15. 2d size, $20.

Township Treasurers' Note Book — Ruling and printed receipt on the back of each note, for endorsements. $1 per book of 100 orders.

Township Treasurers' Receipt Book. $1 per book of 100 orders.

Township School Blanks — Consisting of Election Notices, Poll Books, Tally Lists, Certificates of Election, Census Reports, Treasurers' Bonds, Township Plats. 1 set — enough for one year — 35 cents. 1 package — 3 sets — $1.

School Mortgages. $1 per quire.

Record of Teachers Examined — For the use of County Superintendents. New edition, with printed headings. Bound in half sheep. $3.

County Superintendents' Certificates to Teachers — Two grades, on first quality paper. $2 per 100. First grade extra large size, beautifully lithographed, $10 per 100.

Teachers' Institute Certificates. $1 per 100.

County Superintendents' Note Book. $1 per book of 100 notes.

County Superintendents' Receipt Book — For the receipt of money paid to Township Treasurers. Bound in half cloth. $1.50 per book of 200 Receipts.

Form Required in the Formation of Union Districts. $1 per quire.

TESTIMONIALS.

DEPARTMENT OF PUBLIC INSTRUCTION, }
SPRINGFIELD, ILL., Nov. 23, 1861. }

MESSRS. ADAMS & BLACKMER: It gives me great pleasure to apprise you of the good opinions expressed by the Commissioners in their reports to this office respecting the usefulness and value of your Register and other Blanks.

You are doing a *good work*, for which I thank you. The report from these counties supplied with your Blanks are invariably the most complete and accurate.

With much esteem, yours very truly,
N. BATEMAN, *Supt. Public Inst.*

DEPARTMENT OF PUBLIC INSTRUCTION, }
SPRINGFIELD, ILL., Sept. 12, 1863. }

I am glad to recommend to school officers and teachers throughout the State, the sets of Blank Books and Forms published by Messrs. Adams & Blackmer, of Rockford, and which seem to be admirably adapted to the uses for which they are designed.   *   *   *   These Books and Forms are precisely what is needed to remedy the nameless evils resulting from the general mismanagement of our school interests, and hence I am induced not only to pen for them a formal recommendation, but to *insist upon their introduction* (or others adapted to the purpose) *into every School District in the State.*   *   *   *   *   *

I will only add, that school officers are authorized by the law to appropriate from the school fund, a sufficient amount to purchase whatever books and blanks may be necessary for their use.

JOHN P. BROOKS, *Superintendent of Public Instruction.*

At a Convention of County School Commissioners, held at Bloomington, October 1st, 1863, the following resolution was unanimously adopted:

Resolved, That the series of School Records published by Adams & Blackmer, of Rockford, be officially recommended to teachers and school officers throughout this State, and that the State Superintendent be respectfully requested to call the attention of School Directors, Township Trustees and Treasurers, and all other school officers and teachers, to their great importance, and to adopt such measures as he may deem proper with his official duties for their adoption by all the schools throughout the State.

A similar resolution was unanimously passed at the late meeting of County Commissioners' held at Springfield, January 3d, 1865.

BOOKS AND BLANKS FOR IOWA.

Teachers' General Register — Report of attendance of pupils and branches taught, filed with Township Secretary. $2 per quire.

School District Record — For District Secretary; containing nine different forms, with printed headings, as follows: A Record of the Proceedings of District Township School Meetings; A Register of Sub-Directors, and Term of Office; A Record of the Meetings of the Board of Directors; A Register of Orders on District Township Treasurer; A Record of Rules and Regulations for Government of Schools; a Register of Teachers employed in the District Township; a Summary of Teachers' Report of Attendance; A Record of Annual Report of Township Secretary to County Superintendent; and Plats of Sub-Districts in District Township. $6.50.

Order Book — Filing and receipt on the back of each order. $1 per book of 100 orders.

District Township Blanks — Consisting of Election Notices, Certificates of Election, Bonds for Treasurer and Secretary, Per Centum Tax Certificates, Tax Certificate to Board of Supervisors, Drafts on County Treasurer, Township Plats. 1 set — enough for one year — 50 cents. 1 package — 4 sets — $2.

School Treasurers' Books — Embracing an account with School House Fund, with Teachers' Fund, with Contingent Fund, and Register of Orders drawn on Treasurer. $5.50.

School Census Register — Of persons between five and twenty-one years of age. $5.

Sub-District Record — For use of Sub-Director; containing seven different forms, with printed headings, as follows: A Record of the Proceedings of School Meetings; A Register of the Election of Directors, and Term of Office; A Register of Heads of Families, and Persons between five and twenty-one years of age; A Record of Rules for the Government of Schools; A Record of Teachers' Contracts; A Register of Teachers employed; and A Summary of the Teachers' Report of Attendance. $3.

Sub-District Blanks — Containing Election Notices, Certificates of Election, Tax Certificates, Poll Books, Tally Lists, Contracts with Teachers, and Sub-Directors' Reports. 1 set — enough for one year — 30 cents. 1 package — 4 sets — $1.

Independent District Blanks — For Independent Districts. $1.57. $1.67. $1.77. $1.90.

Commissioner's Certificates to Teachers. $1 per 100.

Among the many recommendations from the Teachers and School Officers of Iowa we have only room for the following:

TESTIMONIALS.

After a careful and thorough examination, and a partial acquaintance with their use, I take occasion, most heartily and cordially, to recommend to School Directors and others interested, the *School Register, Class Books* and *School Ledgers*, as well as all the other *School Blanks* published by Adams, Blackmer, & Lyon.

In my judgment, an average of *40 per cent* would be gained by their general introduction into our schools, and from 10 to 20 per cent with the best of our teachees. And I would call special attention to the advantage of their *monthly report cards* as a most important part of t e system.

A thorough and efficient *system* is what we want; and I know of no greater help towards that end than these books.

The *Blank Books* and papers for the use of school officers, also, will well pay for the investment necessary to secure them, by securing uniformity, and marking out the duties of such officers, thereby securing correctness and punctuality, which we all know to be important under our law, to make sure of its benefits.

GEORGE ORDWAY, *County Supt. Black Hawk Co., Iowa.*

Extract from a letter of J. W. Brainard, Principal of Winnesheik Normal Institute, Decorah Iowa:

In answer to your inquiry, I would say that I have never seen anything, nor have I ever heard any means suggested for awakening a public spirit in school against tardiness, to be compared for an instant with your Tablet. The working of that article is magnificent, and saves me a world of labor and effort.

The set of Record Books, too, is no less a powerful machine. I secure a punctuality and scholarship thereby which I could not by any other known means, and the power of these appliances reaches *every scholar,* save those whom nothing but severity and rigor can reach

----

BOOKS AND BLANKS FOR MICHIGAN.

School District Record — For use of Directors; containing 13 different forms, with printed headings, as follows: Directions for the use of the several Blanks in this Book; Record of the Proceedings of District School Meetings; Register of District School Officers and their Acceptance; Register of the Doings of the District School Board; Printed Rules and Regulations; Rules and Regulations adopted by the District School Board; Contracts between District Board and Teacher; Register of Teachers in the District; Expenses incurred by the Director, Catalogue of Books in the District Library; Census Record; Summary of the Attendance of Pupils; and Financial Report of the District Board. $6.

Order Book — With filing and receipt on the back of each order. $1 per book of 100 orders.

School District Blanks — Embracing Election Notices, Teachers' Contracts, Warrants on Town Treasurer, Reports to Supervisors, and Assessors' Bonds. 1 set — enough for one year — 30 cents. 1 package — 4 sets — $1.

Rate Bill and Warrant — $2 per quire.

School District Assessors' Book — Containing an account with Teachers' Fund, with District Library Fund, with Incidental Expense Fund, and with Building Fund. $5.

District Librarians' Book — Containing an account with Persons Drawing Books, Catalogue of Books, Statement of Fines and Losses. $3.25.

Township Treasurers' Book, Township Clerk's Book, Road Commissioners' Book — $10 each.

School Inspectors' Book — Containing a Record of Proceedings of Board, Record of Examination of Teachers, and Maps for laying out Districts. $5.

Township Clerk's Orders on Treasurer and Highway Commissioners' Orders on Treasurer — Bound in half cloth, with filing and receipt on the back of each order. $1 per 100 orders.

Notices of Examination of Teachers, Bonds of Chairman of Board of Inspectors, Maps for laying out Districts — $1 per quire.

Teacher's Certificates — Three grades; two years, one year, and six months. $2 per 100.

Poll Books — And Tally Lists for General Elections and Annual Township Elections. 70 cents each, including Tally Lists.

Highway Commissioners' Assessment List — For Road Districts. 25 cents.

We also publish all kinds of Michigan Legal Blanks — Warranty Deeeds, Mortgages, Quit Claim Deeds, Land Contracts, Chattel Mortgages, &c., &c.

TESTIMONIALS.

DEPARTMENT OF PUBLIC INSTRUCTION,
OFFICE OF SUPERINTENDENT,
Lansing, December 23, 1863.

I most cordially recommend to School Officers and Teachers the Blank Books for District Records, Teachers' Registers and other blanks prepared by Messrs. Adams & Blackmer for the State of Michigan, and I earnestly advise the District Boards to supply themselves without delay with a set of these books from any moneys in their hands that may be used for this purpose. As these books are such as the District Officers are required by law to have and to keep, the District Boards have full power to make the purchase.

I know of no measure that will do so much to introduce order and regularity into the proceedings of Districts and District Boards, and aid to prevent misunderstandings, losses and litigations as the use of these excellent and instructive blanks.

School Officers and Teachers will find them of invaluable service in making plain and easy a most perplexing and difficult part of their duties; and districts will be delighted with the admirable order and system which these books will introduce into the chaos of their affairs.

By all my love for the good of our schools, I most heartily wish for their universal adoption as the best means of promoting uniformity and regularity in the school work of the State.

J. M. GREGORY, *Supt. of Public Instruction.*

These Books and Blanks are made of the very best material, and are all arranged according to the latest School Laws of the several States. No pains has been spared to make them

The best System of School Records and Blanks ever Published.

We shall be glad to see all Book Merchants and friends of education at our office, Lombard Block, whenever they shall visit Chicago. Teachers and School Officers are especially invited to make our office their headquarters when in our city.

ADAMS, BLACKMER, & LYON.

P. O Box 708, Chicago, Ill.

BRYANT & STRATTON'S

CHAIN OF

BUSINESS COLLEGES.

TWENTY FIRST-CLASS INSTITUTIONS,

ALL UNDER ONE MANAGEMENT.

The Largest Educational Enterprise of the Age.

Scholarships are Issued, good during Life, in all of these Colleges.

The Course of Instruction pursued in this College is so arranged as to give the **student** *Practical* experience, not only in *Book-Keeping*, but in conducting the different **departments** of business, and upon graduation, he is a thorough and experienced accouhtant.

The Actual Business Department

Is the most practical, thorough, and complete, of any in the country.

BRYANT & STRATTON'S

CHICAGO TELEGRAPH INSTITUTE.

Largest Institution of the kind in World — Hall 105 feet long, filled with Telegraph Instruments.

Every facility is afforded for making rapid, practical, *sound* operators. Students have all the advantages of working on a "*Line*," taking charge of an "*Office*," keeping the "*Books*," making up weekly "*Statements of Business*," putting up and taking charge of "*Batteries*," &c., &c. Open all day and evening.

College Office in Larmon Block, N. E. Corner Clark & Washington Sts.

BRYANT & STRATTON'S

CHICAGO BUSINESS COLLEGE

OCCUPIES THREE LARGE BUILDINGS,

Northeast, Southeast and Southwest Corners Clark & Washington Streets,

OPPOSITE THE COURT HOUSE.

1500 Students in attendance the past year. Scholarships good during life in Thirty-five Colleges.

Actual Business Training, Book-Keeping, Business Writing, Correspondence, **Commercial** Arithmetic, Commercial Law and Partnership Settlements, thoroughly taught.

Send for College Paper, College Greenbacks, sample Business Writing, &c.

Address,

BRYANT & STRATTON, Chicago.

ROLPH'S
Normal System of Penmanship,
Complete in Six Books, of 28 Pages Each,
IS NOW READY.

In this series the Reversible Copy Card is kept near the line on which the Pupil is writing.

Directions in BOLD PRINT, and Cuts from actual Photographs, are in sight above the copy.

Each Book contains as much Writing surface as a book and a half with Head Lines.

A Height Scale, showing by COLORS the exact proportions of Writing, is a new and valuable feature.

Liberal terms for introduction. Specimen numbers sent by mail on receipt of 10 cents.

ADAMS, BLACKMER & LYON,

No. 35 Lombard Block, Chicago·

AMERICAN SLATED WOODEN GOODS.

We are prepared to furnish at low rates the following goods, manufactured by the American Slate Company, Norwich, Conn.:

SLATED WOOD COPY BOOKS—3 Nos.

Especially designed for Primary Schools as an introduction to any of the Systems of Writing now in use.

SLATED WOOD DRAWING BOOKS—3 Nos.

Will soon be ready.

THE AMERICAN WOOD SLATE

A light, durable and beautiful article for Primary Schools.

COMMON SCHOOL WOOD SLATES—5 Sizes.

5x7, 6x9, 7x11, 8x12 and 9x13.

The surface of these Slates is the best ever made, and fully equal to that of the Stone Slate.

THE PATENT SLATE PENCIL HOLDER,

A new article, having the hearty approval of all Teachers who have examined it. It is more economical than the common slate pencil, and compels the pupil to hold his *pencil from the first* as he *should* hold his *pen* while writing.

Slate Pencil Points to accompany the Holders.

ADAMS, BLACKMER & LYON,

No. 35 Lombard Block, Chicago,

Exclusive Agents for the West and Southwest

EASTMAN'S

National Business College.

The Proper Training to make Useful, Successful Men.

The Age and Exigencies of the Times Demand the Eastman System of Business Education.

A MODEL COMMERCIAL COLLEGE IN CHICAGO.

There has been built up, in Poughkeepsie, N. Y., by H. G. Eastman, LL. D., the largest and most popular Institution of Learning on the American Continent, numbering Thirteen Hundred Students, and occupying six buildings. He has suggested the best Course of Study for Practical, Useful Education, and the best mode of Commercial College Instruction ever adopted in this or any other country.

Its largely increasing patronage in the West has induced him to extend its usefulness, by establishing a **Western Institution** of the College at Chicago, under the Principalship of Prof. E. P. Eastman.

Its success already has no parallel in the history of Educational Institutions, it having a more extended patronage to-day than any Commercial or Mercantile College in the West.

It is the largest, best furnished, and most complete Institution of the kind in the World, in appointments and facilities.

The Course of Study comprises every variety of Business and Finance, from Retail to Banking Operations, by the great system of Actual Business Instruction. Book-keeping in all its various methods, Business Forms, Terms and Usages, Business Writing, Correspondence, Commercial Arithmetic, Commercial Law, Advertising, Partnership Settlements, Detecting Counterfeit Money, thoroughly taught.

Its **Telegraph Lepartment** is the Best and Most Extensive in the Country.

Graduates are assisted to Situations in Government Departments and the Cities of the Country.

Students are admitted every week-day in the year, without regard to previous education.

Full information may be had at the College, METROPOLITAN HALL, or by addressing the Principal,

E. P. EASTMAN,

D. K. ALLEN,

Sec'y.

CHICAGO, ILL.

815097

Printed in Great Britain by
Amazon.co.uk, Ltd.,
Marston Gate.